TIME AND THE GARDENER

Writings on a Lifelong Passion

ELISABETH SHELDON

Beacon Press
25 Beacon Street
Boston, Massachusetts 02108-2892
www.beacon.org

Beacon Press books
are published under the auspices of
the Unitarian Universalist Association of Congregations.

07 06 05 04 03   8 7 6 5 4 3 2 1

This book is printed on acid-free paper that meets the uncoated
paper ANSI/NISO specifications for permanence as revised in 1992.

Drawings by C. Joanna Sheldon

Text design by Sara Eisenman

Composition by Wilsted & Taylor Publishing Services

Library of Congress Cataloging-in-Publication Data
Sheldon, Elisabeth.
    Time and the gardener : writings on a lifelong passion / Elisabeth Sheldon.
        p.   cm.
    ISBN 0-8070-8556-1 (cloth : alk. paper)
  1. Gardening. 2. Gardeners. 3. Gardens.   I. Title.
    SB455 .S437 2003
    635.9—dc21

                                                              2002151833

For dear Kit

CONTENTS

vii

PART THREE: GARDENERS OF OTHER TIMES

TIME AND THE GARDENER

TIME *and the* GARDENER

While rereading the essays I've accumulated over many years, I've been amazed to see how many plants I've grown, loved—and lost. Most of the things I've written about are still with me, but many are not. I've been saying to myself, "Oh, that was wonderful. I must get it again." Then, as I wondered where I'd put it, I realized that all the places formerly occupied by the dear departed have been taken by new, also beloved, plants. In order to replace those plants lost to beasts, bad weather, or blunders on my part, I'd have to dig an entirely new garden, which, at my age, would be a bit giddy, perhaps.

It's been humbling to see how many plants have disappeared, but I take some comfort in remembering that Vita Sackville-West kept a large collection of plant markers that served as reminders that, as a gardener, she was not infallible.

But if we were infallible, and if there were no beasts or bad weather, and if perennials were all really perennial, how bored we would get looking at the same scene year after year! Either that or we'd have to keep installing new gardens, taking on more territory endlessly. I'd have had to dig a mile downhill to Cayuga Lake, as my husband predicted I would do when, thirty-two years ago, I first started wielding my mattock. Thank goodness he was wrong and I stopped at 250 feet (except for adding raised beds, a woods garden, and a new enclosed garden). Thank goodness, too, for lost plants and new ideas.

For as the garden keeps changing, so does the gardener. In the first place, one enthusiasm follows another: for a while one is wild about campanulas, say, wanting every good species and cultivar one can get one's hands on; then, while not falling out of love with campanulas exactly (one's passion is replaced by a more tranquil affection), one goes completely overboard for astilbes, then nepetas, then rock plants ... It may sound exhausting, but it is actually quite exhilarating.

Then there are the changes of enthusiasm for certain color combinations. In my case, it was for many years my chief delight to combine white, silver, and pale yellow, or greys and pinks, lavender, and lime—all very delicate and tender. Finally, a primitive craving for strong violent color broke loose, causing me to create a garden of hot colors—the greatest thrill of all. Then, having used purple foliage to make quiet spots in the hot garden, I began playing about with purple foliage in the border. In some areas it is now giving depth and importance to pinks, greys, and blues, while in others it is providing a kind of cello accompaniment to the flute notes of chartreuse and pale lemon yellow.

This constant changing of enthusiasms has the virtue of jogging one loose from one's favorite plant prejudices. Just as in making the hot-color garden I was forced into appreciating many genera I had always scorned (zinnias, marigolds, dahlias, even petunias), so, when carried away combining wine and sulphur in the border, I took to my heart plants with yellow leaves, which I had always viewed with strong disapproval. I suppose this is all to the good. Alarming, though: for what if one should be left with nothing to hate?

I should mention, too, the changes that are brought about by the plants themselves. Trees grow and cast more and more shade; plants under them must be moved and others brought in to take their places. Shrubs spread out and crowd their fellows. If we don't keep a sharp lookout, we may be sorry later. I once had a fine colony of apricot tulips under a small magnolia tree. I now have a large magnolia tree and no tulips.

I've been speaking of the changes that take place in the garden as the years roll by and changes in the gardener's interests. But what about changes in the gardener? Alas, although this work affords us all that healthful exercise in the open air, keeps us chugging about when, without our strong motivation, we might be sitting indoors playing cards or looking at television—still, time takes its toll. While the spirit is still soaring eagerly onward and upward, the old bones and cartilage begin to insist that they can no longer handle the demands being made on them. This is obviously unfair and a better system should be devised. We do realize that, as long as babies continue to be born, those of us who have had our allotted time must clear out with as good a grace as we can muster to make room for them. That is acceptable, certainly—we shouldn't be greedy. What I object to is the steady process of gradual dilapidation: now it's the knees, then the back, and in my case the eyes. In the new system I would propose we would all go vigorously full speed ahead until our time was up, then fall suddenly on our faces, finished. Montaigne, the essayist, said he hoped Death would find him planting cabbages. I myself would like to meet Death in the flower garden—falling facedown onto a cushion of *Dianthus gratianopolitanus*, if it's not too much to ask.

I once went to a symposium at which the gardening partners Norman Singer and Geoffrey Charlesworth began their presentation by giving us a figure for their combined ages, as well as a list of their combined physical infirmities. It was very amusing, although we knew it wasn't really amusing for them.

We all deal with the situation as best we can: we use kneeling pads or little seats on wheels, we try planting in raised beds, we work fewer hours. I, who used to work from 6 A.M. to 9 P.M. outdoors, then indoors hanging flowers to dry, now start at 7 or 8 and begin to flag by 4. I try to replace exasperation with gratitude for being able to continue to dig, haul, edge, and weed at all. The trouble is that with my now limited, and only peripheral, vision, even with the aid of a loupe, every job takes much longer than it used to. And no doubt my garden looks shaggier than it used to. I can't be sure. For although I have various vision-enhancing devices that enable me to examine single flowers or small areas of the garden in detail, the garden as a whole, the full sweep, is to me very like a painting by Monet in his late period. There may very well be weeds that I don't see.

I'd like to be as noble about old age and affliction as Lincoln Foster, of rock garden fame, whom I remember, at what must have been the last visit of the American Rock Garden Society to his garden, Millstream. There he was, sitting on a wooded hillside, his white hair blowing in the breeze, receiving his guests like an old Shakespearean king, I thought. Rock gardeners who knew the place well bent down to croon lovingly over the treasures that remained, but remarked sadly that Millstream was not what it used to be.

But should we be sad? We who garden know from the outset that we are working with ephemeral material in what is, in this age of earth-moving machinery, an ephemeral landscape. Do you remember Henry Mitchell's comments on the subject in his first book, *The Essential Earthman?* He has been talking about the outrage a gardener feels when the trees or shrubs that he has, knowing better, planted too close together grow so large that they have to be moved or cut down. He goes on: "On the other hand, I don't see much sense in planting stuff at the proper distance for fine effect fifty years from now. Such plantings will come to perfect maturity just in time for some jerk to

bulldoze the place to sell french fries on." We, in some ways, resemble the Navajos who, beginning at sunrise, make elaborate
paintings with colored sand, which they then destroy at sunset.
It's the *doing* it that counts. It's the work itself, the studying, the
learning, the contriving, the cherishing, the success, and even
the failures. We have not been deceived into thinking that making a garden is like bringing a piece of sculpture out of a block
of marble or like painting on a wall or on canvas. Through observing the yearly, monthly, even daily changes in our gardens
we are prepared to accept the fact that, unless they're grand
enough to be rescued by the National Trust or the Garden
Conservancy, our gardens are bound to grow old and infirm
and to eventually disappear with us, or soon afterwards. And
should we lament? Indeed not, for, as we trudge toward the end
we know that, out of all the people in the world, no one has had
more fun than we have had.

I have only one regret. If I were to start my gardening life all
over again, that is, from the time we first came here to the farm,
I'd take over one of the fields and turn it into an arboretum. The
older I get the more I love *trees*, the more they amaze and impress me. I can understand the ancient people who worshipped
them. I could easily fall on my knees before an old banyan, or
the ancient beeches in Germany. Have you seen the marvelous
trees at Longwood Gardens in Pennsylvania, at Old Westbury
Gardens in New York, and at Scott Arboretum at Swarth-
more College in Pennsylvania? Of course, in thirty-two years I
couldn't have grown very large trees, but they'd be big enough
now to be interesting.

I *did* have sense enough to plant a few trees around the
property. I raised from seed a lot of redbuds that now adorn the
slopes that descend to the stream that runs by the house. Three
dogwoods (bought years ago from Girard Nurseries at three
for $1.25) light up the ravine in spring. A sour gum tree (*Oxyden-*

drum arboreum) in the same area is thriving and giving pleasure, especially when it turns ruby red in the autumn. On the back lawn there now stands a good-sized European linden. Pine, larch, metasequoia, and Chinese dogwood (*Cornus kousa*) are all planted too close together in the woods garden, but still I'm glad of them. Also crowding each other on the front lawn are a 'Dr. Merrill' star magnolia and a fine tall European beech, whose silky grey bark always makes me want to throw my arms around it. My daughter said one day, "Mother, you'll have to cut one of those trees down." I told her I couldn't bring myself to chop down either one of them, so she'd have to do it later on.

I have the loveliest little cercidiphyllum (gift of a friend) coming along behind the perennial border, as well as some amelanchiers and, finally, after three unsuccessful tries, a *Parrotia persica*, now about ten feet tall. It's a multi-stemmed tree with interesting exfoliating bark and glorious autumn color. I've been thinking I'd better put a metal marker on it, for no one will know what it is after I leave, and it might get cut up for firewood.

But by far the best tree on the place is one I got in 1971 as a small sapling *Acer griseum* from Girard's. As it grew, I kept expecting its bark to turn cinnamon-color and to peel off in sheets. Instead, the bark remained the color of mahogany and exfoliated only slightly. It was beautiful, but it wasn't doing the right thing, thought I, and I wondered why the tree formed itself into the shape of a bouquet with many branches spraying out like a fountain from a single dividing trunk, a much finer shape than I'd ever seen in a *griseum*. Then a visiting botanist told me he thought it was a Korean maple, *Acer triflorum*. I looked it up in Michael Dirr's *Hardy Trees and Shrubs* and decided he was right. Some years after that, another expert came along, this one a maple expert, who told me that the tree is a cross between *A. griseum* and *A. maximowiczianum*. It seems that

Girard got *griseum* seed in the late '60s from an arboretum in which the two species were growing near each other and had surreptitiously crossed. I'm so happy they did, for the offspring is, I think, lovelier than either of its parents. I've planted in a circle at its base a carpet of silver *Lamium* 'White Nancy,' which enhances its beauty all spring and summer. In the fall the finely cut leaves of this small tree turn wonderful shades of apricot, flame, and crimson, a torch against the blue autumn sky.

But still, I pore over the tree listings in the Forest Farm catalogue and want three of each. . . . Maybe the next time around.

In the meantime, I've been writing as I gardened and have now brought together essays produced over the last thirteen or fourteen years. They are, in a way, a sort of horticultural journal—observations and comments on what worked out well and what did not, as well as thoughts on the gardening scene in general, on other writers, other gardeners. The occasional footnote indicates where my ideas have changed since I wrote the piece, where my original happy relationship with a plant has turned into disappointment or disgust, or where an undervalued plant grew, over time, to be appreciated. These things happen in the garden, as elsewhere: the faults and virtues of individuals one encounters are not always immediately apparent. It is also the case that vendors of plants are not often inclined (or able) to offer much help to the gardener who is purchasing them. The best recommendation I can give to those who have taken up the delightful, absorbing, intensely gratifying, maddening, and exhausting activity of gardening is to dig, plant, weed, work, and . . . read, read, read. To be glad and grateful when something works out and not to grieve too much when it doesn't. It is to be hoped that these observations by one who has been trying to do just that for many years will be of interest—and possibly some help—to her fellow gardeners.

PART ONE

WHAT I'VE LEARNED

OVER TIME

THE ANXIETIES of SPRING: GROWING PLANTS from SEED

I f you are a gardener who grows perennials from seed you will agree that early spring is a time of joy but also of anxiety, a time of hovering over the seed flats, emitting cries of joy if some tricky seeds have responded to your efforts on their behalf and of disconsolate "damn!"s if they haven't. If you have been engaged in this activity for some years and have been intelligent enough to keep a log of your methods and their results, you may be spared this emotional turmoil. But I, after many years of hit-or-miss seed planting, have only this year set up a file labeled "Propagation by Seed." Having finally made the first step, the next is to write down what I've done and what has happened. Or failed to happen, as the case sometimes sadly is.

Besides not having records, I am further hampered by not having found a seed-propagation guru. The books on my shelves contain many sections on seed planting—there are even two whole books devoted to the subject. My new file contains information from horticultural societies, pamphlets from seed companies, newspaper and magazine clippings, so I'm well supplied with advice. Too well supplied, I sometimes think, as few of the advisors agree on all procedures. Horticultural experts are handicapped by the same problems as those who deal with the psychology and behavior of human beings—it's extremely difficult to draw up really hard and fast rules and analyses, so many unknown or unchartable elements enter in. In the case of perennials, the age of the seed, the method of storing it, the components and moisture content of the growing medium, the temperature at which it is held, the amount of light, the depth at which the seed is planted—all of these things count and most of them are not easy to measure accurately. I may never find my guru and will have to solve some of the mysteries myself.

Certain procedures in seed planting are, thank goodness, clearly indicated. Everyone agrees that the containers used should be clean (I scrub my plastic flats in warm soapy Clorox water) and that the sowing mixture should be sterile. Some pros tell you you can use garden soil if you bake it at a certain temperature for a certain length of time to sterilize it. I tried that once and the odor was so ferocious it was the last as well as the first time I did it. Now I use a prepared sowing medium that contains no soil, hence no harmful bacteria. (When I pot up the babies later I mix in garden soil in order to get them used to their future environment.) The experts agree also that the sowing medium should be moist but not soggy. Some writers then proceed to tell you to soak the flats in water before or even *after* planting—a very good way to make them soggy, I should think. I now put the grow mix into a kitty litter tray and moisten it thoroughly, loosening it and making sure it contains no sticks or big lumps of peat. I then fill the flats, press the mixture gently down with a block of wood, and am ready to plant seeds of ordinary border perennials such as delphinium, veronica, campanula, or balloon flower. If, however, I have seeds of rock garden plants to sow, I mix about one-third coarse sand or, preferably, grit with two-thirds grow mix and put a one-quarter-inch layer of grit and milled sphagnum on top. Chicken grit from a farm supply store can be used for this, if it contains no chemical additives, but I get crushed limestone from a gravel pit. Another rule on which everyone agrees is that very fine seed should simply be sprinkled on the surface of the soil and pressed down. Larger seed should be just covered and no more. The seeds of many perennials require light to germinate and will not even try if planted too deeply. Shallow and surface planting makes it imperative to check the flats often to make sure they remain moist. You can put the flats in clean plastic bags or spray them lightly and often with warmish water from a rubber squeeze-bulb sprayer. When the small plants are well up, I stop spraying and instead soak the flats in tepid water (another kitty litter tray) until the moisture just shows on the surface. This needs to be done every few days or whenever the flat looks dry and feels light. The biggest problem is trying to decide when it's time to administer water; too much of it may cause the young seedlings to damp off. For small plants it's better to give too little water than too much.

Except for watering, this all sounds fairly straightforward, but it is really here that the uncertainty begins. I used to plant some flats in January of those seeds that were said to need freezing in order to break dormancy. I enclosed the flats in plastic bags and set them outdoors on a shady porch. Other flats were planted in March and placed immediately on heating coils under grow lights. The outdoor flats, divested of their plastic bags, joined them under the lights in April. My method was simple and my success rate not very impressive. Since it's disheartening to have seed that one has sown with high hopes and eager anticipation fail to produce plants, and since nowadays one may have paid a high price for what is sometimes a bit of dust that threatens to get lost under the fingernails, I decided to set myself to try to learn the method that would give the optimum chance of success *for each perennial*.

I want to learn which seeds germinate best in the dark, which in light; which want to be cool, which warm; which benefit from a chilling of two or three weeks; which ones need to be frozen and thawed alternately for months, sometimes *years.* (One does, with these seeds, tend to lose interest as the months go by and is apt to develop a fondness for plants that don't fool around, such as dianthus, whose seedlings pop briskly up several days after the seed has been planted.) I'm also investigating and making lists of those individuals whose seed is best sown the minute it ripens, which includes many of the wildflowers as well as anemones, clematis, armerias, and hellebore. Some of these seeds, planted in summer or autumn, will germinate at an awkward time of year and will have to be wintered over in a cold frame or on the back porch; others will not sprout until spring.

Plants have odd ways of managing their seed—I've just read that the reason all of us have so much trouble germinating trollius seed is that it is not mature at the time of harvest and must be kept moist during storage in order to allow the embryo to develop. One assumes the trollius knows what it's doing, but it does seem perverse. This bit of information and lots more on seed germination I found in the spring '87 bulletin of the American Rock Garden Society.

So, as I say, for the first time I'm trying to get organized. I'm determined to follow orders, as much as possible—enough of the casual approach—and to keep records. With some of my seeds this year I'm experimenting with the suggestions of members of plant societies, sometimes professionals, sometimes amateurs, who send accounts of their methods to the society bulletins. Often the recipes from amateurs, like those food recipes donated by readers to cooking columns in the newspapers, prove to be the best. Other perennials I've been looking up in seed company handbooks. I've already had proof that good advice is to be found in seedsmen Thompson & Morgan's booklet, in which I was told to sow aubrieta seed without covering it, to envelop the flat in a plastic bag, and to set it in "diffused" light where the temperature would be around 65 degrees F. I did that, and for the first time, instead of having only a few stray seedlings, I have a flat full of them. A writer in the Royal Horticultural Society's journal *The Garden* persuaded me to plant cyclamen seed shallowly, to cover the flats with foil, and to keep them at a temperature of 60 to 68 degrees F. After three weeks, said the writer, I would have lots of little cyclamen coming up. I did and I have. Ha! I'm on my way!

GARDENING *in* *the* WOODS

P eople who live in residential areas that were established many years ago are inclined to say, when the
subject of gardening arises, "I can't have a garden—our
property is much too shady." Perhaps some of these
people are glad to excuse themselves, thus, for confining their
unimaginative plantings to a few rhododendrons or azaleas, but
others may long to have a real garden and be unaware of the
possibilities shade gardening presents. Books have been written
on the subject, I know, but they apparently have not come to
the attention of many people who, if they garden at all, will have
to grow plants that tolerate or even require shade. Few plants
will thrive in extremely dense shade or directly under low-
hanging branches, but will do well in dappled shade or under
tall trees—even in the shade of buildings where they are in the
open.

For a number of years I've been enthusiastically creating
and tending a large mixed border (a garden of shrubs and perennials) nearly all of which is in full sun. At one end of the border, however, is a little sassafras grove that I have turned into a
woods garden. It is only about fifty-five feet by sixty-five feet—
very small indeed, yet it makes a fine home for a wide range of
shade-loving plants. You can walk into it by one of three paths
that meet in its center where there is a tiny pool.

Years ago someone planted one sassafras tree and since sassafras is stoloniferous, a little glade developed around the parent tree. Because the young trees grew so close together all of the trunks are slim and straight; all I had to do was to remove some of them in order to make room for paths and plants. Nearby I've added a larch, a metasequoia, and a few pines, all much too close together, unfortunately. A triple row of hemlocks, brought up from the woods and kept low and thick, screens the whole area from the road.

Recently I've realized that, much as I love the big flower border, my favorite place is the woods garden. Why, I wonder, since, being closest to the highway, it's the noisiest spot on the property. Yet it seems such a sanctuary—perhaps because we all retain an atavistic sense of being protected when surrounded by trees, perhaps because the predominance of green is soothing, the filtered light a relief, as it certainly is on a day of searing heat and glaring sun. But even on mild pleasant days the woods garden is a comforting spot, so it must be the effect of the trees and that of the plantings under them. The fact that there are very few weeds to cope with must also contribute to feelings of serenity—for the gardener, at least, who when he views his splendid sunny border can't keep himself from running his eye anxiously around, on the lookout for the enemy, thus somewhat marring his satisfaction. While few weeds can tolerate shade, many choice wildflowers and garden flowers love it, and since these plants also love a thick fluffy mulch of pine needles, work is minimal in a wooded area.

Still another element enters in. Sun-loving plants range in type from the very fine compact rock plants of the highlands to huge exuberant individuals that originate in lowland meadows. If one can generalize, woodland plants seem to be, on the whole, more restrained in aspect than most of the sunny border plants—more elegant, more refined even. The large sunny-border plants are very splendid in their way, no doubt, but sometimes one wants understatement as a relief from all that ebullience and bombast.

Another advantage of having a woods garden is that it provides a separate and ideal place for many spring bulbs that are not really suitable for the perennial garden proper for several reasons: They are unsightly when going dormant and are in the way when they've finished that procedure. When they have disappeared completely, they leave an empty place that one tries to fill by setting out more plants, inevitably forgetting about the bulbs and piercing them cruelly with the spade or trowel. Then, too, spring bulb flowers look out of place in a flower border, making little spots of color when the rest of the border inhabitants are just beginning to emerge.

The little bulbs, such as chionodoxa, puschkinia, snowdrops, *Scilla sibirica*, species narcissus and tulips, *Iris reticulata*, and *Anemones blanda* and *nemorosa*, should be grown in great sweeps, as large as one can afford money and space for, and they should all be near one another. What better place than under trees? And when their show is over they can slowly finish their cycle without getting in anyone's way.

Elizabeth Lawrence, author of *A Southern Garden*, wrote often of her friend Mr. Krippendorf who had, in southern Ohio, what must have been the most wonderful woodland garden in the country—Lob's Wood, which included a meadow, a creek, and miles of woods containing thousands, even millions, of bulbs of all kinds, besides other choice woodland plants. Miss Lawrence wrote that you could walk up and down hills for hours and never come to an end of squills and daffodils.* Just the thought of someone's having created such a garden lifts the

*Elizabeth Lawrence, *A Southern Garden: A Handbook for the Middle South* (Chapel Hill: University of North Carolina Press, 1984).

spirits, and while we may not be able to match Mr. Krippendorf's accomplishment, we can derive endless pleasure from
doing the same sort of thing in a very small way.

If I have begun to persuade any novices to start a shade garden I must add that there are two or three prices one must pay
for the above-named felicities—the first, that nearly all woodland plants bloom in the spring, many of them before the leaves
come out on the trees that will later shade them. You will want
to plant as many perennials with good foliage as you can so your
garden will retain interest after the early spring bulbs and other
flowers have finished their performance. If you think you require a riot of color all summer long you must either garden in
the sun or fill in your shaded areas with impatiens or other annuals that don't insist on sunlight. There are some perennials,
of course, that you may use for color later in the season—astilbes, the so-called Japanese anemones (now *Anemone hybrida*),
cardinal flowers, the great blue lobelia, chrysogonum, ligularia,
and a *few* late-blooming hostas, but the choice is limited.

The second drawback, if your shade garden is to be under
trees, is that trees tend to suck up a lot of moisture and nutrients, especially during hot, dry summer weather. Many of the
herbaceous plants go to rest before the battle begins, as the eminent British horticulturist Allen Paterson puts it, some of them
storing their food (and allowing for increasing their species) in
bulbs, corms, and tubers. The plants that remain above ground
will require extra nourishment in the form of old manure, compost, or fertilizer and extra watering all season if you want to
keep the ferns, astilbes, and other moisture-lovers from turning
brown and shabby. I often wish I had a water tap in my woods
garden so that I could simply attach a sprinkler on a short hose
instead of having to drag the long hose out from the house so
often. It would probably be possible to lay plastic pipe just
under the surface of the soil for such an installation. Since it

wouldn't be needed during the winter it needn't be sunk down below the frost level—the water would be disconnected in late fall.

Since it is not only spring bulbs that go dormant in summer but some of the woodland perennials as well, you have to expect empty spots in summer and fall where, in spring, groups of Virginia bluebells, mayapple, bloodroot, bleeding heart, and trilliums made everything beautiful. You can hardly blame the plants for retreating in July and August when you feel so much like doing the same thing yourself, if only it could be managed so neatly. It is, nevertheless, a case of desertion; the loss is felt and coverups must be found.

If you have a woods on your property, or a little grove, or a few trees *that are not surface feeders, such as maple,* you may decide to make a shade garden. Before beginning the physical work on the garden you should, ideally, design your paths, if any, and major underplanting. If you organize the lines of the path or paths and plan the position of shrubs so that all is harmonious, you can later be as whimsical as you please in placing small plants, keeping in mind, however, that as a rule grouping several of the same plant together is more satisfactory than spotting them here and there, especially in a woods garden, where wild plants naturally tend to colonize.

You may want simply to make a path through the trees and place groups of plants here and there along the path—or your project may be more ambitious. In any case, if there is already interesting and attractive undergrowth, leave it as it is and remove only the weeds or scraggly shrubs. If yours is a mature woods with a high canopy of branches, you will have a perfect place for a woodland garden. Your soil, too, will probably need very little or no amelioration. Those of us who have only a group of young trees have to amend the soil.

When preparing my garden I brought up loads of acid

woodsoil and the fluffy remains of dead and rotted trees to augment the peat and manure I used. We are lucky enough to have lots of woodland that includes a hemlock grove. I used to trudge down to that grove carrying gunny sacks, string, a mattock, and a small folding army shovel. I filled the sacks with the wonderful stuff that is made from years of accumulated hemlock needles, gathering it here and there so as not to damage the trees. I tied the sacks and dragged them to a collection spot for my husband to pick up later when he came with the tractor to get logs for firewood.

Back in the little sassafras grove, which had been a calf pasture, my first task was to remove the barbed wire and dig up the fiendish metal posts to which it was attached. Some of them broke off underground so that I still find the occasional piece of metal spike way down under my plants. When I took over the area it was growing burdock, wild black raspberries, an assortment of smaller weeds and was being invaded by sumac. I dug up all the soil in order to get rid of the weed roots and unwanted rocks. The burdock and raspberries weren't too difficult to get rid of, but the sumac kept sending its stolons under and up until I had the idea of painting the cut stumps with poison ivy killer. That caused them to retreat in the opposite direction and the remaining stumps soon rotted enough to be pried out.

If you attack a woodland to prepare it for planting, you will find that it is not easy digging around tree roots. You can't possibly spade it—a mattock is the only tool that works. If you use a systemic herbicide, beware of spraying it around stoloniferous trees because you may kill the parent trees through the young shoots. In any case, the soil should be thoroughly loosened and turned over down to twelve or fifteen inches, at least. If you have your peat, compost, wood soil, or old manure ready you can work it in at this time. Since most woodland plants require or prefer acid soil, you should also work in a generous quantity

of flowers of sulphur (two or three ounces to each square yard).
It would be a good idea to do this work in the fall so that the soil
will be in good shape for spring planting. In the case of bulbs,
of course, they should be put in in the fall, as soon as you have
prepared a place for them.

When it comes to making decisions about which shrubs,
perennials, and bulbs you want in your garden you will have to
decide first how much of a purist you are. Do you want only native woodland plants—or are you going to allow yourself to include immigrants and even hybrids and garden cultivars? I've
drawn up a list at the end of this essay of indigenous wildflowers
and shrubs and have catalogued the interlopers separately, for
purists and non-purists respectively. Myself, I'm in the second
category. I wouldn't want to do without primroses, for one
thing, or cyclamen, or all those Japanese charmers, such as the
little blue and white fan-leaved columbines that have become
available to us. And think of the spring and fall anemones! Besides, Gertrude Jekyll said one shouldn't deprive oneself of
beautiful plants and combinations because of an idea: it is, in
her view, spoiling a garden for the sake of a word. She says a blue
garden may be "hungering" for a few white or pale yellow flowers but not be allowed them because it is called the "blue garden." However, that is a bit different from wanting to see how
good a garden can be made with native plants. For someone
with strength of character that could be a worthwhile project.

But in my garden, East meets West, in what I hope is perfect concord: *Thalictrum kiusianum* from Japan associating with
Chrysogonum virginianum, European ginger with Oregon trout
lilies, London pride with shooting stars, and Spanish bluebells
(white ones) with foamflower. I've used all of the fine native
plants that I can lay hands on, bringing some up from our
woods and ordering others from nurseries—the giant and
small Solomon's seal, woodland phloxes, hepatica, anemonella,

Aquilegia canadensis, Dutchman's breeches, doll's eyes, *Iris cristata*, Oconee bells, many others, but I've also made full use of bleeding hearts, epimediums, anemones from everywhere, and astilbes. Two of the most satisfactory anemones are *A. nemorosa*, from European woodlands, and *A. sylvestris*, from Europe and Siberia. The nemorosa I have is a lovely blue one whose delicately cut leaves are almost as pretty as the flowers. It's spreading itself everywhere, to my delight. Sylvestris, too, has colonized with vigor, putting on a great show with clouds of pure white blossoms in spring and early summer, then a small display in fall, with any luck.

I tried using hostas in my little grove but it didn't work—they're simply too overpowering, the large ones, at least. A few of the smaller varieties remain, notably that little gem 'Louisa', but the larger ones are now making a grand effect behind a wall along the driveway under tall old trees. They need a lot of space to be at their best, space both around and above.

There are any number of shrubs one could use in a woodland—some could be broadleaved evergreens (pieris, kalmia, rhododendrons, and azaleas and their dwarf forms), which benefit from being spared exposure to the blazing sun, and other deciduous shrubs that grow naturally in the forest. The shrubs you choose should look as if they belong in their setting—that is, they should present themselves modestly and not blaze out aggressively, as is the tendency of some "improved" azaleas. Why not use species, rather than hybrid, rhododendrons (*R. carolinianum, atlanticum, arborescens, vaseyi,* or *viscosum*), which come in shapes and colors that would be eminently suitable for the kind of garden we're thinking of. I like too the old Ghent azaleas, especially *narcissiflora* and *daviesi*, which have small deciduous grey-green leaves and sweetly scented pale buff yellow and white flowers.

One could consider planting witch hazel, which tolerates

not only shade but city air and blooms in late fall or winter, or shadbush (amelanchier), whose airy white blossoms are so welcome in early spring. The catalogues always tell you that the berries are good for jelly—that may well be, but the birds and chipmunks get every one of mine just as they ripen, or a little before. The native mapleleaf viburnum is not a very shapely plant, but its leaves turn a most exquisite shade of rosy raspberry pink in the fall. If you live in Zone 6, or even Zone 5 if you're a gambler, you could try corylopsis, the winter hazel, which doesn't mind light shade and produces its pale yellow blooms very early in the year. *Clethra alnifolia*, the sweet pepperbush, grows to eight feet in wet woods or swamps, but will make at least four feet in a drier location. White or pinkish fluffy spikes of bloom appear in July and August above its shiny green leaves. *Enkianthus campanulatus* is a handsome individual that is not seen very often for some reason—strange, since it will grow in full sun or deep shade and has handsome foliage, arranged in whorls, which turns brilliant scarlet in autumn. Maybe people don't plant it because it doesn't have a common American name, being an Asiatic, and they think they can't pronounce "enkianthus." The flowers are dangling clusters of not-very-showy-but-nice creamy bells tinged pink.

We have not yet dealt with the problem of how to decorate the empty spaces left by dormant bulbs and perennials. One of the best solutions is to plant a few well-intentioned, reasonably self-disciplined ground covers, and I am *not* thinking of pachysandra, vinca, lily-of-the-valley, or ivy, all of which would swallow your little bulbs alive. Beware, too, of sweet woodruff, goutweed, or snow-in-summer (*Aegopodium podograria*), which would be a problem anywhere but in a barren strip of earth between cement sidewalks.

Mazus reptans has very shallow roots, yet it forges ahead determinedly, spreading its small neat leaves and lipped lavender flowers over every space available. (Even into the lawn, but no matter.) I was introduced to *Mazus japonicus albiflorus* at the American Rock Garden Society annual gathering in Connecticut one year, brought a pot of it home and am happy to see it beginning to move about under the trees as if it belonged here. The white blossoms on this plant are pure and lovely and larger than the lavender ones on *reptans*. The native partridge berry (*Mitchella repens*) is another pretty little spreader in acid woodsoil and the long-lasting red berries are a joy. (Susan Fenimore Cooper, daughter of the novelist, wrote that children used to gather and eat not only the berries but the aromatic young leaves.) Another aromatic creeper is wintergreen (*Gaultheria procumbens*), as nonaggressive as partridge berry and liking the same conditions. Some of the new, colorful ajugas could be used—'Silver Beauty' or that delicious variegated cream and pink one called 'Burgundy Glow' or 'Burgundy Lace'. These aren't as hard to control as the ordinary old ajugas and are much more decorative. For a very delicate groundcover over small bulbs in light shade try Corsican mint (*Mentha requienii*). It looks almost like moss and has a powerful and most refreshing aroma when stroked.

My impression is that the latest lamiums, 'Beacon Silver' and 'White Nancy', like the new ajugas, aren't the louts that their forebears were. They are stunning in a shady garden and if they should begin to overpower the other plants they could easily be curbed. If they were planted near but not over the bulbs they would spread out and luxuriate in the empty space the bulbs leave during the summer. The pieces that root in the bulbs' territory could simply be pulled up in the fall, possibly to be stuck in somewhere else, possibly to be discarded.

If you are clever enough and/or have the moist, acid soil and cool weather it likes, you might be able to persuade the beautiful bunchberry, *Cornus canadensis*, to grace your garden with its whorls of pointed leaves and white dogwood flowers that are followed each by a large red berry. With me it comes and goes, mostly the latter. Canadian mayflower (*Maianthemum canadense*) is easier and is pretty too with its three-foot tubby spikes of white foam. Moneywort comes in green or gold (*Lysimachia nummularia* or *L.n. aurea*) and likes moisture if it can get it. Even when deprived of it from time to time it never reveals any distress but moves slowly along, keeping its round shiny leaves flat to the ground. None of these plants is out to strangle its neighbors, which is an endearing quality in a groundcover. Since they don't make thick mats of roots, they are compatible with both small bulbs and the perennials that go dormant.

You'll see *Campanula poscharskyana* suggested as a ground cover for light shade, but beware—it means business. Don't put it near anything that can't fight back. Try *Campanula portenschlagiana* or *C. garganica* instead; they are both fine plants and are less boisterous.

If you can contrive to have water in your woodland garden it will contribute a great deal to its atmosphere. If you are lucky enough to have a real stream, it too will add to the number of interesting plants you can grow, as there are those that enjoy being constantly moist. The Japanese are fond of the sound of running water and often have in their gardens a small basin into which clear water runs from a bamboo spout.

I, however, have a modest little pool made unpoetically of a round, iron pig-scalding pot that I found near the barns when we first came to the farm. I measured it, dug a deep round hole for it, and after the ground froze one winter, my husband pulled it with the tractor over the lawn into the sassafras grove and into the hole. It *is* nice to have a bit of water to plant ferns and iris around, and I like it especially because it is home to five small blacky-bronze frogs, some of whom keep me company as I work. Two of them are cowards and jump into the pool when

I come along, but three brave souls sit firmly on the rocks that surround the pool, just keeping their eyes on me over the tops of their heads. They even let me stoop down to enjoy the color of the jade green streaks across their mouths.

Now let us suppose you would like to experiment with shade plants. If you don't have a small grove of trees on your property you might want to make a garden in a shady area around the house, or, if there is room, you might decide to create a grove by planting some suitable fast-growing trees that would turn into a little woods in a few years' time. I have fifteen or twenty redbud trees, twenty to twenty-five feet tall, growing in our gorge that I grew from seed about fifteen years ago. From seed, mind you. What if you were to start with trees of three feet or more? If you have some likely young trees on your own property, or if you have a landed friend who is obliging, you can dig them when they're dormant and replant them where you want your eventual woodland garden. Otherwise, you will have to order them from a nursery. You should get special rates for ordering in quantity. I would try to find native Americans, if I were starting a little woods, but whatever they are they should be trees that grow rapidly and with straight trunks. Ash would be a good choice, or tulip trees. I should think hackberry might do as well. Most oaks are too slow-growing, but pin oak and red oak grow fairly rapidly and tend to be straight. If it were possible to get hornbeam or ironwood saplings (*Carpinus caroliniana*), sometimes called blue beech, it would be wonderful, although hornbeam grows slowly. The silky, blue-grey bark of the fluted trunk makes it, I think, one of our most elegant trees. The little woods could be made of all one kind of tree or of a combination of several kinds. Whatever you choose, you must make absolutely sure that they are not trees with surface roots, such as maple, sweet gum, catalpa, willow, poplar, or birch. The European linden would be a good candidate if you weren't persuaded your

woods should be strictly of native trees. It's a much more refined individual than the American linden, one must admit.

As in the case of an already established woodland the soil
should be thoroughly prepared before any planting is done. If
the soil is poor you will want to add a lot of peat, old manure,
and compost. Then, in order to keep new weeds from settling
in, apply a thick mulch everywhere. If you don't intend to put in
your smaller woodland plants for a few years you might want to
put down landscape cloth under the mulch. Since it is a kind of
mesh, it will let in the rain.

So now the story is complete. A woodland garden cannot
fail to give you pleasure all year round—great joy when it ex-
plodes with bloom in spring, beginning even in February or
March, solace when it provides a green refuge from the heat of
summer, and colorful foliage and sweet smells of earth, pine
needles, and leaves in autumn. Provide for yourself a place to sit,
for in the winter it will be a kind of snow palace, or a snow
room, where you will go to enjoy the tracery of the tree trunks
and branches against the blue and grey sky.

Actaea pachypoda (white baneberry)

Actaea rubra (doll's eyes)

Anemone canadensis, riparia, cylindrica, and *quinquefolia*

Anemonella thalictroides

Aquilegia canadensis, caerulea, etc. (columbine)

Aralia racemosa (spikenard)

Aralia nudicaulis (wild sarsaparilla)

Arisaema triphyllum (Jack-in-the-pulpit)

Aruncus dioicus (goatsbeard)

Asarum caudatum, canadense, hartwegii, etc. (wild ginger)

Caltha palustris (marsh marigold)

Chimaphila maculata (pipsissewa)

Chrysogonum virginianum (golden star)

Cimicifuga racemosa (snakeroot)

Claytonia virginica (spring beauty)

Clintonia uniflora (blue bead)

Coptis groenlandica or *trifolia* (goldthread)

Dentaria diphylla (crinkle root)

Dicentra canadensis (squirrel corn)

Dicentra cucullaria (Dutchman's breeches)

Dicentra eximia (wild bleeding heart)

Dodecatheon meadia (shooting stars)

Erythronium albidum or *americanum* (bulb) (trout lily)

Galax aphylla

Gentiana, various

Geranium maculatum

Gillenia trifoliata (Indian physic)

Hepatica acutiloba or *americana*

Hydrastis canadensis (golden seal)

Hypoxis hirsuta (stargrass)

Iris cristata, innominata, etc.

Jeffersonia diphylla (twinleaf)

Lewisia cotyledon or *nevadensis* (bitter root)

Linnaea borealis (twinflower)

Lilium canadense, philadelphicum, superbum

Lobelia cardinalis or *siphilitica*

Maianthemum canadense (Canada mayflower)

Mertensia virginica (Virginia bluebells)

Phlox divaricata, stolonifera

Podophyllum peltatum (mayapple)

Polemonium carneum, reptans, etc. (Jacob's ladder)

Polygala paucifolia gaywings

Polygonatum biflorum, commutatum (Solomon's seal)

Pyrola asarifolia, minor, etc. (shinleaf)

Sanguinaria canadensis, S.c. multiplex (bloodroot, single and double)

Shortia galacifolia (Oconee bells)

Smilacina racemosa (spikenard)

Stylophorum diphyllum (celandine poppy)

Tiarella cordifolia (foamflower)
Trillium erectum, grandiflorum,
    luteum
Trollius laxus (globeflower)

Uvularia grandiflora, perfoliata, etc.
    (bellwort)
Vancouveria hexandra
Viola, various

NONNATIVE, HYBRID, OR GARDEN CULTIVARS FOR A WOODS GARDEN

Acanthus mollis or *spinosus*
Alchemilla alpina or *mollis*
Anemone nemorosa, japonica, sylvestris
    vitifolia robustissima
Anemonopsis macrophylla
Aquilegia flabellata, pyrenaica, etc.
    (columbine)
Aruncus aethusifolius dwarf
    (goatsbeard)
Asarum europaeum (European ginger)
Astilbe, various
Astrantia major, maxima, carniolica
Bergenia cordifolia, crassifolia
Brunnera macrophylla (Chinese
    forget-me-not)
Campanula persicifolia, garganica, por-
    tenschlagiana, etc.
Cimicifuga simplex (snakeroot)
Coreopsis verticillata (threadleaf
    coreopsis)
Corydalis lutea
Cyclamen europaeum, neapolitanum,
    etc.
Dicentra spectabilis, D.s. 'Alba' (bleed-
    ing heart)

Digitalis lutea, mertonensis, purpurea,
    etc. (foxglove)
Doronicum caucasicum (leopard's bane)
Epimedium, various
Ferns, various
Gentiana, various
Geranium dalmaticum, 'Johnson's
    Blue' *macrorrhizum, phaeum, platy-*
    petalum, sanguineum, etc.
    (cranesbill)
Geum borisii, montanum
Globularia, various
Helleborus niger, orientalis, etc.
    (Christmas rose, Lenten rose)
Hemerocallis, various (daylily)
Hepatica triloba
Hosta, various
Hylomecon japonicum
Iberis, various
Iris gracilipes, reticulata (bulb) etc.
Jeffersonia dubia
Kirengeshoma palmata
Lewisia hybrida
Ligularia clivorum, dentata, stenoceph-
    ala, etc.

Lilium, various

Liriope, various

Lithodora diffusa 'Grace Ward' 'Heavenly Blue'

Lysimachia clethroides (Gooseneck loosestrife)

Oenothera fruticosa (sundrops)

Omphalodes cappadocica, verna

Polemonium 'Blue Pearl' (Jacob's ladder, dwarf)

Polygonatum odoratum thunbergii 'Variegatum' (variegated Solomon's seal)

Primula, various (primrose)

Pulmonaria angustifolia, montana, rubra, saccharata (lungwort)

Rodgersia aesculifolia, pinnata, etc.

Saxifraga urbium, s.u. primuloides

Symphytum grandiflorum (yellow lungwort)

Thalictrum aquilegifolium, speciosissimum kiusianum, rochebrunnianum (meadow rue)

Trollius europaeus, ledebourii (globe-flower)

Tricyrtis hirta, etc. (toad lily)

GROUND COVERS FOR A WOODS GARDEN

Native plants marked (N)

Ajuga 'Burgundy Lace', 'Silver Beauty', etc.

Campanula poscharskyana, portenschlagiana, garganica, etc.

Cornus canadensis (N) (bunchberry)

Dalibarda repens (N) (dewdrops)

*Galium odoratum (Asperula odorata)**

Gaultheria procumbens (N) (wintergreen)

Gaylussacia brachycera (N) (box huckleberry)

Hedera, various* ivy

Houttuynia cordata variegata

Lamiastrum galeobdolon 'Herman's Pride'

Lamium maculatum 'Beacon Silver', 'White Nancy'

Lysimachia nummularia & L.n. 'Aurea' (moneywort) (N)

Mazus japonicus albiflorus & M. reptans

Mentha requienii (Corsican mint)

Mitchella repens (N) (partridge berry)

Pachysandra procumbens (N) (Alleghany spurge)

*Pachysandra terminalis**

Vinca minor periwinkle*

Waldsteinia fragarioides (N) (false strawberry)

*For large area only

Native plants marked (N)

Abeliophyllum distichum (white
 forsythia)
Amelanchier alnifolia (shadbush) (N)
Azalea, various, some (N)
Clethra alnifolia (N) (sweet
 pepperbush)
Corylopsis pauciflora (winter hazel)
Daphne burkwoodii, mezereum, etc.
Enkianthus campanulatus (red vein)
*Hamamelis japonicus, mollis, virgin-
 ianal* (witch hazel)

Ilex, various (holly)
Kalmia latifolia (N) (mountain
 laurel)
Leucothoe fontanesiana, populifolia
 (N)
Pieris andromeda, etc.
Rhododendron, various, some (N)
Viburnum acerifolium (mapleleaf)
 viburnum (N)
Viburnum carlesii

HORTICULTURAL
DISCRIMINATION

When I first went into flower gardening in earnest and began to meet other people who were devoted to the pursuit, I had the impression of having moved into something of a rarefied atmosphere. I felt that somehow my fellow gardeners and I, through our constant association with flowering plants, had undergone a kind of mysterious purification process that had freed us from many human frailties—at least from manifesting them in our dealings with one another. However, I've become aware that, while I had been thinking that we would all be happy guileless gardeners together, children of paradise, in a way, there is strong evidence of one unworthy element that we have brought into our horticultural heaven from the world outside and that is snobbery. A saddening reflection, for surely we should be above it?

This snobbery has two aspects, the first is the simple manifestation of the old human failing of wanting to have something one's friends and neighbors don't have. It makes the gardener cherish his *Corydalis cashmeriana* for the cupidity it arouses in his chums, his androsace for the anguish of longing he reads in visitors' eyes, and his *Arisaema candidissimum* more for the fact that hardly anyone else has it than for the fact that it is strikingly beautiful. This way of measuring the worth of any object, ani-

mate or inanimate, is regrettable but still comparatively innocent. On this subject, by the way, I found an amusing paragraph
in the memoirs of the English novelist E. F. Benson, which follows an affectionate description of a garden he had made:

> There was nothing of the slightest interest or rarity, for this
> garden was not intended to be one where the owner, with
> difficulty deciphering a metal label, solemnly introduces the
> visitor to a minute mouse-coloured blossom and tells him
> that never before has this species flowered in Sussex. . . .
> How I long, on such occasions, to stamp on the mouse, pas-
> sionately exclaiming, "And it shan't go on flowering in Sus-
> sex now."*

But it is the second aspect of horticultural snobbery I find
more disturbing—that of those who concentrate on one whole
group of plants and look down on all others. I don't mean enthusiasts of a particular genus—say those who adore iris,
primulas, or roses—who love these plants especially but appreciate and grow many others. I do mean those who embrace one
group and discount all the rest. The plant hunter Reginald Farrer, who encountered this attitude in his time as well, wrote: "It
is the specialist in gardening that I dread—not the specialist in
himself . . . but the spirit of narrow exclusiveness that special-
ism seems liable to breed."†

Oddly enough, he had just been speaking of people in
Cornwall who concentrated on growing gorgeous rhododendrons and scorned his beloved small plants from the high
mountains. Nowadays that situation has been almost completely reversed, with many sophisticated gardeners sneering at

*E. F. Benson, *Final Edition* (New York and London: D. Appleton-Century, 1940),
p. 264.
†Reginald Farrer, *In a Yorkshire Garden* (Rhode Island: Theophrastus reprint, 1973),
p. 12.

rhododendrons (and other plants that produce big explosions of color) and worshiping only alpines. In fact, it is among these alpine enthusiasts that the biggest plant snobs seem to be found today. Many of them value a plant only if it is very small, very rare, and very difficult to grow. They scorn large lusty perennials and remain unmoved even at the sight of smallish rock plants if they are the sort that are at all amenable. If a plant can be grown by a novice, no matter how pretty it may be, it is beneath their notice.

While it was Reginald Farrer who introduced the fine art of rock gardening to Great Britain, it is Louise Beebe Wilder who is given the credit for bringing it to America. Like Farrer, she adored alpines but regretted the attitude that was quickly assumed by some who became experts in the field and who wrote in defense of *easy* saxatile plants that "seldom receive sufficient credit.... They ask so little, which, instead of arousing our gratitude, seems to engender a faint contempt."*

It is easy to understand a gardener's going overboard for alpines, even to the point of spending a lifetime hauling rock, constructing screes and moraines, and devising crevices made of just the right rock, placed at just the right angle to suit his lewisias, saxifragas, and/or other highland princesses. (I've even heard of an alpine enthusiast who puts all his pots of a particularly exigent subject into the refrigerator every night and takes them out every morning.) Alpines are truly lovely plants, restrained and elegant, and certainly provide challenges to those who need them. Especially if they are trying to grow them at low elevations in America. The fanciest of these plants are also hard to find and expensive when found. The dedicated rock gardener joins alpine societies and raises as many of them as he can from seed-exchange seed. This is all innocent and com-

---

What Happens in My Garden (New York: Macmillan, Collier Books, 1991), p. 79.

mendable activity—even I try doggedly to raise alpines. Even I, as I criticize, am leaving my writing pad to go peer, now and then, at seed flats that I hope are hatching out erodiums, rock yarrows, and androsaces that might miraculously resign themselves to living in my stone wall. I yearn to have alpines as well as easy rock plants from below the tree line.

What I am saying is that rock gardeners and other specialists should keep in mind that Farrer may have had something when he said: "This cult of the separate rarity is the destruction of true gardening ... the true gardener despises nothing. . . . You may ignore, you may leave out, but you must never despise."*

Shouldn't we enjoy plants for their own sakes rather than for their social position? Shouldn't we note the beauties of an ordinary clump of sundrops as well as those of a daphne, value the contribution of a mass of lusty delphinium as well as that of a two-inch *Penstemon acaulis*, of *Aquilegia chrysantha* as well as *A. jonesii*? And when a rock plant, such as aubrieta or *Campanula garganica*, is pretty and easy to grow, we certainly should not scorn it but rather be grateful to it for giving so much to our gardens in exchange for so little effort on our part.

*Farrer, op. cit.

TALL PLANTS

Do you have trouble finding good tall hardy perennials for the back of the border or for the middle of island beds? I've found a few that have proven almost flawless and others that I persist in planting but which are not without their irritating little ways. I will start this discussion by mentioning those plants that are splendid but which have regrettable tendencies and work my way up to those that can do no wrong—at least in my garden.

For many years I've had delphiniums, the big double ones, in the back of the border. There are probably half a dozen reasons for *not* growing them: they must be sprayed to prevent cyclamen mites, red spider mites, and mildew; they suffer from leaf spot and stem borers and are irresistibly attractive to slugs, armies of which throw themselves on the emerging shoots and mow them to the ground; they often fail to make it through the winter and, worst of all, they're the very devil to stake. Even staking each stem and tying it with a soft cord fails when the flower head becomes sodden with rain water. The top half of the spike bends at the cord and dangles toward the ground—a sad spectacle. I must admit I tie each spike in two places only. Now I read that I should tie the flower spike at one-inch intervals from bottom to top! For heaven's sake—a person does have other things to do! Why do we keep struggling with delphiniums? It's all for that brief period of splendor before a summer storm strikes. The sight of four or five fat spikes of cobalt *Delphinium* 'Blue Bird' standing in sunlight against the cream-colored feathery explosion of goatsbeard is worth almost any amount of effort it takes to produce it. Apparently.

The single delphiniums, 'Belladonna' and 'Bellamosum', are beautiful too and bend but don't break during a storm. They do need staking (I never met a delphinium that didn't, no matter what anyone says), but at least it's not a major operation. Two or three light stakes and one cord around the whole plant does it. It's true that these delphiniums too attract slugs, mildew, and mites, but they are longer lived than double ones. They can't be used in the very back of the border as they rise to only four feet, shorter than is needed in most borders.

Another marvelous pure blue is to be had in the Italian bugloss, *Anchusa azurea* or *italica*, which can grow as high as five feet. Its coarse scratchy foliage isn't one of its charms but it produces, early in June, masses of tiny brilliant blue forget-me-not flowers. (In North Africa you can come upon whole *fields* of this plant in bloom, a sea of blue to make you gasp.) However, in your garden, when the performance is over and you cut it to the ground, it leaves a great gap, since just one plant has been taking up a space about equal to that of a wringer washing machine. Anchusa needs near perfect drainage as it has deep fleshy roots that tend to rot. Also, because of those roots it is difficult to move except when very small.

I was reading in Louise Beebe Wilder recently that *Thalictrum glaucum* (*speciosissimum*), the tallest, I believe, of the meadow rues, doesn't need staking. Mine needs three stout posts and two or three rounds of strong twine as it proceeds on its way to six feet or more before erupting into a froth of pale sulphur yellow stamens. The great mass of inflorescences may, in spite of my efforts to prevent it, tip over after a storm. (Perhaps mine is *T. flavum,* which Mrs. Wilder says is even taller and does need staking?) The intricately cut blue-green foliage of this species makes it look like a giant columbine and contributes to the garden picture even after the dead flower stems have been removed. Thalictrum, unlike columbine, preserves its pretty leaves all summer long. No diseases, no enemies for this one, and its pale yellow flowers go well with delphiniums. Actually, I find (also in Wilder) that it's an old favorite combination. I thought I had invented it.

Thalictrums come in lavender and dusty pink as well as yellow. *T. rochebrunnianum* grows almost as tall as *glaucum* and carries light purple flowers with yellow stamens. It doesn't seem to have the rambunctious spirit of *glaucum.*

Another frothy flopper is *Clematis recta*—and *C. r.* 'Purpurea', the latter a form with smoky purplish foliage. This clematis is not a vine but a garden perennial. A full account of *C. recta* is to be found in the chapter "Some Border Clematis."

The British assert that *Artemisia lactiflora* (white mugwort) does not, even when it reaches six feet, require support. I quote from one eminent authority: "It is one of the few tall herbaceous plants that are absolutely self-supporting." Nor do American writers I've consulted mention the fact that two or three strong stakes must be set around it, before it flowers, in order to keep its tall, slim, straight stems from sprawling. They don't curl over but fall straight down. One strong cord attached to the posts suffices to keep the plant erect.

This artemisia is a favorite of mine, not only because it is an imposing presence in the back of the border with its dark green finely cut foliage, but because of the sweet, pervasive fragrance of its small creamy white flowers, borne in tapered panicles well above the mass of leaves. It flowers at the best time of year, when summer is turning into autumn, the oppressive heat is drawing off, the air is tender, slightly misty, gold-spun. The scent of the artemisia blossoms mingles with that of the field asters and the surprisingly exotic perfume of Queen Anne's lace.

If you have enough white mugwort you can cut the huge panicles of flowers before they turn brown, hang and dry them for winter wreaths or bouquets. This artemisia is not an aggressive colonizer, as are so many species of that genus. The clump merely becomes larger every year and is easy to divide—you can have it marching down the whole length of your garden, if you please. No problems, other than the staking.

If you have a damp area where you can use, or where you need, tall subjects, you can plant some of the rodgersias and ligularias. They are becoming easier to find now than they were a few years ago. One garden writer says that the rodgersias are too rarely grown in American gardens, but that just might be because there have been so few of them available, and those few have been—and are—expensive. When they are grown in rich, moist, even boggy soil they display tremendously dramatic leaves—palmate, in the case of the Chinese *R. aesculifolia*, which is probably the tallest one. The leaves are deeply veined and tinted bronze, so splendid that the plant has really already contributed more than its share of beauty before it sends up its huge panicles of small cream to pink flowers.

There are several species of rodgersia in circulation. I've been struggling to satisfy one plant of *R. podophylla*, which never seems to get its required quota of water in my garden. I've finally made it a kind of sunken plastic bathtub which has cheered it up somewhat. It's not very sensible of me to try to accomodate that plant and its companion, *Ligularia japonica*. Both of them just hang in there and visibly yearn to be moved to the edge of a pond, but in a wet summer they're so spectacular that I can't bear to part with them. The ligularia has huge orange-yellow daisies on tall, sturdy stems. The best-known ligularia is probably *L. stenocephala* 'The Rocket' (sometimes listed under *przewalskii*), which shoots its black racemes of lime-yellow flowers up to five feet. A knockout.

On the edge of the same damp spot where your ligularias and rodgersias are growing you can have *Cimicifuga racemosa* as well. When this northeastern native feels adequately nourished, when it has enough to drink, and when the sunlight it receives is filtered—restrained rather than relentless—it will create great clumps, even colonies, of toothed, twice-divided, dark green leaves from which ascend, in midsummer, sometimes to a height of eight feet, tall, dark, smooth, wiry stems that bear racemes of tiny, white, fragrant flowers, like long white candles. The impact is heightened, naturally, if they are grown against a dark background. Cimicifuga certainly needs no stakes and mine have given me no trouble of any kind.

Cimicifuga simplex and its cultivars are shorter plants that bloom late; here in Zone 5 their charming white bottlebrush blossoms are frequently blasted by frost. *C. simplex ramosa* is a good tall plant, but since it and its purple-leaved form bloom even later than *simplex*, I haven't tried them. I'd love to be able to grow them, especially 'Atropurpurea', which is said to be striking.

Angelica archangelica would decorate the same area under discussion and would seed itself freely. All you would have to do would be to remove the volunteers that became too numerous. Both the thrice-compound leaves and the huge umbels of small whitish flowers on this six- to seven-foot plant are attractive. It provides architectural value, as the garden designers say. Angelica will grow happily in sun or part shade, so long as it has enough moisture. Since the seed doesn't remain viable for long, your best bet, if you want to get it started, is to beg seed from someone who grows it and sprinkle it in the fall where you want it to grow. *Angelica gigas*, with burgundy stems and blossoms, is even more striking than *A. archangelica*.

All over the world except in this country, I believe, candied angelica stalks are used in sweet cakes and puddings, much as vanilla is used here. It has a delicious flavor and makes a nice change from vanilla, especially in cheesecake. So far I haven't been able to find it in American stores.

Everybody knows about putting bee balm in the back of the border, and tall daylilies as well, so I won't deal with either of them here. They are a great solace, especially good old *Hemerocallis* 'Hyperion' that takes all kinds of abuse and comes smiling through, holding its perfumed lemon trumpets five feet up into the wind and sun, needing no props, no spraying, no diagnoses of mysterious afflictions. Such a plant endears itself to the overworked, overanxious gardener who by planting lots of 'Hyperion' in his border frees himself to hover uneasily over his exigent alpines.

Goatsbeards (*Aruncus dioicus*, formerly *sylvestris*), the ones standing behind the delphiniums, are superb plants only to be faulted for their tendency to strike back when they feel they are being neglected. Like many of the astilbes, whom they greatly resemble, they cause their leaf edges to brown and curl when their allotment of water doesn't come up to expectations. This, of course, is usually in late summer after their flowering has finished. Still, it's irritating to have fine foliage that one has counted on as a background for other plants fail to carry out its assignment. While they are in their glory goatsbeards are indeed glorious, each plant, about four feet by four feet to begin with, adding another foot and a half of cream-colored feathery plumes on branched panicles.

Some of the delphiniums I was grumbling about in this essay's second paragraph have been replaced by three different plants—and these are the teacher's pets that never behave badly.

The first is Japanese iris, which, while we are still trying to pronounce *kaempferi*, we are now told to call *ensata*. Never mind, we all know what we mean. Those tall, slim-leaved iris that people say are difficult and which must be grown as the Japanese do by a stream with a sluice gate so that they can have water one season and not the next. Is it water when they're blooming or when they're *not* blooming? Or while they're dormant? But the amazing discovery I (and probably lots of other people) have made during the last few years is that they require neither the stream nor the sluice gate. They *do* like soil on the acid rather than the limey side, but after that they seem to be perfectly happy in the border, planted deep, mulched with compost or silage, getting water only when the rest of the garden gets it. Admittedly, they don't grow as tall as they would beside a stream or pond, but they grow tall enough—four and one-half to five feet anyway. *So far*—and mind you I'm not ruling out the possibility that someone will invent a whole collection of Japanese iris diseases—so far, they've been clean and content, busy, in their season, breaking into breathtakingly beautiful blossoms in white, lavender, rose, purple, blue, and various combinations of these, variously spotted, veined, and striped. I can't tell you what a joy they are! They do not get viruses or borers, they do not crash to the ground when it rains, they do not require daily deadheading, and their foliage remains attractive and persistently vertical all summer. If you take seed from a friend or buy it from a seed house you'll be bound to raise some serviceable purple and red-violet ones, at least, and a few very fancy ones. Of course you can buy elegant cultivars from a nursery, but they will be, I fear, less dependable than those grown from seed.

The second of these paragons is a plant that is known in the trade as *Filipendula rubra* 'Venusta'—queen-of-the-prairie, and so it is. If you have a big stand of it (and it does slowly annex territory) you will cut it all to the ground in the fall. In the spring, out of the expanse of wasteland, emerge shiny red shoots that quickly rise to unfurl great, jagged, dark green glossy compound leaves, almost as handsome as those of rodgersia. Up they all go, making a forest, then in July or August, depending on where you live, the fireworks begin, if fireworks can come in pink. On six- to eight-foot stems appear huge, flat-topped panicles of fluffy rose-colored flowers. Spectacular, simply spectacular. If a really bad storm comes, the stems do tend to lean afterwards, but they don't fall to the ground. No disease has appeared on this fine American plant. It does its best in rich, moist soil, but performs heroically even under adverse conditions.

And for the last, and in some ways the best tall plant, and again it is a native—*Veronicastrum virginicum (Veronica virginiana)*. Now, looking at the photograph and description of *Veronicastrum v.* 'Album' in the Clausen/Ekstrom perennial book, I'm beginning to think that, lovely as my species plants are, I haven't seen anything yet.* Mine are certainly not as stout and showy as the cultivar in the picture, whose white flower spikes appear to be four or five times as long as mine. Nevertheless, the species is a fine plant with its straight tall stems providing perpendicular lines and its evenly spaced whorls of pointed, toothed leaves making horizontal ones. Even when, in late summer, it is carrying pointed racemes of white flowers on its four- to seven-foot stems, it never keels over, no matter what the weather does, that is, if you divide it every other year. I wonder if *V. v.* 'Album' will be so brave? I wish I could order it now, but it's only November.

---

*Ruth Rogers Clausen and Nicholas H. Eckstrom, *Perennials for American Gardens* (New York: Random House, 1989). Note that the cultivar, *V. v.* 'Album', three of which I purchased later, proved to be unsatisfactory, having lost, apparently, the vigor and gusto of the species.

A NEW HOME
for ROCK PLANTS

S ome years ago, when our large old elm tree died and had to be cut down, I had what I thought was the brilliant idea of building a stone wall around the three-foot tall stump—a retaining wall, back-filled with earth, that would serve as a home for rock plants. I gathered flat rocks and built the wall, a layer at a time, pounding a special mix of gritty soil in behind the rocks and spreading a one-inch layer of it between each course. I planted as I went, laying small plants in the soil pockets where rocks came together. On top I put lavender and a few other small shrubs that like sharp drainage.

As far as the plants were concerned the construction was a great success—they loved it. The dianthus, lavender, trailing campanulas, pasque flowers, and their companions throve and seeded themselves not only into all the available crevices between the rocks, but even into the woody pieces of stump that protruded at the top. They seemed to need no nourishment at all—only the sun, wind, and perfect drainage. All summer long the stump wall was glorified with plants billowing and burgeoning away, looking strong and cheerful. I told myself it was a fitting memorial to the elm we had loved and lost. But even from the beginning I had a faint suspicion that a round rock garden in the middle of the lawn was, well, *corny*. And although

I struggled against the impression, it reminded me insistently of those fake wishing wells that people put in their gardens. It was a sort of furry wishing well.

On October 1 a few years ago, the fall that I went out of the perennial business, after going down the driveway and enthusiastically bashing down my Ridge House Garden sign, I loped back to the garden, still armed with my tools of destruction, and began to dismantle the round wall. It took weeks to remove the rocks, salvage some of the plants, cart away the fill and debris, and finally get rid of what remained of the elm stump. After I had done all I could with mattock and axe it still looked like something in the Badlands of North Dakota. In the end I had to call in a chap to grind up the remains with a machine, after which I filled in the hole and planted grass. What a relief, then, to have a clean sweep of lawn, both when I was mowing and when I wasn't!

This removal of the wishing well was, however, a double project; at the same time that one habitat for rock plants was being destroyed, another was being created.

It had always been a fault in the design of this garden that there was no separation, either physical or spiritual, between the parking area and the garden. It occurred to me that I could put up a fence and then, against the fence, build a long stone raised bed, similar to one that I had elsewhere, and plant it with saxatile subjects for which I seemed never to have enough room. My husband installed a post and rail fence that I stained grey and planted with vines to make it look less like part of a corral. To make the bed I used stones and fill from the round wall but had to find many more stones and mix much more soil, since the bed is thirty-three feet long, almost four feet wide, and a little over two feet high.

The first long stone raised bed I had planted higgledy-piggledy, simply chucking in plants as I acquired them, wherever I could find an empty spot; but the second one I carefully planned so that colors and shapes would be repeated and nothing would look irrelevant. Comparing the two beds now, I'm persuaded that this is the way it should be done. This, the second summer for the new raised bed, finds it at that happy point when almost every bit of space is filled with budding or flowering plants that have not yet begun to encroach on their fellows—they are merely encountering one another, each draping a tentative tendril over the other, or, in the case of the dome-shaped subjects, puffing up the little mound and moving ever so slowly closer together. Since I didn't make the plants, may I not feel free to say that, at this moment, the bed looks quite perfect? What I attempted to do was to repeat, on either side, the most imposing individuals at approximately the same distance from the center, so that the largest masses of blue, white, grey, or pink would balance, while the smaller plants could be more or less whimsically placed.

At either end of the bed there is a saponaria—or rather there is a whole one at the east end and half a one at the west, the western one having met with some mysterious mishap during the winter. Never mind, even half a saponaria is enough to adequately present a foam of pink. Moving toward the center there are low masses of the grey rock yarrows, geraniums (*dalmaticum* 'Ballerina' and 'Biokovo'), and an absolutely superb campanula called 'Birch Hybrid' (a form of *C. portenschlagiana*?) with deep, vibrant blue-violet elongated bells. Here and there are early pale yellow dwarf iris, the delicate little citron yellow poppy, *Papaver fauriei*, single and double *Silene alpestris*, and the dramatic *Arenaria montana*, whose large bright white flowers are such a pleasant shock when they appear on the fragile thready plant.

There's one spread of a fine-cut silvery potentilla (perhaps *P. nevadensis*) whose sulphur blossoms are close in color to those of the *fauriei* poppy. Aubrieta, pink and purple, and starry grey-lilac *Campanula garganica*. A couple of nifty silver hedgehogs called *Astragalus angustifolius*—much too regal a name for such a jolly plant. There are two hanging curtains of pink creeping baby's breath and one silver, intricately designed centaurea (*C. simplicicaulis*). One of the 'Birch Hybrid' campanulas has sent a traveling branch down through the soil to emerge as a garland of upright violet bells from between the grey rocks below. Above, the smooth, flat, candy-pink, five-petalled blossoms of *Geranium dalmaticum* combine with the campanula to make a picture that is almost too pretty.

Which are better, I ask myself, the flowers of the single or double *silene alpestris?* The single ones look like small watch wheels, with little cogs all around the outside, except that they are cut almost to the center into five sections. The doubles are charming, having three or four rows of petals, and they do bloom longer. The white that they produce in early summer is furnished later in the season by an eight-inch American aster called 'Niobe'.

Anyone who goes in for both rock and grey-leaved plants will sooner or later start collecting the rock yarrows. The only problem with them is sorting them out—and *keeping* them sorted out. I have two kinds in the raised bed that look identical to me—mats of slender, very finely toothed one and one-half inch downy leaves growing in close-packed tufts. The only difference between them is that one plant is a lot greyer than the other. I believe them to be *Achillea ageratifolia* var. *serbica*. Perhaps one of them is simply a better form? *A. clavennae* has three and one-half inch pinnatifid leaves—that is, lobed halfway to the spine. Looks like a fluffy grey chrysanthemum. *A. kellereri's* leaves are cut to the midrib as if it were a silver-white fern. It's a real beauty with pointed leaves that are seven inches long, if you count the petiole, or leaf stem, but not much more than one and one-quarter inch wide.

These plants all produce chalky white daisies, either on separate stalks or in yarrowy corymbs, holding them above foliage that ranges in height from two to six inches.

I think it was from Rocknoll Nursery that I got a veronica whose foliage rises to no more than an inch and a half. This is not a creeper but a clump-forming plant that carries its flowers in tubby two- to three-inch lavender blue spikes that are starred with tiny white anthers. There must be one hundred spikes on each plant. This veronica was sold simply as *V.* 'Amethyst Gem', but it is probably a form of *V. spicata* 'Nana'.

Across a mat of pink pussytoes is *Geranium* 'Ballerina', whose blossoms (lilac, veined wine red) are hanging beguilingly over a clump of that best of all sedums, *S. cauticola*, the grey of whose rosettes is suffused with purply rose tints. If I had combined the two plants on purpose I'd be proud.

What I *did* do on purpose—or inadvertently I should say—was to put that classy *Arabis ferdinandi coburgi* 'Variegata', with its glossy cream and green leaves, right next to the white and green variegated aubrieta, the result being that they cancel each other out. One of them will have to find a new perch.

Penstemon hirsutus pygmaeus next to *Veronica* 'Waterperry' isn't bad, although the penstemon's pinky-lavender tubular blossoms are only a bit deeper in color than those of the veronica. I had thought, by the way, that the creeping 'Waterperry' wouldn't live through the winter here, so potted some up last fall to bring indoors. When spring came the mother plant outdoors looked less peaked than the indoor ones. Early in the spring this veronica has deep red-purple tones in its shiny round leaves. When the one-quarter-inch flowers first open they are a definite lavender, making a rich combination with the leaves. Later in the summer, the leaves become greener and the flowers paler. Right now, in June, they are milky white with fine purple lines on their upper petals. The new pairs of leaves and the tips of the old ones are stained dark red.

Crammed into corners are two Japanese succulents that are not classed with sedums and sempervivums but strongly resemble them—a chartreuse one called *Orostachys aggregatum* and a grey one (much the prettier of the two) called *O. furusei (iwarenge)*. For most of the year they are simply fat little roses, hugging the ground, but when they get ready to bloom—or their equivalent thereof—they rise in conical turrets that remind me of nothing so much as the temples of Angkor Wat.

Have you seen the grey scabiosa that goes under the name of either *Scabiosa pterocephala* or *Pterocephalus parnassii (perennis)?* You've probably been growing it for years, while I just discovered it last year. It seems such luck when a Mediterranean plant will put up with 20 below zero! And when it's a charmer like this, we're doubly grateful. It forms mats of crisp scalloped grey leaves that would certainly suffice even without its shaggy pale pink summer flowers. Actually the leaves are of two types—one set a smooth oval on long stems, while the other is compound, having one large oval at the end, then opposite ovals, getting smaller as they go toward the base of the stem. Very decorative, especially in frosted grey-green. It seems to be easy to please, given full sun and gritty soil, and it gradually creeps outward, industriously making new divisions that can be scooped up and planted elsewhere.

Of campanulas there are at least seven different species or cultivars in the bed. Two of the *turbinata pallidas* are next to a penstemon, their light, lavender-grey flat blossoms picking up that same color in the penstemon. One of the best qualities of this campanula is that, while it has the same rounded growth habit as the plain *C. carpatica*, unlike *carpatica* it does not grow so large that it flops open when it blooms.

'Blue Gown' is a trailing clump of crimped and ruffled dark green leaves decorated with open blue-violet, white-throated bells, while the western American *C. planiflora* sits stolidly on its gritty bed, pressing its hard, dense green leaves close to the four-inch stem. The most unlikely purple cups have appeared on this pygmy, seeming much too large for the rest of the plant. (I have some *planifloras* with white bells, as well.) Lincoln Foster says this campanula has a distressing tendency to die off the second or third year, unless divided—or—it may begin to grow tall and turn into *C. persicifolia!* He thinks *C. planifora* may be a Mendelian recessive form of *C. persicifolia.** That may explain why, from a packet of seed-exchange seeds I planted, I got some plants that look like the ordinary border *persicifolia* campanulas and some of these queer dark leathery green dwarfs. I was *wondering* what was going on.

Aside from a strange, congested little hump called *Arenaria tetraquetra*, whose name, so far, appears to be more interesting than the plant itself, only one other subject deserves mention and that is *Bellium cahruliescens*, which must be the world's smallest daisy. The one-third-inch flowers are white, yellow-centered, held three inches above the round flat mat of tiny spoon-shaped leaves on long petioles. The books say the plant should be divided every year. Mine made many babies last summer that I potted and took inside for the winter, but the mother plant, undivided, is still performing famously in this, its second year.

In this new bed there are only two kinds of dianthus, the

---

*H. Lincoln Foster and Laura Louise Foster, *Cuttings from a Rock Garden: Plant Portraits and Other Essays* (New York: Atlantic Monthly Press, 1990).

first a small, very tight grey bun that makes one-quarter-inch pink flowers at the proper time. I've lost track of its name, unfortunately, but it is almost sure to be a species since its self-sown offspring are all exactly like the parent. The other is *Dianthus crinitus*—a bristly green six- to eight-inch hemisphere that resembles a sea urchin. When it decides to flower it sends, straight out in all directions, one-foot wiry stems that explode at the ends into minuscule white spiders that release a strong scent of gardenias. Amazing. How is it that a rock plant can produce the same fragrance as that of a jungle flower? There are always these surprises.

SHRUBS
for the MIXED BORDER

I n the days when British horticulturists William Robinson and Gertrude Jekyll were laying down the law, "herbaceous borders" were created and planted with perennials only, masses of them. Money and space were no problem for most leisure class landowners, and cheap skilled labor was so easily available that Gertrude Jekyll once fired a gardener for leaning on his hoe at 10:30 in the morning (though, since he had been at it since 6 A.M., his fatigue was understandable). But now, when skilled gardeners are hard to find, and when found must be highly paid, many gardeners have discovered that the so-called "mixed" border is more practical than the glorious herbaceous border that was brought to such artistic heights by Robinson, Jekyll, and their disciples. In a mixed border compatible shrubs are combined with herbaceous plants (perennials). Since the shrubs don't need dividing, staking, spraying, or cutting back (except, perhaps, for an occasional pruning) they do save time and labor. Furthermore, they add structure to the garden all year round, unlike the perennials.

When I started digging and planting my mixed border I included many shrubs, some of which I had later to remove and replace with more appropriate subjects. Since digging up shrubs is neither amusing nor easy, gardeners who are contemplating including them in their perennial borders or island beds would be well advised to think carefully before they begin and perhaps avoid making some of the mistakes I made.

Choosing Shrubs Wisely

Shrubs for the mixed flower border or island bed need to be carefully chosen; it is not every shrub that is a good candidate for such a position. What are some of the qualities it should have? First, it should be deciduous—at least so it seems to me. When I started my garden I tried to use evergreens such as yews and dwarf conifers, but they looked so irrelevant I had to take them out again.

Shrubs for a sunny border should have an airy quality not found in evergreens in order to mingle successfully with the other plants. This is only a personal opinion—many other gardeners use evergreen shrubs in mixed sunny borders quite cheerfully. For me, dwarf conifers make good companions for other evergreens such as heaths and heathers, bearberries and little boxwoods, but not for perennials such as dianthus, campanulas, and cranesbills.

Second, border shrubs must not become so large that they crowd out the perennials. A ten-foot-by-ten-foot beauty bush (*Kolkwitzia amabilis*), for example, wouldn't leave room for many perennials in most gardens. Nor should they be surface rooted or have colonizing instincts or underground stolons or swiftly multiplying suckers. Beware of stephanandra, that fiend that uses every foul device in the plant kingdom to take over the earth. It even tip roots, like a wild bramble. Beware of hippophae, the sea buckthorn, whose stolons send up, as far as five feet away from the parent plant, fiercely armed shoots that remind one of the warriors that sprang from the earth when Jason sowed the dragon's teeth. No one tells you of hippophae habits. Beware of forsythia, too. It doesn't carry two-inch thorns, but by means of new shoots and tip rooting, it can make almost an instant jungle. And beware also of big old-fashioned lilacs whose matted surface roots deplete the soil around them of all moisture and nourishment besides making it almost impossible to pull out grass and other weeds from around them.

For the job we have in mind we need shrubs with handsome foliage and with flowers that are of a size and color that will combine well with perennial flowers and not overpower them. I should think that *Hibiscus* 'Southern Belle', with its ten-inch brilliant red flowers, might knock the stuffing out of a neighboring cranesbill that was modestly presenting its small, pale pink or lavender blossoms smaller than a communion wafer. And it would be the rare perennial garden that could serenely accept the presence of some of the more strident modern azaleas.

Among shrubs that answer our purpose three of the smallest—lavender, santolina, and helianthemum—come first to mind. Except for their inclination not to put up with especially severe or capricious winter weather, they are perfect companions for the smaller perennials. They never grow taller than one and one-half feet; they have small leaves and flowers that blend beautifully with those of their border companions, besides having similar tastes as to cultivation and environment. The sweet spare soil, sunlight, and perfect drainage they require are also demanded by dianthus, armerias, nepetas, and other plants that are often used for the front of the border. They have no nasty habits and require no attention at all except for a covering of evergreen boughs in winter and a thorough pruning in late spring. The feathery grey foliage of *Santolina chamaecyparissus* and the slim grey one-inch leaves of lavender and of some of the helianthemums make peace between the variously colored flowers of their companions, while the green foliage of *Santolina viridis* and the tiny, slender, pointed leaves of the green helianthemums, even though evergreen, are delicate enough not to look out of place in the border.

There are some lovely dwarf spireas whose slender leaves and fragile-looking flowers go perfectly with perennials. I have been growing, and enjoying, a little bush I got as *Spiraea lemoinei* many years ago. It does sucker, but it is not too hard to control. Because *S. lemoinei* remains at a height of around one and one-half feet it is quite satisfactory; but now I'm trying some new ones. One of the prettiest is *Spiraea bullata*, a fifteen-inch native of Japan whose dark leathery one-and-one-quarter-inch blue-green leaves are most attractive even without the deep rose flower clusters it produces in July. This little shrub doesn't have the loose arching habit of many of its better known relatives but holds its branches quite upright. Grey-foliaged plants such as lavender and some of the small artemisias, if planted nearby, would bring out the fine color of its leaves and flowers.

I'm afraid the spirea situation is in a sad state of confusion. Several years ago I ordered from different nurseries three plants, all of which were labeled *Spiraea japonica* 'Alpina'. They are now all of different heights and have different growth habits. One that has reached only ten inches is probably the true 'Alpina', since it is spreading out along the ground (as it is supposed to do) rather than growing up. Catalogues and reference books disagree as to what its ultimate dimensions should be, but the most trustworthy authority says twelve inches by thirty inches. The plant starts producing its clusters of pink flowers in late June and will keep on producing them until fall if dead-headed. It makes a good front-of-the-border or, better yet, edge-of-the-woods-garden plant; small bulbs could live happily among its low, slender, trailing branches.

Beguiled by the jazzy catalogue photographs of a three-foot spirea called variously 'Shibori' and 'Shirobana', which is presented as carrying corymbs of pink, white, and dark rose flowers all at once, I ordered one. When it bloomed a solid dingy white, I ordered two more from two different (and more reputable) nurseries. One of them bears dim pink blossoms while the other tries desperately to live up to the advertisement by making small whitish flowers, a few pink ones, and, when it can manage it, one in dark rose. Last spring, when my so-called 'Shiboris' produced hundreds of seedlings it occurred to me that possibly there was a pretty Japanese cultivar that posed for a picture but is being propagated in this country by means of seed rather than by the proper method of cuttings or division. 'Shibori'/'Shirobana' is sometimes listed as *S. japonica* and sometimes *S. bumalda*. The woody plants expert, Michael Dirr, says it's japonica. *S. bumalda* is an old cross between *S. japonica* and *S. albiflora*.

I had put these shrubs in the border but decided that even though they were the right size and had good foliage (two-and-one-half-inch toothed and pointed leaves on graceful branches) their blossoms did not make them worthy of a place in my garden where real estate is at a premium. I've moved them over to a spot near the house where, from my window on bitter days in October, November, and even December, I can enjoy their marvelous gold-orange-apricot autumn color. The leaves and decorative seedheads hang on through all the early winter storms.

One more spirea in my garden is *S. nipponica*, 'Snow-mound', a four- to five-foot upright specimen whose small blunt leaves are dark blue-green—very attractive. As you may have surmised, its flowers are pure white. This is a shrub that could be used almost anywhere, including the back of a large border—combined with shrub roses, perhaps? It's really spectacular in autumn, when a fire starts at its center, orange-scarlet, that slowly moves out along the blue-green leaves until the whole bush is aflame.

Not being daunted by the disordered spirea scene, I plan to order two new pink japonica dwarfs next spring—one with the slightly off-putting name of 'Gumball', the other with the more reassuring, if banal, name of 'Little Princess'. From their descriptions they sound like perfect border shrubs.

There are lots of two- to three-foot spireas with variegated foliage in yellow, copper, and orange, but they would be for sites other than that of the usual pastel perennial border, it seems to me.

The two- to three-foot shrubby potentillas are a natural choice for mixed borders. Their branches arch out over their neighbors but can easily be clipped and kept from doing harm. My favorite was *P. fruticosa* 'Abbotswood' until I saw *P. f.* 'Gold Star' a couple of years ago. Actually, if you are looking for a shrub with white flowers, 'Abbotswood' can't be beat with its little grey-green leaves and snowy white flowers. It blooms over such a long period that the flowers are a real contribution. I have it near the pale yellow *Helianthemum* 'Wisley Primrose', a white helianthemum, a white single peony with gold stamens, and a pale yellow Ghent azalea. Now I want *Potentilla* 'Gold Star' to finish the composition. 'Gold Star' has the largest, most elegant, back-curving blossoms I've ever seen on a potentilla. Pale yellow. These shrubs come with red- or tangerine-colored flowers as well, although I understand the colors aren't durable or dependable in full sun or during hot weather.

A standard border shrub is the polyantha rose 'The Fairy', and no wonder, since it never grows over three feet, never allows its shiny little leaves to become diseased or to drop, never gets mildew, and tirelessly brings forth its generous clusters of tiny, double pink roses from early summer into late fall. One could complain of its lack of fragrance, I suppose, but that would seem niggling after the performance I've described. The dark-blue globe thistle, *Echinops bannaticus*, grows behind 'The Fairy' in my garden, and beside it is a cloud of *Artemisia* 'Powis Castle' with *Geranium endressii* 'A. T. Johnson' repeating the clear pink of the rose. I've tried a lot of roses in the border—they've come and gone. 'Michelle Meilland' was delicious and I cherished it for the five or six years I had it before it succumbed to a bad winter. 'Golden Wings', 'Nevada'—so many just couldn't make it over the long haul—but 'The Fairy' goes on forever. I'm trying one now that's said to be similar in size and performance—'Sea Foam'. It's a bit lower and broader than 'The Fairy', has exquisite creamy flowers, even in November, and has given me, as yet, no trouble, except for taking up too much space horizontally. I'm obliged to prune it severely every spring.* There's another almost carefree rose called 'New Dawn' that clambers around (or falls off of) posts on either side of an exit from the garden. If all the Japanese beetles in the world would only drop dead this rose would go on blooming more or less all summer, after its initial gala presentation in June. Well, it does go on blooming—to no purpose at all, unfortunately. I hate to see it wasting its time and effort making food for beetles. Next summer I plan to take a tip from the organic gardeners and try to keep the beetles away by planting garlic under the rosebushes.

I keep meaning to put some of the small deutzias in the border. They have excellent foliage, no unneighborly tendencies, and seem to answer the job requirements. They're low, neat, and refined, not greedy, not raucous. *Deutzia gracilis* is a slender, graceful, two- to four-foot Japanese shrub that has narrow, pale green, alternate leaves and trusses of single white or pink scentless flowers in late May. I do have several of the new import *D. gracilis* 'Nikko', in the sunnier section of the woods garden. They are really unusual little creatures. Mine, in their third

---

*'Sea Foam' was later evicted from the border because of its determination to sprawl all over its bedfellows.

year, are about four inches tall and twelve inches wide, but they are supposed to be heading for two feet by five feet eventually. My catalogue says that 'Nikko' is cold hardy for Zone 6 (minus 10 degrees F) but mine have shown no sign thus far of having suffered in my Zone 5 (minus 20 degrees F). I cover them well with evergreen boughs, looking forward to their pure white flowers in spring. I'm thinking of ordering *D. elegantissima* 'Rosalind' for the center of a large loop in the border—it grows four or five feet tall. It's a deutzia from Ireland, has deep rose blossoms in June, and should be hardy. It looks great in the catalogue—but what doesn't?*

Another possible shrub for the mixed border is kerria—not, however, the common one whose dark green leaves and bright orange flowers don't blend well with most perennials. Choose, instead, *Kerria japonica* 'Picta' or 'Variegata', which has, admittedly, orange flowers but they are single delicate little things whose color impact is much mitigated by the fact that they are floating (and for only two weeks) on a haze of pale green and white produced by slender variegated leaves on long graceful green branches. It grows only to two or three feet and is very nice indeed.

One could try small Korean lilacs (*Syringa palibiniana* or *S. meyeri* 'Palibin') with perennials. They might tend to take up a lot of moisture and nourishment but one could plant around them perennials such as lavender, *Salvia memorosa*, or yarrows that don't ask for much in the way of food and drink. They are wonderful shrubs with very small leaves that do not mildew in summer and their little trusses of lavender-pink blossoms, which appear a week or so after ordinary lilacs are finished, are wildly fragrant. The foliage on these five-foot to six-foot lilacs turns a good pinky beige in the fall. *Syringa patula* 'Miss Kim' is

---

*'Rosalind' arrived, was lovingly planted and tended, and died the first winter.

an even smaller shrub and has inflorescences described as bearing pink buds and "icy lavender" blossoms.

The last and possibly the loveliest shrub I have to suggest is three-foot, August-blooming *Caryopteris clandonensis*. Of all the cultivars or selections, I especially like 'Black Knight', though I must admit I haven't seen them all by any means. The one most often planted, one that I saw swarming all over gardens in Hamilton, Ontario (where it seeds itself), is C. c. 'Blue Mist'. This one has grey, pointed, opposite leaves, fuzzy delicate grey-lavender-blue flowers and a rather unrestrained way of floating its branches about. Grows to two and one-half or three feet. Very pretty, certainly, but 'Black Knight' takes a more definite upright shape, has deeper green-grey leaves with grey undersides, and darker violet-blue flowers. I got a nice inexpensive little specimen last spring that grew to its full height of three feet and gave such pleasure, especially while it was blooming with *Sedum* 'Autumn Joy' and *Lespedeza* 'Pink Fountain', that I'm going to tuck it well in for the winter and order three more.*

---

*I didn't order more because my dear 'Black Knight', not being as hardy as 'Blue Mist', perished during its first winter.

To the PLANT BREEDERS—
THANKS and NO THANKS

P eople have been working at controlling plants since the beginning of civilization, at first using the only method they had, that of selection and elimination. They were aided in their work by the fact that no two plants are alike and sports occur in nature. Over the centuries they produced cereal grains from wild grasses, fat succulent root vegetables from field plants with edible but stringy roots, and all the brassicas from wildlings on seashore cliffs. Not a mean feat when you consider that it was all done without laboratories and scientific knowledge. As civilization marched on (as we wistfully put it) gardeners and farmers continued their efforts to produce desired changes in plants—size and flavor in vegetables and fruit, doubling or changing of color in flowers, variegation in the foliage of decorative plants. They experimented with various methods such as controlling light and shade and changing the soil mixtures—old gardening books are full of recipes thought to be helpful in altering plant forms. However, the ability to predictably bring about changes has developed only quite recently.

The biggest leaps forward began with Camerarius's discovery in 1691 that plants, like animals, reproduced sexually. Apparently his contribution was considered to be of intellectual rather than practical interest, for it wasn't until 1719 that one

Fairchild produced the world's first man-made hybrid by crossing a carnation with a sweet william. Still, people seem to have remained unimpressed until the early 1800s when Thomas Knight set forth the results of his hybridizing of vegetables and fruit, and lo—the ball started rolling. Its impetus was greatly aided by the work of Gregor Mendel who, in 1866, published the results of his first experiments with garden peas and his theories of heredity, which in time became known as Mendel's Law. Charles Darwin's *Variation of Animals and Plants under Domestication* (1868) also had a great effect on plant breeding.

Even now, however, not everything is known about the laws of heredity and their application to plant breeding. Certain species of plants may look uniform but are far from it, thus complicating matters for the breeders. Plants reproduced vegetatively (by cuttings or division) are less prone to variation than those from seed. Even plants grown from seed of a self-fertilized plant can vary widely since the plant has inherited qualities from forebears that it may not demonstrate but can transmit to its descendants. Hence, the good qualities of the original plant may in time be completely lost.

Breeders now use many methods other than that of selection and elimination. They cross plants through hand pollination and obtain variations through the use of X-rays and chemicals such as colchicine that bring about changes in the cells of the plant body or generative organs. They can change the color and form of flowers in wild, wonderful, and sometimes woeful ways.

Although doubling of flowers can occur in the wild, it is also brought about in the laboratory. A flower is said to be double when the number of petals is increased, or when the normal disc florets are replaced by ray florets, or the disc florets are greatly enlarged. Often the number of petals is increased at the expense of other organs, especially the stamens—which would explain the sterility of most double flowers. Sometimes the petals are increased without altering the stamens and carpels.

So, how does all this interference by human beings in the plant world add up? One would have to say that the good has far outweighed the bad. We regret that the breeders of fruits and vegetables have, especially in recent years, tended to stress size, appearance, shipping, and keeping qualities over flavor. We've all read about the tomatoes that are bred to be impervious to being bounced. And isn't there a plan—or is it just a funny story?—to make them *square* so they'll take up less space in a packing crate? Plastic tomatoes. Some of us never eat tomatoes until they ripen in the garden or are available at the local farmers market. Same goes for strawberries, peas, corn. But we certainly wouldn't want to have to scout around the fields for wild grass seed in place of wheat. And try peeling and cooking the roots of skirret, an old edible herb, and be grateful for parsnips, carrots, and turnips as we know them today.

There is no doubt that breeders of flowers have also contributed many delights to our gardens—consider roses (especially old roses), delphiniums, and dianthus and compare them with their humble progenitors. Through the crossing of species within genera we have such splendid garden plants as *Achillea* 'Moonshine' and 'Coronation Gold', *Artemisia* 'Powis Castle', *Geranium* 'Mavis Simpson', and many many others. Almost all of our astilbes were bred in Germany, and the garden asters, most of them a real improvement over the field asters, are the result of much work in England, Canada, and the United States. A Swiss breeder produced *Asters frikartii* and 'Mönch'. Wild columbines are beautiful indeed, but we perennial gardeners enjoy all the tall garden hybrids as well—'Snow Queen', 'McKana', and others. Phlox comes in colors much prettier than its original dull pinky mauve and there are improved forms of campanulas, especially of *Campanula persicifolia* and *C. lac-*

tiflora. And don't forget Japanese anemones (*Anemone hybrida*) that give such pleasure in late summer and fall.

Now, having expressed gratitude for all favors bestowed, I have arrived at the *however* stage of my comments and will be thundering out again with protests at what appear to be mistaken priorities among many flower breeders. They are doing two very wrong things: First, they are making fleeting appearance more important than health, strength, and fragrance. Second, they are destroying distinctive flower forms while wantonly creating boring repetitive monstrosities.

In the first category, consider bearded iris, hostas, and hemerocallis, becoming more gorgeous and more disease-prone every year. One trembles for Siberian and Japanese iris as the breeders' interest in them increases. We don't need any more beauty queens to win prizes in flower shows while their siblings back in the garden are keeling over in the first rainstorm, their stems no longer able to support them, their rhizomes succumbing to viruses, borers, and root rot. Consider, too, hybrid tea roses, many of them with no fragrance and no strength to fight back when attacked by disease. And greenhouse carnations that smell like cucumbers or nothing at all—it seems almost criminal to deprive a flower of perfume that has solaced and delighted people for centuries and has been more than half the reason for their having been grown at all. The same can be said for mock orange (philadelphus), now dwarfed, doubled, and often scentless—who would deliberately plant a mock orange with no fragrance? Next they'll be leaching lilacs of their principal claim to garden space. Lilacs get fifty-two weeks of garden space a year for the sake of two weeks of fragrance. Well worth it, too.

In the second category we have the frantic production of flowers, not only in increasingly hectic, unbelievable colors but doubled to the point where one has to search for the legend under the picture in plant and seed catalogues to see whether the mop-headed, globe-shaped pouffe one is looking at is a begonia, a dahlia, a marigold, a chrysanthemum, a hollyhock, a china aster, a poppy, a petunia, or, now, God help us, even a daffodil. The whole point of being a daffodil is to be a trumpet—don't you agree?—but I ask you to look at something called 'Erlicheer' (the name an added offense) in some of the current catalogues. Then there is that fright 'Nora Barlow' that claims to be an aquilegia but looks more like a confused thistle than a columbine. Snapdragons now come with their insides on the outside, some of them closely attached to bush-shaped plants rather than to graceful spikes. Even calendulas are beginning to puff out, and there's an alarmingly fat new coreopsis called 'Early Sunrise'. What's going on? Is more always better, even now when we are supposed to have grown beyond that concept?

The doubling of flowers is not always a disaster. Nature did a splendid job of it with double bloodroot and trilliums—although I refused to believe it of the latter until I saw some. Man-created double feverfew is charming and so are garden dianthus. Where the shape and character are retained and are only enriched by another row of petals, the change is also successful, as in the cases of platycodon and *Anemone hybrida* (*japonica*) 'Whirlwind', both of which are as elegant as the single versions.

Single flat shasta daisies are always effective—clean and forthright, but I don't think many people could fail to be entranced by some of the doubles that are *not* fluffy powder puffs but are merely embellished by crested centers and an extra row of flat petals or by having their petals fringed. *Chrysanthemum maximum* 'Wirral Pride' is one of the better crested types and *C. m.* 'Aglaya' is a lovely fringed one. They are still beautiful because they have not been transformed into non-shastas. The same could be said of the so-called double pyrethrums, which are simply extra-nice painted daisies with a double layer of petals, sometimes with slightly crested centers.

It's hard to make a decision about double helianthemums, but I really do prefer the singles, in this case, because they allow the sun to shine through their translucent petals. The only advantage the doubles have is that they don't drop their petals at noon as the singles do.

So. What right, you may be asking yourself, has an individual to pass judgment so summarily, so high-handedly, on the whole plant breeding industry? Who is to say what is beautiful and what is not? There's the rub. Still, one is certainly not alone in believing that the distinctive character of each plant should be preserved. If changes are made, surely they should be made to enhance that character, not destroy it. If enough people fail to plant the results of the misguided efforts of the breeders, no doubt they will turn their energies to more worthy aims, such as giving us fragrant roses that are hardy and are not debilitated and defaced by black spot. But if masses of gardeners really do like, buy, and plant the distortions I've been damning, of course the breeders will continue on their headlong course. In that case, all we can do is hope that someone will preserve specimens and seed of all the charming old plants we love before they disappear irretrievably.

SHADE GARDEN
REVOLUTION

I t was the summer heat that brought about a change in my
approach to one aspect of shade garden design. Because it
was too hot to work in the sunny border, I took my spade
and wheelbarrow to the woods garden, where it was rela-
tively cool. Things had been running wild there for some time.
I had been happy to have the Virginia bluebells, bloodroot, columbine, anemones, and small bulbs spread themselves around
wherever they pleased and had been merely shoving them aside
a bit when I wanted to add new plants. That deep-rooted fiend,
brunnera, had not been adequately restrained either and was in
a fair way to take over the place.

This summer, as I coolly (or warmly) assessed the situation, it struck me that plants as lovely as *Astilbe* 'Sprite', helleborus, English painted fern (*Athyrium otophorum*), and the 'Roy
Davidson' pulmonaria deserved better treatment than they
were getting. The form and texture of fine plants cannot really
be appreciated, I decided, when they are closely surrounded by
the foliage of other plants, especially the disreputable-looking
foliage of those spring bloomers that, as summer wears on,
abandon any attempt to keep up appearances. The tattered
yellow remains of bloodroot, the limp, dusty August leaves of
that beautiful April flower *Pulmonaria angustifolia* (*azurea*), and

worst of all the bleached, chewed-up rosettes of primulas, don't add a thing to the midsummer shady-garden scene.

So, with the zeal of a reformer, I've embarked on some big changes, liberating the handsomest plants from their detracting or distracting neighbors and making a dramatic frame for them by surrounding them with a layer of fine dark fluffy mulch. There is now a wide area separating the large clump of *Acanthus spinosus* from the rest of the garden. Suddenly it looks regal, impressive. What chance did it have for dignity with waves of big brunnera leaves lapping close around it? And now the delicately incised fronds of 'Sprite' and the long, elegantly silver-splotched leaves of 'Roy Davidson' are given full value against a solid dark background—or should I say underground? No raggle-taggle irrelevant stuff to weaken the impact.

The only problem with this reform movement is where to put the primulas. I can easily sacrifice bloodroot, which, in its zeal for colonization, has been making itself awfully cheap the last few years. Brunnera I'm mining and composting by the bushel, still leaving plenty to cover the dry spots where scarcely anything else will grow. But the primulas?

Do other people's primulas stay tidy all summer? If so, how do they do it? Mine become spotty and yellow, quite hideous, during July and August, before sending up a nice neat set of new green leaves in the cool of September. Can I learn how to keep them from blighting the place in midsummer? Must I spray for red spider? They're already getting more than their share of water and are divided and replanted in enriched soil every year or so. What more do they want? I may have to devise a system of planting them where they can be seen in early spring but not in summer. That would be quite a trick, since they are so low that they need a forward position in order to be enjoyed when they're blooming. If I had a team of gardeners I'd have all primulas hustled out of sight for the hot months, then brought back and replanted in early fall. Some of the British gardeners wag their perennials back and forth, you know—but I'll bet they've got help with the job. Perhaps I'll just cut the primulas to the ground and wait for the better days of September.

Aside from having not yet solved the primula problem I am having fun creating new spaces in the woods garden. I've taken masses of astilbes out from under a pine tree where they were not happy and have replanted them in a damper, more appropriate spot. Someone suggested that instead of replanting the area under the tree, as I had planned to do, with shade-lovers that don't need as much water as astilbes, I should leave the round space covered only with thick pine needles. No plants. I'm thinking it over. It might be as restful as the dark shapes of mulch. Quiet places and planted places—like pools of water and the shore. Serenity. It seems a revelation. Heavens, if this idea runs away with me, what will happen to my great, long, romping perennial border? If I keep going in for quiet places I'll end up like the Japanese with raked gravel and a few rocks.

MAIL-ORDER PLANTS

When a gardener is looking for a certain plant or plants, and they are to be found growing in a nearby nursery, surely it makes more sense to go there and pick them out than to send away for them. Gardeners can see what they are getting and if the plants happen to be growing in real earth the gardener will probably get a big clump of whatever it is for less than the price of a single plant from a mail-order nursery. There are also shipping costs to consider. But if the nearby nursery doesn't have the right plant, the gardener may decide to order it from a mail-order nursery.

I have often thought, as I sent in my own orders, that it must be a very difficult job, that of being a mail-order nurseryman. It's hard enough to grow a great number of different kinds of plants, with all their varying needs, but to then undertake to send them to customers all over this large country with its different climates seems to me a daunting assignment. And think of the complaint letters, fair and unfair!

Most nurseries ask you to tell them when you want the plants delivered. If you give no date they say they'll send them at a time "appropriate for your area." That means they have to have a pretty good idea of what the weather will be like, during the spring and fall months at least, from Maine to California and from Louisiana to Minnesota. And, since most of them ship UPS, which makes no deliveries on Sunday, they have to juggle the shipments so that the boxes won't arrive just before the weekend, when they might have to sit in either a freezing or an overheated storage area before being delivered.

Wrapping live plants for shipping so that they reach their destination in good shape is another tricky task. The nurseries that confine themselves to container-grown plants usually send them, if they are small, in their plastic batteries or growing units, putting excelsior, moss, or plastic packing chips on top or between layers of plants to protect the leaves. Some nurseries remove the plants from their pots and make a round package of each one with newspaper (which system allows the recipient to catch up on what's going on in Ohio, Connecticut, Oregon, or Saugatuck, Michigan). The newspaper swaddling rises up to form a collar that protects the neck and foliage of the plant. It's a pretty good system. Crownsville Nursery in Maryland does the best packing job of all, enclosing *each plant* in a carton of its own so that not a petal or leaf is crushed.

Nursery people who grow plants in the field (and they are becoming fewer every year) send them bare root, either in plastic bags or lying between layers of damp moss or moss and excelsior. These plants, although they may get a bit mashed, are usually larger and lustier than those that are container-grown. They soon recover from their arduous experience and send up strong growth shortly after being planted, unless they were kept in cold storage too long before being shipped. Nurseries used to dig field plants in the spring for spring shipping. Now, apparently, they find it more convenient to dig them in the fall, store them in refrigerators all winter and ship them out in spring, by which time many of them have lost their will to live. Trees and shrubs are usually sent with their bare roots swathed in damp moss, heavy brown paper, or cardboard enveloping them to make a long sturdy package.

Considering all the hazards, it appears to me, after having acquired many thousands of plants by mail through the years, that the nurseries generally do a fair job. It is true that they've sometimes sent the wrong plants, or have canceled my orders at the last minute, or have sent plants that I was sure hadn't even started their trip in good health. But with the exception of only two companies, they have never failed to replace or give credit for unsatisfactory plants that were reported immediately. That's a pretty good score.

So let us suppose you are considering sending away for plants. Should you order in the spring or fall?

Those of us who live in temperate areas of the temperate zone, where summers contain lots of 90 degree weather and winters can provide 20 below and worse, have a hard time deciding when to order plants. Dare we "get a head start on spring" by choosing fall, as the catalogue suggests? "Optimal time ... ground warm and workable. . . ." One may take the plunge and then wait through all the warm and workable golden days of Indian summer, looking for the UPS truck in vain, only to have it surge up the driveway after five days of chilly freezing rain. The same thing can happen in the spring, of course—it might even be snowing when your shipment arrives. "Which is worse," you wonder as you unwrap the travel-weary little plants, "setting the things out in mud or making them wait days for the ground to dry out?"

In the fall it's really serious, since, if the plants have been much delayed, there may be no more warm weather in which they can establish themselves before the long winter battle begins. You cannot afford to hold them very long.

Whatever the season, the first thing to do upon receiving

a plant shipment is to unpack everything immediately. Any plants showing green top growth should be set upright in a cool but not cold place, with their leaves in the light but not in the sun. Examine each one individually to make sure the roots are being kept damp in their soil, moss, or newspaper. You should then carefully cut off any damaged or dead foliage, any flower stems or seed heads, reducing the plant to only the foliage it will need to feed its roots. If you have received perennials in pots they can be held for some time before planting (unless cold weather is on the way), but if they are bare root they should not be forced to stand in their box for more than a day or so.

There is one preservation device I have used when I've received more plants than I could handle at once, and that is to put them in plastic bags in the refrigerator. If they don't have a lot of soft foliage that might turn mushy this works very well—the plants will keep for several days to a week. It's an especially useful solution in the case of plants with no foliage at all. Nurseries often send gypsophila, platycodon, and other perennials with tuberous roots straight from storage where they have been kept dormant, so they have no leaves. In this condition they'll keep in the refrigerator as long as if they were carrots.

You will not have to choose between setting your plants into mud or making them wait indefinitely if you have been forehanded enough to dig holes for them while the weather was yet dry and to store a supply of dry earth under cover. (You can and should dig holes in the fall for trees or shrubs that you are ordering for spring delivery. Prepare your fill-in soil as well and keep it dry.) If the plants are to be lined out you can, by laying down boards, navigate over the mud to their holes without compacting the soil too much. If they are to go into the flower border you will do well to stand on flat rocks or something similar.

But what if you have *not* dug holes while the weather was

dry nor laid away dry soil? If it is fall and time is pressing, I would suggest you dig large holes in the mud and use prepared soil from a garden center for filling in. If you have sandy loam you might be able to get away with using the wet garden soil, but if the soil is heavy clay it will be in big lumps that will be hard to break up. When you finally do manage to batter them to bits the soil will plaster itself around the plant roots, seriously impeding their growth. As one who has jammed a lot of perennials into wet clay with disastrous results I speak with authority when I say, "Don't."

If you haven't dug holes and it is spring with rain or snow coming down or if the soil is saturated, you might solve your problem by putting everything into pots in which they can peacefully wait for better times before going into the ground. When you do eventually plant them, try not to disturb the roots a second time.

There is yet another method for holding plants that you are unable to deal with immediately and that is to heel them in. I've had spotty success using this method with perennials. It seems to work better with shrubs or trees, probably because they are always (or should be) sent in a dormant state and thus have no leaves to be dessicated by the wind and sun. What one does is to dig a shallow trench in the shade, lay the plants side by side with their roots in the trench, then cover the roots loosely with a thick layer of soil. I cover the perennial leaves with pine branches, but still they seem to object to this heeling-in treatment and I am apt to lose some of them. An added hazard is that if the perennials are a bit tender they are sometimes nipped by a late frost when they are not really actively growing. It seems to be harder on them than it would be if they had been properly planted.

Here it might be appropriate to discuss this problem of receiving plants in spring when there is severe weather yet to come. It really is a problem because often the plants come from a region warmer than one's own or they have been raised in greenhouses so must be introduced to the real world gradually.

In the case of trees or shrubs there is really no risk if they have arrived properly dormant. If they have sprouted leaves or buds either before being shipped or en route they are in grave danger. You should promptly notify the company that sent them and tell them you will expect a replacement if the specimens subsequently die. You can plant them and try to protect them from hot sun, wind, and/or freezing temperatures but your efforts may be in vain.

In the case of perennials, if the ground is in proper condition for planting—dry enough and friable—I would advise setting the plants out immediately while the setting out is good, even though a possibility of late frost remains. If they have leaves on them, cover them with pine branches or branches from shrubs or with straw—whatever will keep off most of the sun and wind for a while (a week?) until they become accustomed to their new situation. If a heavy frost is predicted, remove the boughs and cover each plant with a large flower pot, container, or basket to give them more protection, throwing the branches back on top for good measure. I don't think I've ever lost any newly planted perennials from a late spring frost when I've remembered to cover them in time.

It's another matter setting out plants in the fall. Nursery plants from Ohio or Connecticut—to say nothing of North Carolina—are not going to take kindly at first to the winters they'll have to endure farther north. If they are hardy enough perennials for your region (you will have ascertained as much through the nursery itself, garden books, or your local cooperative extension, or all three) it still might be better to get them in the spring so they'll have time to settle in before the cold weather hits them. Here, in what we like to think of as Zone 5,

I order the slightly tender things such as helianthemums and shasta daisies in the spring. Also, the small plants that may easily be flipped out of the ground by freezing and thawing if they haven't had time to get a tight grip on the soil with their roots.

One more thing. Container-grown plants usually arrive with their roots coiled up like watch springs. Sometimes they are visible but sometimes not, being encased in peat moss or gro-mix. One has heard so much about not disturbing plant roots any more than necessary that one hesitates to poke at the little brown bundle. However, poke one must, delicately, with a plant marker or table fork, perhaps, in order to liberate the roots that may be tangled around each other or pointing heavenward. Earthward is where they must point, and it's up to you to help them. In their pots they've been able to survive, even thrive, thanks to constant feeding by the grower. In your garden they're going to have to go searching on their own for nourishment, so they must be prepared to forage. Be sure you see that they get off to a good start.

HELP!

Overwhelmed as we all are these days by statistics on growing crime, pollution, and the general deterioration of the planet and people's morals, we take great pleasure in learning of the growth of worthy, as opposed to unworthy, activities. News of the surge of interest in and involvement with flower gardening all over the United States must cheer those who have deplored the attitude of most of their fellow middle-class citizens who have for long confined their gardening activities, if any, to mowing the lawn and perhaps to "landscaping" their properties, that is, getting some landscaping firm to install foundation plantings in the form of Japanese yews and possibly to plant somewhere on the lawn a clump birch, a dwarf red maple, and/or a pink dogwood. To this display the more ambitious homeowners have sometimes added circles of tulips around the trees, for spring, and for summer, strips of garden-center annuals down either side of the walk to the front door.

People who have had a chance to drive and walk around Europe in a leisurely way have come home to look at American gardens (quite properly called yards) with dismay. Why, they ask, do the Swiss, British, Germans, Dutch, and Scandinavians grow flowers in gardens large and small, in containers on the street, and in window boxes attached to houses, barns, and even department stores, while we, on the other hand, confine ourselves mostly to maintaining large areas of stone, brick, cement, shrubbery, and lawns? Why are flowers sold for little money on the street corners of Europe and for a lot of money in florists' shops here? Why does the European housewife shop for food and *flowers* as if the latter were a staple, while here we buy food as a staple and flowers only for special occasions? It would require considerable sociological research to answer those questions, to find out what happened to the Swiss, British, Germans, Dutch, Scandinavians, and others when they crossed the ocean. What divested them, over time, of their interest in flowers? Was it that simple survival was all they could handle? No time for frills?

We know that many people, women especially, brought bulbs, roots, and seeds with them when they came from Europe and lovingly planted dooryard gardens of herbs and flowers—but for many years now such gardens have been exceptional. An old woman I knew told me that the men in her family objected to her using any space for a flower garden. "You can't eat flowers!" they told her. But we mustn't blame it all on the men. We might blame the climate, which is surely rough enough in most parts of America to discourage all but determined gardeners, and on the wildlife, which becomes more of a problem rather than less as the years go by.

Yet, in spite of these two deterrents, more people every year are now discovering the great satisfaction that comes from caring for, developing, and working out harmonious combinations in real perennial gardens. It is important that these newcomers to proper gardening be given the help and encouragement they need, which brings me, in a roundabout way, to the point of this piece.

In order to help people make up for their lack of gardening experience, many articles and books on gardening are being printed these days. The latter generally fall into two categories—either they are great glossy books containing heartbreakingly beautiful pictures of established gardens (usually in England) or they are businesslike, how-to books full of diagrams, charts, and figures. Books in the first category inspire those of us who, although we have not inherited stately mansions complete with mellowed brick walls, ancient yew hedges, a team of gardeners, and a gentle climate, are sane enough to cheerfully settle for less. We study the pictures and texts, culling ideas from the old hands, using what we can in a small way.

But it is the books and articles in the second category that I am about to discuss. Some of them are extremely helpful to beginning gardeners, giving sensible, simple information about soil preparation, garden design, maintenance—all the basic stuff. Others, I fear, may be losing new recruits either by making gardening sound too easy or, oddly enough, too difficult. There seem to be two currents in modern garden literature. One writer will tell you it's a breeze, while another terrifies you with large amounts of scientific information and complicated requirements. There is the writer who says that a "cottage garden" is the solution to your gardening problems. For this you take up the sod (nothing to it!), then till sand and "organic matter" into the area, install tough perennials, mulch with chipped pine bark, and relax. No more hard work. All you'll ever have to do from now on is enjoy your colorful garden and occasionally divide your plants.

Then there's the writer who recommends planting a "meadow," surely the most difficult gardening project of all—as if you could sprinkle a can full of wildflower seed out in a field and expect masses of beautiful flowers to result. Even if the area is made free of weeds and tilled before planting, the weed seeds already in the soil and those that will be deposited by birds and the wind will produce tough unattractive weeds capable of winning the battle against most wildflowers, which generally make up their own minds about where they want to live. Cornell University did a study on meadow gardens and found that even when the previously prepared "meadow" was weeded for two years after planting the wildflower seed, very few wildflowers remained for long.

It is understandable that vendors of seeds and plants would want to make "meadow" or any other kind of flower gardening sound easy, but what many people don't realize is that many magazine editors want to do the same thing in order to please the seed and plant vendors who will be buying advertising space in their publications. Their writers must accentuate the positive and all but eliminate the negative.

Then why is it that I say that some horticultural writers frighten novice gardeners by making gardening sound too complicated and difficult? I think, actually, that most of the authors who err in this direction are authors of books. You have to say a lot to fill a book.

I remember becoming quite irritated by the authors of books on raising animals that my young daughter used to read. They told her that her horse had to have a wooden floor in his stable, that he had to have expensive equipment, food, and medicine; her dog had to have a special diet, regular visits to the veterinarian, and a battery of pills administered at regular intervals. I realized (but she did not) that the experts who wrote those books were describing what would be optimum conditions for the horse and dog but that the animals didn't necessarily require 100 percent perfection as to care and nourishment in order to thrive—any more than people do. Or plants.

When a writer tells me that "bulbs need a neutral well-

drained soil with a high phosphorus content and these nutrients should be at their root zone or just below it," I would
never—if I took him seriously—put a bulb in the ground. In
the first place how could I ascertain that the soil was neutral
without having a sample tested from each area where I planned
to plant bulbs. No doubt, in order to get the largest, happiest
tulips the author's instructions should be followed, but perfectly lovely tulips, daffodils, squills, and other flowers can be
had by simply chucking the bulbs down into what appears to
be reasonable garden soil. A child could (and often does) do it
without testing the soil or adding phosphorus.

There's a big book on color in the garden that might persuade you that you don't dare put two plants together in your
border without first checking the position of their colors on the
color wheel. I've talked to novices whose self-confidence has
been all but destroyed by taking such material too seriously.
They are afraid they've designed their gardens badly, have chosen the wrong plants and have put them in the wrong places.
They fear their color combinations are crude. When a plant
dies they feel guilty, instead of feeling cross with the plant, as
we old timers do. What *is* this? Gardening is supposed to be
fun.

We should certainly read constantly and search for information on the plants we are trying to raise—find out their place
of origin, their preferences as to soil, light, temperature, moisture—then do our best to accommodate them. We should have
our soil tested, too, if it appears to be lacking in nutrients or to
be inhospitable to the plants we're trying to grow. But since
there are so many variables and inexplicables in gardening, it's
sometimes hard to say what went wrong—or right. It's well
known that a plant may grow for someone but not for the person next door, even when the environment and treatment seem
to be the same. We can but do our best and not grieve too much

over our losses. I did that for a long time until my husband cured me of it with the old saying, "You can't win 'em all!"

And as to the design of your garden and the way you combine colors—again, read lots of books and use your eyes. After that—it's *your* garden. Design it in a way that pleases you; grow the plants you like, combining forms, colors, and textures that are beautiful in your eyes. That's what it's all about.

PROBLEMS *in the* TAPESTRY
BORDER

I
t begins to appear that my favorite kind of gardening has its drawbacks. I've always worked to create what is sometimes called a tapestry border and have steadily ruled out using the current all-American labor-saving system that calls for each plant to stand alone, surrounded by a thick layer of chips or some other heavy mulch. Instead, I've grouped plants close together, chummily, so they can consort, mingle, blend, or contrast with one another—and crowd out the weeds at the same time. When this is properly done it looks wonderful and I don't intend to switch systems; but it does, as I say, have its drawbacks.

In the first place, one daren't set a new smallish plant in the border before it's in fighting condition or one will surely lose it, especially if it's put anywhere near a slob of a plant like *Geranium psilostemon* or *Artemisia* 'Lambrook Silver'. The new plant must have a season of training, of bodybuilding in a holding bed where it can develop strength and self-confidence before being subjected to the battle of life in the border. I've known that all along, but the last year or so I've been finding that even stout seasoned subjects actually do better when left in the holding beds than they do in the border. I have hated to admit it, but it's true.

For one thing they are more likely to remain vertical.

Growing alone in a raised holding bed *Veronica* 'Saraband', for example, makes a fine silver clump, from which the spikes of lavender flowers rise straight up—no flopping, no messy twisted stems. When 'Saraband' is simply one of the mob in the border it's another story. And last summer a stout double helianthus stood by itself in a holding bed, massive and solid, admirably upright, while two clumps of the same plant, in the crowded garden, keeled over and had to be staked to prevent them from smothering their companions.

Can it be that plants behave differently in those two different sites because the holding beds, surrounded by big old railway ties and raised six inches, provide better drainage? Is it a question of drainage or the close proximity of other plants? Or both?

As to proximity, what about the theory we hear so often that plants set close together hold one another up and are less likely to need staking? In this garden it seems to be the other way around. My plants seem to have no notion of comradely mutual assistance; instead of holding one another up they seem interested only in knocking one another down.

Drainage must certainly enter in—but I can't very well raise my whole long border. I do add fresh enriched soil every time I divide plants or move them to new positions, so the garden level is very gradually rising. (Perhaps in another twenty years it will be high enough to please even the lavenders, santolinas, and all the other plants that hate to have soggy roots.)

Several years ago I had in the nursery a gorgeous Siberian iris called 'Swank', of a most splendid, almost true blue (and just before dark it *is* true blue). After selling off the nursery plants, I put the last clump of the iris in the border where, sadly, it proceeded to dwindle away to a few weak leaves. In the nick of time I whipped it out and tucked it into a carefully prepared spot in a holding bed where it cheered up and began to pull itself together. Then one early summer evening a year later, while I was weeding the holding beds, I became conscious of an intense blue glow. I looked up from my labors and discovered that 'Swank' had produced, not only a stout sheaf of leaves, but a flock of divine blue flowers. What a miracle! Now—do I dare move it back into the border?

SEED GATHERING

Do you ever gather your own seed?

We know that most hybrids and some other garden cultivars will not come true from their own seed and must be propagated vegetatively, that is, by means of division, layering, rooted cuttings, or by the use of seed that has been produced by hand pollination under controlled conditions. Other means must also be used to propagate plants that don't set viable seed—plants such as lemon verbena and French tarragon—and most of those with double flowers, which are often sterile.

However, there are many perennials (and annuals) that will reproduce themselves perfectly from home-gathered seed. No need to buy seed year after year for these plants when your own would be just as good—in fact, it will often prove to be more viable than that found in a commercial packet, if that packet has been sitting on a shelf too long. The satisfaction that comes from using one's own seed cannot be accounted for as coming merely from the joy of saving money or having fresher seed. It makes one feel more a gardener, more truly part of the growing process.

Nevertheless, one doesn't go to the trouble of gathering seed and sowing it if the plants one wants more of can be multiplied quicker and easier by some other method. Some perennials are easily divided (some of them, such as chrysanthemums and asters, even *require* frequent division) so it would be foolish for a gardener to try to propagate them by any other means. One stout yarrow will, when wiggled apart, yield fifteen to twenty plants. Veronicas, although they may have to be separated by force and the use of a knife rather than by persuasion, benefit from the operation, and the gardener acquires several plants from one. But there are many perennials that resent disturbance—primarily those with long tap roots—and do not lend themselves to division. Platycodon, the balloon flower, is one of these. Linum (flax), aquilegia (columbine), *Oenothera missouriensis*, some erodiums—and there are others. Delphiniums, while they don't form a taproot, seem never to thrive after division, at least not for me. New plants from seed do much better.

Other plants from which seed might be gathered are those one either does not wish to lift and divide or cannot do so because of their location. There may be an enormous *Clematis integrifolia* in the border that will go on thriving without division and which looks too splendid to touch. One wants to keep it just the size it is. In that case gathering some seed is the preferred way to have more. Or there may be a *Campanula garganica* in a dry wall that not only is looking lovely spread all over the rock face but could not be dug out alive even if one had the heart to try. One can gather the seed, in these cases, and have blooming plants by the second year. Another group of plants from which it is advisable to gather seed are the biennials. Their system of making a plant that doesn't flower until the second year and then dying is fine for their purposes but is less than satisfactory for the gardener who wants flowering plants every year. A gardener who plants seed of digitalis, clary sage, or Canterbury bells for two successive years, thus having one-year-old and two-year-old plants, then makes sure that the seed from the flowering plants is sown every year will have blooming plants every year instead of every other year. Some digitalis and salvias that are listed as perennials *behave* like biennials, so it is a good idea to gather their seed too—the dusty pink *Digitalis mertonensis,* yellow *D. grandiflora,* and the *Salvias haematodes* and *argentea.*

Some perennials self-sow generously—columbines, malvas, feverfew. Usually there is no need to gather seed of these. Other perennials will sow themselves occasionally, especially after a summer of adequate moisture—flax, delphinium, certain dianthus, aruncus, baptisia, lobelias, and sidalceas. But if you want to be sure of having an ample number of new plants the following year you should gather seed even of these enterprising individuals. You cannot really depend on their contributing on their own. Some perennials, of course, never sow themselves at all.

There are a few things to learn about gathering seed, the first of which is to get it when it's ripe but before it has scattered. I usually keep a list on my refrigerator—CHECK SEED OF—then I name the plants that are about to mature seed. The rule of thumb is to wait until the pods are dry and are beginning to open. Time to swoop in with your scissors or pruning shears and a paper bag. Cut off the stems that hold the seed pods or heads, then invert them into your paper bag. Leave the bag open and put it where the contents will dry out thoroughly. *Do not fail to label the bag.* You may say to yourself, "Oh, I'll recognize that—no need to write it down." But several weeks later you may be completely baffled as to its identity, especially if you have many bags of seed. It will look maddeningly familiar but you won't be able to remember what it is. It's not much fun to plant a flat whose label reads "?"

By the end of August my back porch is full of these bags, which are ready to be dealt with. I spread newspapers on the kitchen table and take care of one bag of seed at a time. Some of the seeds are easy to handle, others are more difficult. Some are simple, such as the interesting pods of the so-called Missouri primrose (*Oenothera missouriensis*), whose flat wings pull open like the ends of a Ziploc bag to reveal ribs packed with smooth, easily identifiable seeds. Other plants have a more complicated system; some cranesbills, for instance, have an arrangement that enables long split segments of the crane's bill—the central column—to curl back, then shoot the seeds out from their little compartments, or carpels, at the base of the column. Puzzle— find the seed. I usually have a magnifying glass handy for this work.

Goatsbeard (*Aruncus dioicus*) bears large panicles of creamy white flowers that form two different kinds of dried "seeds." Some of the panicles are delicate with tiny grains along the curled stems and some panicles make heavy broom-like sprays of large grains. For several years I was gathering and planting the little grains that contain no seed at all. With a magnifying glass I finally discovered that the larger grains were actually small seed pods and could be opened to reveal their contents. I, in my ignorance, hadn't known that aruncus is dioecious and that this is its way of handling the fertilizing process.

Flax seeds are contained in tiny round balls that look like coriander seeds. When they are ripe the balls can be pressed or rubbed open to expose the shiny flat seeds packed neatly in their globe-shaped container.

Dianthus holds its seeds upright in elongated urn-shaped pods formed from its tubular calyces. These will be open at the top when the seeds are ripe and can, as a rule, simply be shaken out. This seems to be true especially of mat-forming dianthus. The taller *D. plumarius* often makes you work harder, tearing the pods apart to search for the seed.

Amsonia seeds are amusing—they are packed into long

pointed needles and look like miniature cinnamon-colored logs of wood, several of them, end to end in each needle.

Red valerian seed you must catch before it floats off on its bits of fluff. So, too, the seed of anemones such as *Anemone sylvestris*, *A. magellanica*, *A. pulsatilla*, of asclepias, which is a kind of milkweed, and that of the non-climbing clematis, all designed to be airborne.

When the pink flowers of Persian candytuft or stonecress (*Aethionema grandiflorum*) have disappeared, the racemes that remain produce lots of flat scale-like seed containers, each with one seed inside. Draba, another rock garden plant, has the same arrangement. These seeds are easy to manage but there are others, such as lavender seeds, that are troublesome to try to separate from the fluff and debris that result from rubbing them free. I take a fresh sheet of newspaper and shake all of the material through a sieve. If I'm lucky the seed comes through first and most of the trash stays in the sieve. However, one would like to get completely clean seed, especially in the case of lavender, which shouldn't have any organic matter around it when it's germinating, owing to its tendency to damp off.

The seed should be put in labeled packets and kept in the refrigerator until needed. Be sure all moisture is kept out by means of either plastic bags or jars.

Some annual seeds need not be stored but can be sprinkled about the garden when ripe. Thousands of seeds can be shaken out of the big capsules of the tall glaucous broad-leaved annual poppies such as *Papaver somniferum*. The capsules are just like pepper shakers with little holes around the top. These seeds you can toss around the garden in autumn to have masses of poppies in the spring. Or in the spring to have masses of poppies in late summer and autumn.

However, seed that is to be started indoors should be

planted in early spring in a sterile, moist but not soggy sowing mixture in clean flats or pots. The sowing mixture should be one-quarter to one-half inch from the top of the container as, for some reason, seed germinates better when it is not set down low in its receptacle. Very fine seed, such as that of the campanulas, should be sprinkled on top of the soil, pressed firmly down (I use the back of a soup spoon) and left uncovered. Larger seeds should be pressed down and *just* covered with some of the sowing mix or a combination of milled sphagnum and vermiculite.

Everyone has his own pet system but I've worked out a watering routine over the years that consists of using a fine spray from a rubber spray bulb before and after the seeds germinate but later, when the seedlings begin to grow and send down long roots, soaking the flat from the bottom instead. One must use restraint with both processes, not spraying too heavily and long and not soaking the flat too often. Also, it should be well drained after the soaking. Seedlings always seem hell-bent on suicide through damping off. If your seedlings start to look pale and droopy, chances are you're watering them too much. The agonizing question always is what is too much and what is not enough? You have to work it out through trial and, I am sorry to say, error.

Books often say, "Cover the flat with glass or plastic and put it in a warm dark place." When I obey them the flat mildews forthwith. I *do* put in plastic bags the flats containing seeds of rock garden and some recalcitrant border plants—aquilegia, delphinium, lavender, for example—but those I plant in November and winter over in a shady spot out of doors. The freezing and thawing helps to break the seeds' dormancy. When I bring the flats in in April I remove the bags immediately and put them on heating coils under grow lights. Other seeds that don't necessarily benefit from the cold treatment—veronica, gypsophila, dianthus, and the like—I plant in March or April and put, uncovered, over coils and under lights. The heating coils are supposed to make up for the temperature of the cold draughty room. If the room stayed at 65 to 75 degrees F I wouldn't need heating coils for the perennials. Annuals, most of which are from tropical or semitropical countries, need additional heat in order to germinate.

Some perennials have seed that doesn't retain its viability for long and is best sown as soon as it ripens, even if that leaves you with a bunch of babies to get through the winter in some way. Among these I would include *Armeria caespitosa (juniperifolia); Anemone sylvestris, A. pulsatilla, A. palmata,* and other anemones in their group; and *Clematis integrifolia* and *C. recta.*

I have always waited to plant seed of *Clematis integrifolia* until it was thoroughly dry on the plant, but last summer I read that it was liveliest right at the point when you could, by tugging a bit, detach it from its mop-head cluster. It should then be planted immediately. I planted a flat of seed I'd gathered at that stage and over a period of weeks nearly every seed germinated—a much better score than I'd ever had before. Of course, then I had a tray of potted infant plants to help through hard times in my cold house until April.

These short-lived seeds can, if you wish, not be planted right away but be kept dry in the refrigerator and planted in March. The germination score will be somewhat less in this case.

Delphinium seed loses viability fast, too, so I always gather and plant some 'Bellamosum' seed early in July and have new plants that are big enough to stay in the cold frame all winter. I save enough seed to plant more flats indoors in early spring.

Obstinacy in germination of certain seeds can be handled, as I have indicated, by subjecting them to changes of temperature (sometimes called stratifying), either by using the freezer or by planting them in flats that are kept outside all winter. You can also sow seeds directly in a cold frame or in a raised, prepared seedbed outside.

For real determined obstinacy I would cite trollius (globeflower), astrantia, dictamnus, and acanthus. I believe I've been really successful with trollius seed only once. Otherwise I've had very very spotty results or no results at all. Astrantia, like acanthus, prefers to sow itself and does not often accept human—at least this human—assistance. After coddling, begging, and wheedling astrantia seed for several years, usually in vain, I now have self-sown plants coming up all over the place. I'll be weeding them out next. I can't say the *Acanthus spinosissimus* is that prodigal of its progeny but it has tossed a few babies out of the nest (into awkward places such as the middle of a heather plant); whereas, after crucifying myself year after year extricating the seeds from their thorny coverings and carefully planting them in yummy mixtures, freezing and thawing them and keeping them moist, I have never caused a single seed to germinate. With dictamnus I had one triumphant season— about twenty little gasplants popped up in the coldframe one May. Since then my record has been zero. You live but you don't necessarily learn.

In collecting seed the question always is whether or not it will "come true," that is, produce plants that will be exactly, or almost exactly, like the plant from which they were taken. If you gather and plant seed of such species as wild lupine, creeping gypsophila, *Veronica gentianoides*, or London Pride (*Saxifraga umbrosa*) you know that your babies will turn out to be replicas of their parents, but this is not always the case. Some plants are notorious for their promiscuity, aquilegia being a prime example. If you want to keep the seed of *Aquilegia canadensis* pure, for example, you daren't plant it near A. 'McKana Hybrids' or A. *caerulea* or any other aquilegia for they will all happily interbreed. You will get some beautiful plants but they will not be of pure blood. Dianthus have the same happy-go-lucky attitude, which I didn't realize until I had sold some plants I had raised from garden seed and labeled "*D. caesius (gratianopolitanus)—pale pink.*" When some of them that I *hadn't* sold bloomed I found that they were of a dark intense pink, having crossed with some Thompson & Morgan hybrids I'd had in the garden, called (unfortunately) 'Elfin's Hat'. The cultivar had corrupted my demure little cheddar pinks, and while I was sorry I had sold them under the wrong name, I couldn't help thinking they were prettier than the pure species.

I find that when I sow seeds of the single *Delphinium* 'Bellamosum' and *D.* 'Belladonna' most of the plants come out the dark blue of 'Bellamosum'. All of them are beautiful, so that's all right, but to be sure of getting the single pale sky blue you would have to buy commercial seed labelled *D.* 'Belladonna'.

When I planted garden seed of the balloon flower, *Platycodon grandiflorum*, from pink, white, and blue plants they did not come true. Although I had marked the seed and the young plants according to the color of their parents, they made their own decisions about what color they were going to be, from which I deduce that the bees mixed them up in the flower border. If I had kept the parents far enough apart their descendants might have come true.

Primulas, too, mingle to a degree. The tall oxlips (*P. elatior*) with the low *P. vulgaris* or *polyanthus*. But not *P. sieboldii* with *P. vulgaris* or *veris* or *elatoir*. And not *P. japonica* with *P. denticulata* or *P. denticulata* with *P. pulverentula*. They do know where to draw the line.

The campanula species keep to themselves except for the rare digression, so if you gather and sow seeds of any of the species—*carpatica, garganica, poscharskyana, portenschlagiana, persicifolia, raddeana*, and so on, you will be sure of the offspring's being true to their forebears. This would, of course, not apply to cultivars such as C. *carpatica* 'Wedgwood Blue', C. 'China Doll' and others. The species veronicas, potentillas, and digitalis give no trouble either.

PLANTS FROM WHICH I USUALLY GATHER SEED

Achillea, rock garden species
Amsonia
Anemone magellanica, palmata, pulsatilla, sylvestris
Aquilegia
Asclepias
Campanula species
Centranthus ruber
Clematis integrifolia, recta
Delphinium
Dianthus
Digitalis
Draba
Erigeron
Erodium
Gaura

Geranium
Gypsophila repens
Hibiscus palustris
Iberis jucunda
Lavender
Linum
Lupine species
Oenothera missouriensis
Potentilla nepalensis 'Miss Willmott' and *megalantha*
Primula
Salvia argentea, haematodes, sclarea
Saxifraga
Scabiosa
Veronica gentianoides

AUGUST

Augustis usually a month to be endured, to be got through somehow, but this year it's different. In the first place we've had enough rain for a change. Every time we've started hauling hoses around a rain has come, at least in time to make it unnecessary to haul them to every last part of the garden. In the second place, the Congo weather has been kept to a minimum; there were very few days in which we thought seriously of moving to British Columbia.

As a result of the benign weather conditions, the phlox hasn't even got mildew and is now, on August 21, when it is usually disgracing the garden, looking very fresh and pretty in white and all shades of pink and lavender. I've found it's really true that heat and humidity, *combined with lack of water on the roots*, are what cause mildew on phlox. Heat and humidity don't seem to result in mildew if it rains often and thoroughly.

Since one always complains loudly about August in the garden, I feel an expression of gratitude is in order for this year, and perhaps some comments on what is blooming now, beginning with that never-say-die lythrum, whose performance must have started more than eight weeks ago. Admittedly, by now the blooming ends of the five-foot spikes tend to be only two to four inches long, but they're still very showy—there are so many of them. 'Morden's Pink' has less blue in it than either

'Morden's Gleam' or one that came as 'Dropmore Purple'. There's precious little difference, actually, between the last two, both being a pretty strong, hot purply pink. I've got so I like it, finally—how can one resist a plant that performs so faithfully through the long hot days of summer?

To continue with the pinks, a great find this year has been cleome. Hardly original—my father used to grow it, everybody has grown it, but it didn't really hit me until last summer when I saw it in another garden and realized that it's one of the few annuals that really associates harmoniously with perennials. These that I raised from Stokes seed were called 'Rose Queen' and were robust enough to survive being put as seedlings in the back of the border, where, instead of being overwhelmed by their big tough bedfellows, they went quickly to work and surged up to flaunt their huge blossoms, just where and when they were needed after the delphinium and goatsbeards had left the scene and just before the veronicastrum and cimicifugas began. The two latter plants and the cleome did a lovely job together, and now that the veronicastrum and cimicifugas have finished, the cleome is triumphantly carrying on with the frothy white (really cream) mugwort (*Artemisia lactiflora*).

The blossoms of 'Rose Queen' make loose globes five inches in diameter that occur on upstanding branches, sometimes twelve or more of them on one plant. They appear to have three horizontal stripes because the long pointed buds on the top row are deep salmon pink, the just-opening petals around the equator are paler pink, and the petals on the bottom, beginning to fade, are so pale as to be almost white.

Cleome is sometimes called spider plant because the two-and-one-half-inch stamens protrude far beyond the petals and as the stem elongates and the flower moves up it leaves long, slender seedpods sticking out all the way around, radiating, some of them over six inches long counting their stalks. This gives the flowers a fragile daddy-longlegs look in spite of their size. The plant has handsome, palmately divided leaves.

I feel more than a little embarrassed to be rhapsodizing over cleome, which is a kind of kindergarten plant in horticulturally hep circles. I won't dare show my face at gatherings where other gardeners are talking about edrianthus and cortusa. Still, since one can hardly keep cleome in the closet, it's probably best to come right out and put a brave face on it.

Cranesbills are easier to admit to, even sloppy old *Geranium endressii* 'A. T. Johnson', which is tolerated, even cherished, for the good clear pink of its blossoms and for the fact that it never stops making them. On and on—May, June, July, August—it flings them around wherever there's space and especially where there isn't. Much 'A. T. Johnson' cares what gasps its last under the pink blanket. If there are plants that can be cherished with reservations, G. e. 'A. T. Johnson' falls into that category.

There are still a few mallows (*Malva fastigiata*) that are indefatigably producing pale pink flowers—and *seed* that they are just as indefatigably sowing. I look at them as I look at 'A. T. Johnson', appreciatively but severely.

The flat *Geranium striatum* never does anything reprehensible and has a few delicate veined blossoms here and there all summer after the heavy bloom in June. 'Russell Prichard', a low but not flat geranium, chugs away at full speed the season long, not smothering its fellow plants, merely decorating them with cerise blossoms that keep appearing on long delicate tendrils. Its fellow plants are, ideally, grey-foliaged.

I really cannot decide whether or not I like those big rough pink echinaceas. The ones whose petals stand out horizontally from the cone are certainly prettier than the droopy-petalled sort—the latter look so discouraged, like rhododendrons in winter. It doesn't help much to remind oneself that it's the plant's natural behavior and not a sign of stress. If you have a mass of *Echinacea purpurea* with either horizontal or vertical petals they make such a brave show during the dog days that they might be forgiven for being such coarse plants. However, I'm going in for *E. tennesseensis* next year, having seen it in a friend's garden. A brilliant thing with clear pink *horizontal* petals.

Right now I'm looking appreciatively at the long slim wands of *Linaria purpurea* 'Canon J. Went' that are decorated all up and down the sides with very small baby pink dragonhead blossoms. A double light pink balloon flower and a few rosy dianthus are still putting out, along with several pink roses. 'The Fairy', 'Ballerina', and 'Queen Elizabeth' are getting their second wind just as the double and single pink chrysanthemums are beginning their show.

Little colonies of *Astilbe chinensis* 'Pumila' are huddled in shady places. The muted, somewhat melancholy rose of their short furry spikes is not quite so lugubrious as the murky lavender of their parent, *A. chinensis*, but you couldn't call their color clear, clean, or bright, could you? Nevertheless, this astilbe is valued by a great many of us simply because it waits so long to bloom. If it were to choose June or July for its performance instead of August it would find a place in very few gardens, I imagine, being outclassed at that time of year by all its gorgeous relatives.

The pink Japanese anemones always open long before the white ones, perhaps because they are hardier and don't have so rough a time getting started in spring as the white ones do. At any rate, they are all out in force now in various shades of pink—the single ones, that is. The doubles, such as 'Prince Henry' and 'Margarete', are a bit later.

The color lavender occurs in the border now mostly as a forest of *Verbena bonariensis*, but also, delicately, in *Clematis jouiniana*, in some purple linarias, and—oh, a great gathering of the tall, blue lobelia, *Lobelia siphilitica* which I had the good luck to plant this side of a colony of the above-mentioned Japanese anemones on the edge of the woods garden. What a wonderful combination! The anemones, leaning this way to reach the light (not knowing that they are supposed to prefer shade), are surrounding and peeking through the lobelias like people posing for a group photograph. The red lobelias (*L. cardinalis*) are, fortunately, off to the side.

Two groups of lemon yellow daylilies are still performing, both of them very tall. There are fountains of gaura and lots of *Campanula carpaticas* in blue and white. Some Missouri primroses (*Oenothera missouriensis*) are tirelessly producing a few of their huge pale-yellow cups and, to match them, are small new blooms on the *Achillea taygetea*, which I cut back when it began to look very ratty a few weeks ago. It's still looking less than glorious. Christopher Lloyd takes his *taygeteas* right out of the border when they've finished their main show, replacing them with something else. Not a bad idea if one can manage it.

Caryopteris 'Dark Knight' and that superior globe thistle *Echinops bannaticus* are looking their best, both of them with deep, violet-gray-blue blossoms.

Some of the double feverfews are blooming again, but even more charming are the sprays of tiny white stars on *Euphorbia corollata*. I *do* wish the thing would stand up! By the time it starts to bloom I've just about had it with staking, so it is allowed to lounge around and lean on adjacent plants. It's such an airy-fairy thing that it's not much of a burden on them, however.

Blues, real blues, are found in the annual forget-me-not, *Cynoglossum amabile* 'Firmament' that I sprinkle down the border every fall, and in that dazzling *Salvia patens*. This year there is a lighter, October sky blue one as well as the familiar deep electric blue one. The paler one is called Oxford blue, I believe, but it is almost exactly the blue of *Mertensia virginica*. I've already started saving seed of both kinds when I cut them back. *Salvia chamae-*

dryoides (which, of course, must be wintered in the house) is valuable in the border as a small silver shrub. It's an undisciplined creature, going in for long, twisty, adventuring branches and its cobalt blue flowers are exasperating because you want *more* of them. Perhaps there is a way to wheedle it into being more generous—I haven't yet learned what it is.

But the best spot in the garden at this moment is the place where two very stout plants are manifestly luxuriating—a four-foot-by-four-foot *Clematis heracleifolia davidiana* and, behind it, a four-foot-by-four-and-one-half-foot chelone. Both of these were gifts that I haven't thoroughly appreciated until now. The chelone has handsome, opposite, toothed, dark green five-inch leaves mottled with pale green. The clusters of deep rose turtle-heads are very fat, with light pink showing in their open mouths. Out of the curved top of each mouth protrudes one down-curling white style, looking almost like a tooth. The blossoms are clustered in groups of four to six, occurring, as in candelabra primroses, in intervals up the stem, in this case not forming a corolla but emerging from the leaf axils.

Clematis heracleifolia davidiana (for more, see some "Border Clematis") has the same architectural growth habit as the chelone—with differences of color and detail. The clematis leaves are opposite, large, and toothed and are divided in three with the central one on a long petiole or stalk. The flowers start way down in the center of the plant and recur at each leaf axil up to the top of the stem, where there is a cluster with no leaves, then perhaps, another, and another in an excess of enthusiasm. (The chelone's leaves go on framing its blossom clusters right to the top.) The clematis flowers, in groups of six or more, have blue-grey-violet curled-back petals resembling those of hyacinths and are delicious, heavily scented. The leaves are fragrant as well, especially so when dried, having the same odor as sweet woodruff.

I'm not sure of the name of the chelone, which came to me from a friend who had it from her mother who had it from a friend. It is probably a form of *Chelone lyonii*, although it doesn't answer exactly to the descriptions in books, being taller and having somewhat variegated leaves. Furthermore, the books say it wants lots of moisture and cannot tolerate full sun. My plant (in full sun) never shows any sign of distress during dry hot weather and is not watered any more frequently than the other border plants. Since it grows in a fine shrubby form, holds itself perfectly upright, is of no interest to insects, suffers from no diseases, and blooms for very nearly two months during the most difficult time of year for the garden, it is a real treasure, whatever its name may be.

AUTUMN

Having just about given up on hybrid chrysanthemums except for a few old faithfuls, I decided this last spring to try planting seed of the daisy-form Korean sort. Years ago I raised some of them but later tossed them out in favor of the fancier fluffy hybrids that are called "hardy mums"—hardy in Carolina and Kentucky, perhaps, but not in upstate New York. Now, much chastened, I'm opting for less jazz and more dependability. The Koreans I used to grow made it easily through our winters; let's hope this "Korean Eriso Mixed" seed I planted produces plants as tough as the old ones. They are certainly beautiful.

There seemed to be nearly 100 percent germination of the seed but, with space in mind, I kept only fifteen plants, all of which are blooming this October, having begun in mid-September. Although they're planted out in raised beds that are used as trial and holding areas, rather than in the borders, they've provided a pretty exciting season. Making mounds two feet tall, on an average, their flowers vary as to size, form, and color, ranging from one-half to two and one-half inches across, single or semi-double, in colors that go from pure white through cream, shades of pink, peach, orange, and rose to a dark rusty red. Except for a couple of the pale pinks that are not very distinguished, I love them all and wish I'd saved more.

There is one place in the raised beds where the most extraordinary combination has come about. There is an old mass of *Pycnanthemum muticum*, that delightful aromatic mountain mint that, just as it sets about producing at its apex the amusing little knobby pinkish circles it calls flowers, acquires a hoary white bloom over all its top leaves, a bloom like that on a Concord grape. This phenomenon makes the plant look silvery grey-green. Against it, then, three Korean chrysanthemums, all jammed together, have burst into masses of bloom—one plant apricot, one apricot-orange, and one dark henna red. This side of the chrysanthemums are two low clumps of grass, both of which are short because of having been moved in the spring— a ribbon grass (*Phalaris arundinacea* 'Picta') in pale green and white, and *Imperata cylindrica rubra* 'Red Baron', the dark red Japanese blood grass. Wow. I keep visiting this spot, feasting on the marvelous combination of colors that I never could have planned myself. One's own color arrangements do become such a bore.

I'm also padding up and down the borders with my notebook and pencil, deciding what to take out and replace with the best of the Koreans. *Chrysanthemum* 'Clara Curtis' has done so poorly the last few years that it may be on its way out to make room for the newcomers—that is, if they turn out to be winter hardy, which, of course, remains to be seen.

Some of the 'Alma Potschke' asters are coming out too—I think I've had it for a while with that particular shade of pink. Funny, what you adore for one year, or two or three, sometimes ceases to appeal. It's like having a series of love affairs, luckily not so costly in the way of emotional wear and tear.

There's another new chrysanthemum that I'm going to move from the borders into the raised beds, instead of the other way around, one I begged from British horticulturist Allen Pat-

erson in Ontario one fall. It is *Chrysanthemum arcticum* 'Red
Chief'. It's a superb plant.

I put the chunk I was given in a six-inch pot to winter over
in the cold frame. This spring I divided it and planted two small
pieces in the front of the border where they took off so fast, the
mounds growing bigger and bigger, that, in spite of my trying to
hold them off with stakes, they managed to submerge a *Salvia
chamaedryoides*, a 'Hidcote' lavender, various alpine-type asters,
dianthus, and two big semicircles of lawn. The mounds were
three feet by five feet (surely they were only fifteen to eighteen
inches in Canada?), and about one-third of the flowers were
open when I first sat down to describe them. The open, semi-
double daisies were one to two inches across. The smallest tight
shiny buds gleamed silver in the sun, standing out against the
dark green, elegantly cut foliage. The larger buds were deep
Chianti red before opening to become rosy pink, yellow-
centered flowers. These chrysanthemums are so sweetly fragrant that the bees have been having a September–October
festival among the thousands and thousands of blossoms, flying
frantically from one to the next, unable to settle down to steady
work amidst such an *embarras de richesses*.

Just the same, I mean to make a special place for these chrysanthemums in opposite-facing ends of two raised beds so that
they can expand all they like without doing any harm. Not that
I'll really mind having to resow parts of the lawn after such a
magnificent show.

PUTTING *the* GARDEN *to* BED

hy is it that autumn is for many of us gardeners our favorite time of year? Surely it should
be spring when the big drama begins, at least
for those who live in the North. The long winter
is being forced to relax its grip on us, no matter how reluctantly;
green shoots are emerging through the half-frozen mud, and
we're exhilarated by the sight of buds beginning to split their
winter jackets. This should be the season we glory in; we love to
garden and we garden the most feverishly in spring. But that's
just it—it's so feverish. We love our children, but as I think back
on the days when mine were young, I have the feeling that bed-
time was the nicest time of the day—the last story read, the last
song sung, the last drink of water drunk and lights out. At last.

In spring everything needs to be done at once—now—and
can't wait. We dash about, frequently intending to perform a
certain task, then finding ourselves dealing with five or six others on our way to the first. For example, the list of "Spring Jobs"
says: "1. Divide chelone. Put division in empty space by 'Sea-
Foam'." Good. You get your tools and pry out the chelone, trot
with it down to the designated spot in the border where you
discover that a double saponaria has sneakily moved in to annex
all the ground around 'Seafoam'. You go for a large plastic bag

and fill it with saponaria you've forked up. Where to plant it? You notice an empty space by a shed, near a clematis—but oh! The clematis has fallen and needs attention. Back to the house for hammer, hooks, and twist ties. On the way, you notice that the weeding and edging must be done immediately if there is to be a garden this year at all. The day had started off cold; now it's hot. You must go in to take off your wool tights and put on black-fly repellent, a hat, sunscreen (on top of or under the insect repellent?), and dark glasses. The sun is searing now, but rain is predicted, or possibly snow. But good heavens! Where did you leave that chelone? In order to make it through spring the gardener needs strength and courage.

But ah, the fall! It's the time for leisurely gardening, for pottering about in the warm sun, in the cool golden air. No bugs, no perspiration, no frenzy. No dear plant is calling out for attention now—they are all being quiet and good. The work of dividing and replanting was done long ago in order to give the plants time to settle in and get a firm grasp on the ground before the freezing-heaving-thawing routine begins. Now you go about serenely cutting back spent stems and foliage, digging out dandelions and pulling up chickweed (both of which go on growing all winter), and perhaps gathering seed of important annuals and of perennials you'd like to share without having to dig up your plants. You insert stakes to mark the late risers, such as Japanese anemone and platycodon so as to protect them from damage during the frantic spring cleanup. You write down new plans for the coming year. You might even sit on a bench and savor the scented air and the flaming colors of leaves against the pure blue sky. Catch any gardener sitting on a bench in spring!

This day it's past the middle of November but we're having fine Indian summer weather. I've been tidying up and cut-

ting back delphiniums, feeling, as usual, a bit guilty because—
should I? Some books say "always cut delphinium stems to the
ground because they're hollow and will trap water that will rot
the crown." Other books say: "Never cut back delphinium
stems because they help prevent the crown from rotting." I cut
them back, thinking I might as well be tidy while I risk crown
rot. Actually, I've never been able to tell that it makes any difference; I always lose a few plants whether I remove the stems or
not. I think it's generally not advisable to leave cutting back and
tidying up until spring when there's already too much to do. I
don't, however, cut back the branches of woody Mediterranean subjects such as lavender, thyme, sage, santolina, or helianthemum no matter how scraggly they may have become;
as you probably know, pruning stimulates growth in woody
plants, and if these tender individuals should be encouraged to
stop hibernating and start growing during a warm spell in fall or
winter they might subsequently be killed by severe cold. I wait
until late spring to make them neat.

With a clear conscience I've been removing the brown
shriveled foliage and stems of chrysanthemums and the dried,
stiff stalks of phlox, making sure to cut the phlox at ground
level; hard, sharp phlox stems inflict cruel wounds on the heed-
less gardener in spring. I attack forests of goatsbeard and that
great glorious oaf, *Euphorbia pilosa*, whose stout red stalks are, at
this time of year, the color of the reddest rhubarb. The plant is
surrounded by the several stout posts that are needed for the
heavy cord I use to hold up this most exuberant individual. In
spring it surges out of the ground green, looking like a bundle of
asparagus, then shoots up and up, never stopping until it's made
a five-foot bush, a dome-shaped construction with each straight
unbranched stem clothed in four- to five-inch smooth, oblong
leaves. These stems are quickly crowned with large cymes of in-
significant flowers that are, however, surrounded by extremely

flashy, chartreuse bracts, each inflorescence making a spring bouquet.

My euphorbia was given me by a friend, and so far I haven't been able to find it on anyone's nursery list. I can't think why not. A plantsman told me that it may now be classified as an outsize form of the common *Euphorbia polychroma*.

One of the late-season jobs that really does consist of tucking in plants for the winter is that of spreading a thick blanket of pine needles around the azaleas, rhododendrons, and heathers. Such a gratifying activity—the soft needles look and smell so good! And the knowledge that they will acidify the soil, conserve moisture, protect the surface roots, and, later on, as they disintegrate, provide nourishment for the plants, makes one feel like a ministering angel.

One year, I cut pieces of that fine black mesh they call landscape cloth and put it around my azaleas under the pine needles in an effort to smother the roots of sweet woodruff that had crept in. What a mistake! The following fall I found that new azalea shoots had been coming up and banging their heads against the cloth all summer long. The poor things were bent, pale, and exhausted by the time I, with many apologies, released them.

Another kind of mulch I lay down in late fall is composed of the leaves I've raked up. Some of them I jam in around the base of shrubs, some I pile behind the low stone wall that backs the perennial border, and some I pile on top of the long triple row of hostas that line the driveway. Before dumping the leaves on the hostas I mark the plants with tall stakes so that I can find and liberate them in spring when they begin to send up new shoots. The purpose of the leaf layer in all three places is to keep down the weeds—and, of course, eventually to contribute organic matter to the soil. Because they pack themselves in slimy, slug-infested layers I never use leaves on or around ordinary perennials for fear of smothering their crowns. Even chopped, I should think they might cause crown rot. Since hostas grow from underground rhizomes, I figure they're safe.

I do cover tender perennials, but with evergreen boughs (which allow the air to circulate) rather than with leaves. The boughs help shield plants such as lavender, santolina, heather, helianthemum, and dwarf boxwood from the searing winter winds as well as trapping snow for added protection. The fact that pine boughs also protect mice, voles, and rabbits is a trade-off I have to live with. Since our cat, Sam, has improved his hunting skills, the winter damage caused by rodents and rabbits has decidedly decreased. Still, since rabbits start making more rabbits when they're about two weeks old (I exaggerate, but not by much), steps must be taken to thwart them.

The pine needle and even the leaf operation is certainly more fun than the one of constructing anti-rabbit devices. Around fair-sized trees one can wind that special paper tape, but shrubs and baby trees require fences, and chicken wire is such nasty stuff, rolling and unrolling on its own and viciously attacking you and your plants the moment you drop your guard. I always come in from this job dripping blood and with my temper severely tried. It is nice to walk around later and observe the young trees and shrubs, each safe in its individual cage, even if it does remind one of a zoo.

Aside from mounding earth around the base of the roses (with soil swiped from my husband's vegetable garden) that's the extent of my fall assignments. My neighbors, who have fancy shrubs planted near the road, have also the job of wrapping them in burlap to prevent their being splashed with salty slush. It must help, but—I always wonder—what about the salty water that soaks the ground around their roots? I hope it won't be too late when the highway authorities finally wake up to the fact that salt is dangerous to the health of plants, and that plants matter. Don't they remember that, when the Romans decided to defeat once and for all the troublesome Carthaginians, they covered the Carthaginians' fields with salt?

Another bit of history we seem to have forgotten is that much of North Africa was green and fruitful until the Arabs came with their sheep and goats—browsing animals that destroyed all the young seedling trees that would have replaced the trees the people cut down—and thus changed the climate and made desert out of land that had formerly been productive. Deer are also browsing animals and here in the Northeast and in many other parts of the United States where we have eliminated their natural enemies and have fostered their health and well-being with grain that the mechanical harvesters leave behind, they are not only damaging our crops and gardens but are destroying millions of young trees as well. They must be controlled if we are to save our woods and gardens. All that we gardeners can do at this point is battle doggedly to protect our small bits of paradise. For years, I, like other gardeners, hung out bars of soap and cheesecloth bags of hair begged from a local beauty parlor (my husband said it would be the smell of the shampoo and lotions that would repel the deer, if anything could). I sprayed ugly smelly stuff on the most precious shrubs and laid chicken wire over shorter treasures, and knew that all my efforts were sure to be only partially successful. The herds of deer in our neighborhood are never satisfied with stuffing themselves with the young trees and shrubs in the woods and with the huge ears of corn that the farmer's harvesting machine leaves lying in the fields all winter but must vary their diet with rhododendron buds, the delicate branches of red Japanese maples, and with perhaps a few daphnes and dogwoods thrown in. I grieved not only for my own losses but for the damage deer were doing to the whole horticultural scene; just when Americans are finally becoming serious gardeners they're having to struggle against such odds that those who can't afford expensive deer fencing sometimes give up in despair.

My own problem was pretty much solved when the multiflora rose branches that my husband had stuck into the ground one spring, all along one edge of our garden, grew into such a thick thorny barrier that no deer could penetrate it. Around other garden edges he erected barriers of crossed poles and piles of branches so the whole area is quite safe from deer except for the occasional one that might climb up from the gully or wander up the driveway from the road. Because the ground is cultivated on both sides of the multiflora hedge, the roses are not spreading, and only occasionally do I find one of their seedlings in my garden.

So now, as I look about me, I feel reasonably safe from the perils of winter. The perennials are cut back and the weeding has been done. Pine needles and leaves have been spread and the wire cages are in place around vulnerable trees and shrubs. All the evergreen boughs I could scrounge on our own property have been laid over tender plants and I'll be able to finish covering them after Christmas when we collect discarded trees from in front of houses in town. All the evergreens have had plenty of water and the nonhardy plants have been potted and brought indoors. I gaze out over my handiwork and at Sam, on patrol among the pine boughs, and am content.

FALL *and* WINTER
COLOR

When we talk about fall colors we are usually thinking of the red, orange, and gold foliage of trees and shrubs that make autumn in this country so dramatic. We all look forward to the transformation—almost transfiguration—of the green forest and wayside trees into great flaming torches, and feel a bit cheated if the season hasn't been propitious for the production of much brilliant color or if heavy prolonged rains knock the leaves from the trees before we've had a chance to enjoy them. But there's more to autumn than New England calendar colors, if we open our eyes and look.

Many garden flowers go on blooming into late fall, providing more bright color, but last year I noticed for the first time a more subtle change in foliage and the wonderful color combinations it produced. I had remarked, in other years, a phenomenon that has been observed by gardeners before, that of the rose, pink, and purple flowers intensifying their color as the weather becomes colder. As I walked along the perennial border last October, I saw, without surprise, that the astrantias were much pinker than they had been during the summer; the 'Apricot Nectar' roses that had been cool creamy pale apricot were now almost orange, and the pink cranesbills were certainly coming out in stronger shades. But what suddenly struck me was the change in the greys. They seemed all to have taken on blue tones, or, if some were blue-grey to begin with, the blue was now stronger. The cushions of fine spiky dianthus foliage, the narrow needles of *Lavender* 'Hidcote', and the leathery leaves of a dwarf sage had acquired a bluer look almost overnight. Even the silver and gold-edged grey thymes were really purplish at the ends of their branchlets. The most striking changes were in *Ruta* 'Blue Beauty', whose intricately stencil-cut leaves were bluer and more luminous than I had ever seen them. (The rues were to go on gaining beauty way into December.) In a dark corner, *Lamium* 'Beacon Silver' had taken on a strange frosty-blue glow and had decorated the edges of its leaves with purple embroidery.

I took note of some of the plant combinations these changes had produced or enhanced. In one section of the border there was a splendid rue. In front of it were the white felty foliage and purple spikes of a veronica whose seed I got as *Vitalanata* (but can't find in any reference book). To the right of the veronica was a mound of blooming dwarf *Aster* 'Royal Opal', which has pale, pale lavender daisies with golden or dark rose eyes. Behind the rue stood, or I should in honesty say *sprawled* that glorious troublesome individual *Salvia pitcheri* whose leaves have some blue in them and whose labiate flowers are pure cobalt. Beside the salvia were tufts of the now blue-grey feathery foliage of *Achillea* 'Moonshine'. Behind all of this rose many dark purple and blue spikes of delphinium, putting on their autumn performance. The whole composition was done in related, slightly differing shades of grey, blue, lavender, and purple.

Across the path from this group were several low *Artemisia stelleriana* whose leaves are so pale grey as to be almost white. Next to one of them was a low, three-foot-wide prostrate mound of close-packed opposite, blue-grey, small, ribbed and pointed leaves—*Helianthemum apenninum roseum* (*rhodanthum carneum* or 'Wisley Pink'), one of the handsomest plants I know but looking its most spectacular in cool, fall weather. There was *Santolina chamaecyparissus*, whose grey was somewhat less blue than that of the helianthemum. Between two of the artemisias were a few green-grey *Papaver fauriei*, crimped and compact, and an ebullient tri-color sage (dark grey and grey-rose with touches of cream) and a small bush of *Cynoglossum* 'Firmament' covered with tiny, sky blue forget-me-nots. *Gaura lindheimeri* was spraying airy pink and white blossoms over the whole affair. Behind all of these, the pink was repeated by *Geranium endressii* 'A. T. Johnson' and the low pink rose called 'The Fairy'. Winding off along the front of the border were more artemisias, blue-grey dianthus, silver-edged purply thyme, and some pale pink phlox. More 'Firmament'. That group made harmonies of blue, grey, white, and pink.

What wonderful things a garden can do all by itself and what endless pleasure it gives as it makes all its changes! The variegated dogwood (*Cornus alba* 'Argenteo-marginata') intensifies the red of its stems in fall, which red is picked up by *Sedum* 'Autumn Joy' whose pink flowers turn dark red at almost the same time. The grey-green, white-edged leaves of the cornus seem to accentuate the feathery grey of a froth of *Artemisia* 'Powis Castle' this side of it. The foliage of the sedum, some nearby santolina and lamb's ears repeat, with subtle differences, the color of the artemisia.

As winter moves in we lose the colors we've been enjoying during summer and autumn, but others take their place. In northern gardens, winter color must be provided by bark, berries, and evergreens, as the herbaceous plants have either died back or have been covered by snow or evergreen boughs laid over them for protection. These days, many people use tall ornamental grasses, principally to provide winter interest in the garden. But both inside and outside the garden winter in the north, especially early winter, is in many ways more beautiful than summer; rich earth tones replace those of the flamboyant garden flowers and autumn leaves. We are returned to the essential forms and hues. Now that the trees are no longer simply masses of green their individuality appears. The intricate designs of twigs and branches are traceable against the sky; the many varied shades and textures of bark are apparent once more. Dogwood shrubs with brilliant red or yellow stems can be appreciated.

Walking down the lane in December I look for color and texture. I see that the blue-grey fluted muscular trunks of the ironwood (*Carpinus caroliniana*) are now revealed and the dark gleaming satin stems of black birch (*Betula lenta*) growing by the stream. A clump of aspens display their straight, tall trunks of cool Corot green, striated in black. The young hop hornbeams (*Ostrya virginiana*) have bark of dark purply red that appears to have been rubbed with grey wax. Nearby, black seedheads of rudbeckia, standing out sharply against a background of beige, look like musical notes on an ancient manuscript. The floor of the woods is orange-brown, covered with oak and beech leaves.

The far-off maple woods are silvery below with a rosy swath of twigs above—the buds all ready for next spring. In the middle distance, the red is repeated in the plum-colored arching stems of black raspberry bushes, the dark plum being covered with the grey bloom that is found on grapes and some other fruits.

Cedar trees (*Juniperus virginiana*) that close-up are a dingy, repellent yellow-green, look an elegant bottle green, almost black, in the distant maple woods. Behind the woods rise hills and fields of buff, beige, dun, and terre verte, outlined with hedgerows and interspersed with woods that alternate between being pale lavender-grey or dark—what is called in artists' colors "Payne's grey"—a smoky, inky blue-grey, depending on whether the sun is shining on them or not. Above all, the sky is three or four different shades of grey with one slice of blue and a luminous gold streak. Against it are silhouetted the black and umber trunks and branches of closer trees. In the hedgerow there is every shade of brown, from pale buff through burnt sienna to deep rich darkest burnt earth color.

Later, when walking through the fields after snow has fallen, one sees that each blade of dried grass, each twig, each burdock and teasel has been glorified, taking on the elegance of the brush strokes in a Chinese painting. Queen Anne's lace, whose dried seedheads have curved upward to make small filigreed goblets, are full and brimming over with snow; an abandoned slope looks like a field of cotton or a meadow full of winter flowers, white, gold-stemmed against the dark blue-grey woods. The dangling willow branches are dark yellow and the corn stubble in the fields shines golden ochre in the long slanting theatrical winter sunlight. The sky behind it is bluer than it is at any other season—a deep endless blue. It is, as Willa Cather put it, "a blue to ravish the heart—a limpid, celestial holy blue."

PART TWO

TIMELESS PLANTS—SOME

OF MY FAVORITES

COLUMBINES

When I was about ten years old I wanted a gift to take to a teacher I loved. My mother generously ravished her garden of several dozen long-stemmed, long-spurred columbines in shades of sky blue, mauve, pale pink, light yellow, and white. As she lifted them to lay them in the box she said: "Look at them—they're more beautiful than orchids!" So, for the first time, I really looked at them. She was right. Above their scalloped, slightly grey-green foliage, they hung like butterflies, like dragonflies, hummingbirds. They flew, they floated. They were delicate, almost ethereal, with their translucent petals, their long slender spurs, their pale lovely colors, their fragility. They seemed to be barely attached to their stems, barely earthbound. No wonder they were named "aquilegia" for the eagle and "columbine" for the dove.

No doubt my mother's columbines were 'Mrs. Scott-Elliott's Hybrids', which came in pastel colors only, as I recall. That strain seems to have been replaced by 'McKana Hybrids' and newer ones of more intense color—'Red Star', in bright red and white, 'Spring Song' ("extra large flowers . . . in bold colors") and 'Music', of medium height and "striking" combinations of color. Of the newer hybrids I have had only the 'Mc-Kanas' in my garden—bicolors they are, and very beautiful, especially one that combines a deep plum color with smoky lavender.

I have had for years groups of *Aquilegia chrysantha*, a three- to four-foot native of New Mexico and Arizona. One expert gardener calls it gawky and says it should be grown among shrubs but horticulturist Graham Stuart Thomas and I think it elegant. It's pale yellow and not only long-blooming (through all of May and June until the heat of July knocks it out) but also long-lived for a columbine. I must have had the same plants for six or eight years.

I wish the Colorado columbine, *A. caerulea*, were half so sturdy. I nourish myself with its beauty while it lasts; a summer or two of its creamy white petals and grey-lavender-blue sepals is all I get, then I must start again. No doubt it misses the cool, dry mountain air. Both *A. chrysantha* and *A. caerulea* have been used to breed many of the tall columbine hybrids.

Another yellow native that has contributed to the modern hybrids is *Aquilegia longissima*, a three-foot plant from Texas and Mexico. Its spurs are from three and one-half to six inches long, making it attractive to breeders. I've been wondering whether the big yellow aquilegia sold, both as seeds and plants, under the ill-chosen name of 'Maxi-Star' is really *longissima*? I cannot now find the old catalogue in which I read that 'Maxi-Star' is a native of Texas. It's a splendid subject, flashier than the yellow *chrysantha* but neither so long-blooming nor so long-lived.

Hybridizers have used *Aquilegia formosa* as well, this one from the Northwest. Its petals are yellow and its spurs and sepals coral to bright red. It must be somewhat similar to the wild columbine we're familiar with in the Northeast, *A. canadensis*, except for ours being smaller and daintier, with more slender blossoms. *A. canadensis* loves rocks, often hanging from cliffs in the gorges hereabouts, but I have a friend with a paved court into which this plant has moved and seeded itself in all the available interstices. It's a pretty sight in spring, and later, too, as the foliage remains dark and thrifty-looking all summer, unlike that of the big border columbines.

Aquilegia 'Snow Queen' vies with *chrysantha* in both length of blooming time and in longevity. I no longer have it in my border but I did for many years and must start it again. It's tall, pure white with medium long spurs, obviously developed in Germany since its alternate name is 'Schneeköningen'. I've also grown 'Mrs. Nicholls', a deep blue strain, no doubt derived from *caerulea*. It seems to have disappeared from seed lists along with 'Mrs. Scott-Elliott'.

The British are very sentimental about what they call granny's bonnets, *A. vulgaris*, a vigorous three-foot native of the Welsh valleys and parts of Europe. The purple or pink flowers on this species look dumpy compared with the ones I've been describing, being wide of girth and short of spur. Nevertheless, since some have come up in my woods garden I, like the British, have found it hard to pull them out; there's something appealing about them. If I don't harden my heart, they'll crowd out plants that I like better, since they're determined self-sowers. There's one *vulgaris* I'd like to get hold of—*A.v. nivea*, called the 'Munstead White'. It's said that in a contest of glaucous-foliaged plants it would win with the greyest leaves of all. It has pale stems and buds and pure white flowers. Of course, I think if Miss Jekyll liked it I would like it. (But it's not necessarily so—I dislike her beloved yuccas, for example, except in a semi-tropical setting.)

Long ago *A. vulgaris* was crossed with *A. alpinus*, a ten-inch blue or blue and white plant from Switzerland, producing the 'Hensol Harebell', another cottage garden favorite. This one is usually deep Wedgwood blue, but sometimes blue and white and even plum, pink, lilac, or white, on account of its granny's bonnet blood. It has handsome dark foliage and seeds itself about generously, filling in bare spots, especially bare rocky spots.

Among the new columbine hybrids there are some that one might wish hadn't been created. I haven't seen the 'Biedermeyer' dwarfs (ten inch) in bloom but some discerning critics have called them ungraceful and stumpy. Certainly, from the pictures, the new fifteen-inch 'Fairyland' hybrids deserve Graham Stuart Thomas's comment that they're an "abomination." He says they have lost all beauty of floral shape. I've been fretting about *Aquilegia* 'Nora Barlow' since I first saw it advertised— the flowers have been doubled to the point where they look nothing like aquilegias but something like thistles or astrantias. If they were astrantias I might like them. My antipathy is partly outrage that anyone would commit such violence on a flower with so uniquely lovely a form.

There are about seventy species of aquilegia, most of them from mountainous regions in the northern hemisphere. (They are of the buttercup family, *Ranunculaceae*.) Some of them are natural dwarfs that are cherished by rock gardeners. Most of them, actually, seem to be more yearned for than cherished, as the Alpine sorts are extremely difficult to console when deprived of their perches on screes, crags, or stone deposits near icy streams. Many a rock gardener has nearly broken his heart trying to compensate a tiny individual from the American West called *Aquilegia jonesii* for such a lack. It is described, almost tearfully, in rock garden books as having a one- to three-inch spread of downy silver foliage and one small, rich deep-blue flower to each two-inch stem. When it has flowers, that is.

Linc Foster says that not only do most alpine columbines take two years to germinate but, when raised in a rock garden, they either "grow fat and wheezy, short-lived and pale, or they intermarry with the undistinguished to gain longevity and awkwardness."* Furthermore, it's difficult to find seed that is really that of the alpine offered unless it was gathered in the wild, the besetting sin of columbines being their willingness, even eagerness, to breed with any other columbine of whatever species that happens to be growing nearby.

Some of the alpine species are less demanding than others and are certainly worth a try. From the Altai Mountains in Siberia there is eight- to ten-inch *A. glandulosa* that, if planted in a sunny, sheltered, humusy spot, will celebrate with large, bright Oxford blue and white flowers. There's a white variety of this, *A. jucunda*, that the Royal Horticultural Society dictionary says is almost sure to come true from seed.

There are two from the Rocky Mountains in Utah, *A. saximontana* and *A. scopularum*. *Saximontana* is a little gem with grey, twice-divided leaves ("crinkly, bluish foliage") and pale blue and white nodding flowers on four-inch stems. It wants coarse limestone soil in sun or light shade, and I am actually growing it in a raised bed. It's not easy but easier than *jonesii*, says Walter Kolaga, somewhat bitterly.† *A. scopularum* has three-lobed glaucous leaves growing in tufts and carries pale blue flowers with long slender spurs. It wants coarse limestone, like *saximontana*, but full sun.

It is apparently not impossible to harbor the ten-inch *Aquilegia alpina* (mentioned earlier), which is also blue and white, with short curved spurs. There's a slightly larger variety of this, *A. a. superba*. One from France and Italy, called *A. bertolonii*, is about a foot tall when flowering, its two-inch rich purple, short-spurred blossoms rising over a tuft of greyish foliage. Kolaga cheerfully calls this one "a dandy."

---

*H. Lincoln Foster, *Rock Gardening* (New York: Bonanza Books, 1968), p. 137.
†Walter A. Kolaga, *All About Rock Gardens and Plants* (New York: Doubleday, 1966).

I once bought seed for *A. pyrenaica* but am not sure that's what I received, for it wasn't particularly pretty and Foster says that in its true form it is one of the most beautiful columbines. Deep blue, short-spurred flowers on six-inch stems above dark green foliage.

Lots of us raise the Japanese *Aquilegia flabellata*, a plant with thick, creamy blue-grey fan-shaped leaves. Its chunky blossoms have purple-blue sepals and spurs and white petals, the colors and shapes combining perfectly. For a while *A. f. nana* 'Alba' grew here—it's a shorter one with lovely pure icy white flowers. *A. f. pumila* is the same as one sometimes listed as *A. akitensis*, a six-inch version of the ten-inch *flabellata*.

I grow a Chinese plant with the amusing name of *Semiaquilegia ecalcarata*, which I now find goes around sometimes as plain *A. ecalcarata*. It's a dear thing with miniature brownish-purple or dregs-of-wine colored spurless columbine flowers above lacy darkish columbine foliage. Mine are usually eight to ten inches or less, but the books say they can attain twelve inches. I haven't yet tried another murky one with green and brown flowers, twelve-inch *A. viridiflora*.

Considering columbines as a whole, you might ask yourself if they are worth growing. Their shortcomings are many. They interbreed, they are subject to crown rot and are quite short-lived. The border varieties care nothing for their appearance after they've finished their show for the year and allow all their outer leaves to turn yellow. Unless steps are taken to prevent it, their green leaves are defaced by leaf miners, and the last few years they've become the favorite food of armies of small green worms that cleverly creep under the leaves where they can't be seen and chew them to the bone overnight. (I am told the insecticide Dipel will take care of them, but when I remember to sprinkle systemic granules around them every few weeks I have no trouble with either miners or worms. My organic daughter is teaching me to use Bt—*Bacillus thuringiensis*—to combat the worms.) Columbines don't like to be moved, can't be divided or reproduced readily from cuttings, and, while they come up enthusiastically from seed they have sown themselves, they take the devil of a time to germinate from seed you have planted in a flat, even when you've done it properly, just pressing it into the surface and not covering it.

As to virtues—ah, well, the virtues far outweigh all the faults. Yes, they are short-lived, but better a short life and a good one than a long, dull haul. Better a brief dancing columbine than a permanent stodgy pulmonaria say, or an old faithful, boring hosta. As to their interbreeding, it should be possible to keep separate species far apart, if one's garden is large enough.

To non-purists like me their proclivity for promiscuity has an advantage I appreciate, that of producing surprises every spring, color combinations I've never seen before. I had a group of the red and yellow *A. canadensis* in my woods garden, far enough away I thought, from a few 'McKana Hybrids' introduced later. But no—they all mingled merrily, probably adding a few genes from some dark blue *vulgaris* in another corner, until now there is a columbine festival every spring at that end of the garden. Columbines in pink and white, blue and white, dark solid red, pale yellow and blue, wonderful peach colors and apricot, even a semi-double pure blue. All of this with no trouble on my part. Could one ask for anything more?

LYSIMACHIAS

It is frequently the case that owing to the misbehavior of some members of a family the whole family acquires a bad reputation—especially among those who know only the black sheep. As with people, so with plants. Take veronica, for example, whose good name has been ruined by *Veronica filiformis* and *serpyllifolia*, those relentless invaders of lawns, causing beginning gardeners to steer clear of the whole genus. Thus those amateurs who have been presented with fat clumps of *Lysimachia punctata* by generous neighbors may well feel somewhat apprehensive when considering the acquisition of any plant whose first name is lysimachia. They will learn in time that there are both ruffians and aristocrats in many families, and that each member must be judged on his—or its—own merits.

Actually, the roughneck lysimachias have their virtues and are very fine plants for special places—none of which is, in my opinion, the perennial border.

Lysimachia was so named by Dioscorides after King Lysimachus of Thrace. I don't know what he did to deserve the honor and only wish that Dioscorides had picked someone whose name had fewer than five syllables. My reference book says it is to be pronounced "Lye-sih-MAK-ee-uh," but I go on saying "Lih" instead of "Lye." Surely there is room for personal preference in these matters?

Unfortunately, the common name for lysimachia is "loosestrife," which is also used for the genus lythrum. Now lysimachia belongs to the primrose family or *Primulaceae*, while lythrum is of the Lythraceae or loosestrife family—they are not related at all. Hence lysimachias, some of which are commonly referred to as loosestrife, have no connection, botanically, with purple loosestrife (*Lythrum salicaria*), the troublesome immigrant that is invading our wetlands. Sometimes it seems as if people have deliberately created confusion where none need exist.

Of the 165 lysimachia species that can be found in all regions having what is loosely referred to as a "temperate" climate, I will deal with only six, beginning with those that are best known.

All of the tall lysimachias grow in sun or part shade, and while they all do best in a wet location, they are all too willing to put up with ordinary garden conditions. In many years of experience growing these plants I've never known them to suffer damage from disease, insects, or four-footed predators.

Undoubtedly, the one most planted is *L. punctata* or yellow loosestrife, which quickly forms stout straight stems, one and one-half to two feet tall, clothed with leaves three to four inches long, crinkled and lance-shaped, either opposite or in whorls. From the axils of these leaves appear, in midsummer, starry one-inch bright yellow flowers. Although it comes from Europe, yellow loosestrife feels very much at home in America and will with the slightest encouragement advance in all directions, adjusting to almost any situation in which it finds itself, never succumbing to disease, insect attacks, drought, or poor soil. It *may* be vanquished by weeds eventually, if it is in a dry place and is utterly neglected. But with the minimum amount of attention, you may grow this plant on the edge of a woods, against a fence, or in some other semi-shaggy spot that you'd like to decorate. By a pond it would be completely happy, growing taller and taking on more territory without restraint. Fat clumps of *Rudbeckia* 'Goldsturm' (or better yet, that prettiest of all black-eyed Susans, *R. triloba*, a biennial whose masses of small blunt-petaled orange blossoms will delight your eye for many weeks) could be planted nearby, as well as some of the more interesting grasses. The rudbeckias will be beginning to bloom just as the yellow loosestrife is finishing, so you'll have a long season of color.

Another candidate for the edge of a pond or stream (although it will grow in dryer locations) is the Asian *L. clethroides* or gooseneck loosestrife, an intrepid individual that manages to combine most undisciplined behavior with an aspect of perfect elegance. It stands almost a foot taller than *L. punctata*, its stems carrying smooth leaves that come to a point at both ends. Its common name is very apt, for its tiny white blossoms are closely packed on a tapered terminal spike that curves gracefully over and down, very much in the manner of a goose's neck—or better, that of a swan. The blossoms last well in water and provide marvelous material for flower arrangers. If grown in the sunny wet locations it loves it will attain four to five feet in height and will bloom from July to September. The leaves turn to rich gold in autumn.

If you can keep the lysimachia from overrunning them, you can install Japanese iris (which will enjoy the same sunny, damp location) as companion plants—although I'm not sure that "companion" is a word that can be properly applied to these lysimachias, plants that are more interested in the survival of their species than they are in friendship. With such individuals one must decide whether one loves them well enough to struggle with them or not. If gooseneck loosestrife is planted by itself near a stream or pond it will be able to take care of itself and will cause the gardener no concern. If, however, it is used as one element in a mixed planting, either by a pond or in the perennial border, constant care will be required to keep it from creeping into and eventually demolishing its neighbors. Each spring the gardener will have to attack the clump or clumps of loosestrife, either lifting and dividing them before resetting pieces of them or, by going around each clump with a spading fork, lifting up the traveling roots and cutting them off. The first method is more effective, obviously, and will slow the plants down for a longer period. Some gardeners sink these and other aggressive plants into the ground in bottomless containers, but I've found the method unsatisfactory—in fact a lot more strenuous than the two solutions mentioned above, since, eventually, the ingenious plants will either go over the top of the container or roots will go out through the bottom to work their way quite swiftly to the surface. I've found that, with *Artemisia* 'Silver King', at least, the plants do not remain baffled for long and the whole contraption has to be dug up by the summer following its installation—a much more difficult job than digging out an unconfined plant.

If you decide to take on this species, you will be paid for your pains by the sight of its gracefully arched and tapered racemes of white blossoms—especially if you plant them against the wine-dark foliage of *Clematis recta* 'Purpurea' or the cimicifuga with similarly colored leaves—*Cimicifuga simplex ramosa* 'Atropurpurea'. Smashing.

A native of the northeastern United States, *Lysimachia ciliata* doesn't seem to me to be worth growing anywhere but in a wildflower collection. Its slender, tapered, four- to six-inch leaves are pleasant enough, but its small, nodding pale yellow flowers, borne in the leaf axils, don't compensate for all the space it quickly appropriates in the garden. However, the purple-foliaged version of this plant is another story. Those of us who love to work with purple foliage are willing to put up with the unbridled enthusiasm of *L. ciliata* 'Purpurea' because of its glossy wine-colored six-inch leaves that combine so well with silver, sulphur, and cadmium red. Admittedly, the handsome ruby tuffets that appear in spring, both where you planted them and where you did not, grow taller and exasperatingly greener as the season progresses. One writer says they can be cut to the ground in midsummer, after which they will surge up red again. I plan to be brave and try it next summer, even though it will surely leave a great gap in the border between the time of the chopping operation and the rebirth. Because the foliage of this plant is most dramatic in early spring, I have used the lemon yellow *Trollius europaeus* and *T. cultorum* 'Lemon Queen' for color contrast. Some dark velvety red—almost black—*Primula* 'Cowichan' grow nearby, picking up the red of the lysimachia leaves and intensifying it.*

But of all the tall lysimachias, *L. ephemerum* is unquestionably the queen. This noninvasive individual is seldom seen in our gardens—I can't think why, unless it is because it is designated for Zones 6 to 7 by the writers of reference books. Actually, it does very well in Zone 5 here in upstate New York, only occasionally failing to come through the winter. It seems to be

---

*When *Lysimachia ciliata* 'Purpurea' had been growing in several places in my garden for several years, confining itself to making colonies of an acceptable size, it underwent a character change. Suddenly, the colonies began to spread sneakily underground. Last spring I found them cheerfully flaunting their red rosettes (attached to stout hairy roots and stolons) among the phlox, delphinium, and monkshood—all the plants that grew nearby. Enough is enough, thought I, and went to fetch my two-pronged mattock. I did what I thought was a thorough job of destruction, but later in the summer I found red rosettes settled in comfortably among all the new plants with which I had replaced them.

more averse to heat than to cold, for plants in full sun during a hot, dry summer may very well dwindle or even die. The best location for them is in a spot where they will be sitting in fairly rich, moist, well-drained soil and receive filtered or only morning sun. There they will luxuriate, displaying their tall rosettes (if there is such a thing) of glaucous, stemless leaves, some of them as much as ten inches long. These leaves are grey-green with a golden undertone and an ivory midrib—the rosette effect being produced by their occurring in opposite pairs pointing in opposite directions up the one and one-half foot stems, of which there are usually three to a plant. From this most attractive foliage rise, in June, straight slender spires covered all around with small white outfacing flowers. These will endure for many weeks and seem never to flop over, even when it storms.

Finally, I'd like to mention two good little creepers. The first, *L. nummularia*, creeping jenny or moneywort, makes a fine ground cover in semi-shaded areas where it will gently blanket small bulbs such as scillas and species tulips which would be overwhelmed and extinguished by stronger ground covers such as vinca, English ivy, or pachysandra. Its small round one-inch leaves do resemble coins, making it quite appealing. It will naturalize in shady places along a stream, running and rooting from prostrate stems. In fact this European native has gone wild in some parts of America. Golden moneywort, *L. n.* 'Aurea', is the same thing in yellow, that is, the leaves are yellow rather than green. Both moneyworts carry cheery yellow flowers in their leaf axils from May to September, if they are pleased with their location.

An even smaller creeper, as you can tell by its name, is *L. japonicum* var. *minutissimum*, so small it's almost moss-like. It produces tiny yellow flowers and is a gem of a plant for the edge of a woodland garden, keeping company, perhaps, with its fellow countryman, delicate four-inch *Thalictrum kiusianum*, and possibly a spread of hardy cyclamen.

Against a grey shed I have created what I tell myself is a very classy composition with a group of *Lysimachia ephemerums*, tall, pearly, pale creamy yellow daylilies, helictotrichon (a mid-height, blue-grey grass), and pale lavender-blue and white campanulas (*C. carpatica*) as well as blue *Festuca glauca* and the intricately incised grey *Glaucium flavum* in the foreground. Floating over and around the whole affair are the lacy white leaves of *Senecio leucostachys*. Up the shed, behind these lovely things, clamber two clematis, one lavender and one yellow (*C. tangutica*). I look at this little garden and think that James McNeill Whistler would have approved.

SOME BORDER
CLEMATIS

If you say "clematis" to the average citizen, the picture that will undoubtedly come to mind will be that of a vine, covered densely with large, flat, purple flowers. This is perfectly reasonable since *Clematis x jackmanii* must clamber up more American trellises and front porches than any other of the hundreds of clematis that exist. People who have gardened for a while will have discovered that large-flowered clematis, single or double, come not only in purple but in white and many shades of rose and blue, some of them with striped petals. These gardeners, like me, may even have learned, with a feeling of faint dismay, that what we take to be petals are really sepals. And they will have found that there are many small-flowered clematis, most of them species rather than cultivars (that is, nature-made rather than man-made or propagated) whose blossoms are frequently urn-shaped or in the form of little shredded bells. The next stage for those who become interested in clematis is to discover that not all of them are vines. Some are semi-woody climbers (or trailers) that go as high as six to eight feet and some are simply herbacious perennials with no tendency at all to travel onward and upward.

In my garden, the one plant visitors are sure to ask about is a non-climbing clematis—*C. integrifolia*. While we are always being urged to acquire whatever might prove to be a "conversation piece," it is not for that purpose that I grow this clematis and urge others to do the same. It is simply a very fine plant, as are the other border clematis discussed here. They are not vines, although it's true that three or four of them seem to *wish* they were vines and make no effort whatsoever to stand on their feet after the first month or so of the growing year. One of them even sprawls on the ground from the beginning—but they are herbaceous perennials and not vines, all the same.

The conversation piece comes from southern Europe and grows to no more than two and one-half feet in my garden, although those who must know say it can go as high as five feet. What it would take to make it do that I can't think, but since I don't want it that tall I'm not going to start dousing it with Rapid Gro. The plant has what one book calls "wiry, vining stems," which is a perfect description of them. Dozens of these stems emerge in spring, and as they grow and produce their slender, undivided, veined and pointed pairs of leaves, these do a most endearing thing—the two on the top of the stem cup together, pointing up, like a pod, or more like a pair of praying hands. When they open, they reveal another pair, set in the opposite direction. This goes on until some time in June when the last pair of hands to open contains a flower bud that looks like a dark blue pointed pod. As it opens, it turns itself upside down so that its urn-shaped flower, consisting not of petals but of four slightly twisted, upcurving, indigo-violet sepals, shyly conceals its center—a compact wad of cream-colored cottony stamens. A strange and wonderful flower. The plant bears its blossoms for many, many weeks, and when the fluffy seed heads take their place, they are almost as attractive as the flowers until the plumed seeds gradually float off on the wind.

I have several plain C. *integrifolia*s and one C. *i.* var. *caerulea*, whose flowers are a bit bluer than the others. I wish I had one called 'Hendersonii', which is sometimes listed as an *integrifolia* cultivar and sometimes as *C. eriostemon* 'Hendersonii', *eriostemon* being a cross between *integrifolia* and *C. viticella*. Whatever its parentage, it's similar to the species except that the flowers are larger, deeper blue, and are produced over a longer period. It's probably just as hard to make presentable as mine, whose "wiry, vining," semi-woody stems collapse as soon as they've attained one inch in height. One is told to prop them up with pea sticks. So far I've been using various kinds of metal hoops but am far from satisfied with the effect. If it were planted among some of the floppy cranesbills they could all just let everything go together. Maybe I'll try that next.

That's the system—or non-system—they use at the Cornell Plantations with *Clematis recta*. They give it a circle of space about five feet in diameter and let it collapse when and where it wants to. It looks something like an unmade bed, or perhaps an ostrich's nest.* There's something to be said for not fighting a plant's natural inclinations. The only trouble with giving *C. recta* its head in my border is that I don't have a slope and I'm not willing to spare it a five-foot circle all to itself. I've found that if it is moved in the spring it behaves perfectly when grown through a tomato hoop—it just surges up and froths over, hiding the hoop with its cascades of small white blossoms. You can even get away with that treatment the second year, but by the third season you're in trouble. It goes up and up, way past the hoop and subsequently sags awkwardly down to the ground, presenting a most disheveled appearance and covering up its neighbors into the bargain. Nevertheless, it's a great plant, so

---

*A better siting of this plant at Cornell is at the bottom of a slope where six or eight of them cascade down toward the road, looking marvelous.

I've resigned myself to surrounding it with stout stakes and re-taining it, as it grows, with strong cord. That beats digging the blessed thing up every other year.

Clematis recta, as you may have gathered, bears panicles of small white flowers. They are starry and fragrant, similar to those on the autumn flowering vine formerly called *C. panicu-lata*, now *C. maximowicziana*, unless the name has been changed again. The leaves, too, are similar to those of the vine, being small, smooth, and pointed. It will grow to five feet and will need a three-foot-wide spot in the garden before you've had it very long. *C. r.* 'Purpurea' has beautiful dark burgundy-colored foliage, especially colorful in the spring. Mine becomes greener as summer progresses, but the color varies from plant to plant, apparently.

C. r. mandshurica makes no attempt to be a proper border plant and should be draped over rocks or on the side of a raised bed, where its cascades of white froth would be a delight rather than a problem.

The deciduous subshrub *Clematis heracleifolia* has been en-joyed by gardeners since some time after 1837 when it was brought back from China to the Royal Botanical Gardens at Kew by one of that establishment's many plant hunters. The variety *davidiana*, which has fragrant flowers and is thus supe-rior to the ordinary *heracleifolia*, arrived in the West some years later, in 1864. The one I have was supposed to be *davidiana* but I wasn't sure it was, for a while. Even when a plant has come la-beled from a nursery one cannot swear to its identity, but when it is a gift from a friend who got it from a friend, identification becomes even less certain. My plant grows about two and one-half feet tall, a good mid-border height, but since it will gain ground sideways, spreading to three or four feet eventually, I made sure to install it between plants that don't mind being moved. (Of course one could move the clematis if the situation became desperate. I am told it is divisible.) The leaves on this species are divided into three sharply toothed leaflets, the large central one about five inches long. The tubular one-inch flowers that cluster in the upper leaf axils and on the stem tips look like blue hyacinths. Authorities say that *C. h. davidiana* grows to four feet and has *deep blue* flowers. Mine are medium blue. Allan Armitage in his book *Herbaceous Perennial Plants* says that *davidiana*'s foliage is "heavily scented when dried and may be used in potpourri."* I didn't have to dry the foliage. While I was weeding near the plant, one autumn day, I noticed a marvelously sweet perfume, as of almond blossoms, and eventually traced it to the dried lower leaves of *C. heracleifolia davidiana*! Perhaps that's one way I can find out which plant I have—I'll dry some of its leaves next summer.

There are several other *heracleifolia* cultivars (mentioned in reference books if not on nursery lists); two of them, 'Crépuscule' and 'Côte d'Azur', are described as having lavender-blue flowers. One called 'Wyvale Blue' sounds alluring, as its clustered flowers are said to be larger and of a deeper blue.

I have a cultivar *C. jouiniana* 'Mrs. Robert Brydon' (also going around as 'Robert Brydon'), that was made by crossing *C. h. davidiana* with *C. vitalba*, the wild vine called traveler's joy. This creation is not exactly a herbaceous perennial and not exactly a vine but something in between. It certainly is woody, but its long strong enterprising stems, which shoot up to eight or ten feet during the summer, die back in the winter to about one inch from the ground. During the growing season, I tie it to a small trellis and encourage the stems that surpass the trellis to adventure among the branches of a *Euonymus europaeus* that

---

*Allan Armitage, *Herbaceous Perennial Plants* (Athens, Ga.: Varsity Press, 1989).

backs it up. The leaves on this clematis resemble, on a larger scale, those of its *heracleifolia* parent, being divided into three large coarsely toothed leaflets. They complement nicely the fluffy panicles of small bell flowers of pale yellow and greyish lavender-blue that appear in July and August. Very elegant, restrained manifestations, they seem, for such a rambunctious plant.

There are two other semi-woody climbers that could be used in mixed borders—one a native of eastern America from New York to Georgia—*C. viorna*. It sounds as if, like most wildflowers, it is quietly appealing rather than flashy. Its nodding, pitcher-shaped, solitary flowers range in color from yellow to a dull reddish purple. The fruit has a dark yellow plume and the seed propagates readily when sown in gravelly soil in autumn. All of this information about *viorna* is straight out of the books for I have never been lucky enough to encounter *C. viorna*, either while out hiking or prowling through a nursery or nursery catalogues. Now, I understand, a few nurseries offer it.

C. durandii is another trailer, although not properly a vine, and usually dies down to the ground in winter. It was created by crossing *C. integrifolia* with *C. x jackmanii*. It's next on my list of wanted plants, since Graham Thomas calls it a superlative plant with "wide handsome blooms of intense indigo-violet lit with cream stamens." Think of it, draped over a small tough border shrub, perhaps, blooming away for six weeks or more! The flowers, which are three to four and one-half inches across, have white centers. A variety called *pallida* has paler blooms of violet rose.

All of these border clematis will do their best if they are grown in soil that contains lots of organic matter in the form of old manure, compost, or leaf mold and peat. There is no need to shade their roots nor to barricade their lower stems according to instructions given for clematis vines.

As to hardiness, *Clematis heracleifolia, integrifolia,* and *recta* are hardy through Zone 3 and *jouiniana* and *viorna* through Zone 4. Nice that they don't mind the cold.

We've been told for years that clematis need lime but lately the word is that they don't care whether their soil is limey or not. Moisture, they want, and nourishment, and good drainage and they'll be satisfied.

LEGUMES *for the* FLOWER BORDER

D uring the last few years I've discovered some lovely legumes that merit an introduction to those gardeners who may not yet have made their acquaintance. All of us know about sweet peas (*Lathyrus odoratus*), and those of us with the right climate may even be growing them. Readers of Gertrude Jekyll must certainly have taken note of what she called the "White Everlasting Pea," *Lathyrus latifolius albus,* a floppy European perennial half-vine that she liked to plant behind subjects such as delphinium that had to be cut back mid-season. The vine was then pulled forward to decorate the empty space. I tried her trick several times but never managed to pull it off; either the delphinium smothered the lathyrus in early summer or the lathyrus the delphinium in late summer. However, the blossoms on this sprawling pea plant are, although scentless, of great beauty, being large and of an exceptionally pure white. Having failed in trying to grow them as fillers I now plant them where they can scramble up into rose bushes. Both plants being enterprising and resourceful they manage to solve their own problems and end up looking very good together. The lathyrus can be used on fences or embankments, of course—in fact the magenta form, having settled down comfortably to life in the United States, is to be seen growing wild on many a roadside bank.

The Hardy Plant Society seed exchange lists seeds of *Lathyrus latifolius* that will produce flowers of many colors other than magenta or white—pale or deep pink, flame, or two colors together on the same flower.

A pea of a more retiring nature is European native *L. vernus* or spring vetchling, which makes a many-stemmed clump only six to twelve inches high. I have two kinds, raised from seed— the species, whose blossoms are red-violet and crimson, and *L. v.* 'Variegatus' (*albo-roseus*) in pink and white. The two plants are wonderful growing next to one another and would do well in the front of a well-drained border, keeping company with dianthus, nepetas, armerias, and the like. One eminent gardener writes that they are lovely with daffodils and red tulips. The charm of *L. vernus* lies in both the racemes of silky, nodding, wonderfully colored flowers and in the shiny, tapering leaflets that appear in pairs on the wiry stems.

As is obvious from the name, this plant blooms in spring. The books say it goes dormant in summer but mine have never done so. Books also say that it is very deep rooted, so I'm wondering, dare I move them next April? They want poor, gravelly soil and plenty of sun, although to look at them, with their delicate leaves, you'd think they'd cook to death in hot sun and would prefer a woodland site. There are several cultivars other than 'Variegatus' that may or may not be available in America. I'd like to get seed of some of the many other lathyrus species. Once you find a genus you like you want to try them all.

That is what's happening with lespedezas. This is a group of more than one hundred species native to North America, Australia, and Asia. They were named by a French botanist for a Spanish governor of Florida, unfortunately—although, come to think of it there *are* more cumbersome names. Before seeing a slide at a garden lecture I had thought lespedeza was a forage or green manure crop. While it's true that farmers use the annual *L. striata* and a few other species for such purposes, those working-class plants have a few distinguished relatives that make fine ornamentals. After seeing the lecture slide of it, I sent to Montrose Nursery for *L. thunbergii*. It was such a knockout that I subsequently ordered *L. t.* 'White Fountain' and *L. t.* 'Pink Fountain'.* If there are any other good species or cultivars floating around I want those too.

The first virtue of these plants is that they bloom in late August, September, and sometimes into October, when most of the border perennials have long since wound up their performances. There's something tremendously exhilarating about seeing a plant burst into bloom just when it seems the show is finished. Besides, the season is perfect for enjoying the garden. In spring one is feverishly digging, weeding, and transplanting and has to remind oneself to stop and look at the flowers. (In this part of the country one is also swatting black flies.) In summer it's often unbearably hot and humid, but in autumn—ha!—the big push is over, with only tidying-up jobs remaining. The heat and the bugs are gone. A benign sun and dry, cool, golden air make everything look heavenly, and it's now one can wander slowly about feeling one has earned a bit of leisure. There's time to make assessments and to thoroughly relish the late bloomers. And there stand the lespedezas.

The three specimens in my garden are all shrubby plants that die to the ground in winter but surge up and fill a largish space by summer's end. The species (*L. thunbergii*) is the smallest so far, attaining only two and one-half to three feet, although it is said to be capable of reaching six feet. The pink and white 'Fountains' have grown to four feet and five feet respectively and the white one is almost as wide as it is tall. 'Pink Fountain' grows

*Nancy Goodwin of Montrose Nursery (now closed) first called this plant *L. japonica* but now believes it to be a white form of *L. thunbergii* (not, however, *L. t.* 'Albiflora'). *L. japonica* also has white flowers.

up more than out. None of them, so far, has had any problems with insects or diseases nor do they need special attention such as staking or dividing.

The species makes a mass of feathery arching stems bearing five-inch oval-lanceolate, blue-green leaves, from the upper axils of which emerge five- to six-inch wiry threads carrying racemes of two-color satin butterfly flowers, whose keels are lilac, their wings and standards deep plummy rose. They are small but so numerous that they make a big splash. The plant should, if possible, be grown on a gritty bank or large raised bed so it can cascade with more effect. Mine is looking as good as it can on level ground, surrounded by asters, including *A. frikartii* 'Mönch', and dusty rose chrysanthemums. Nevertheless, I mean to plant divisions at the ends of two raised beds and surround them with low grey somethings—perhaps the non-blooming lamb's ears?—onto which they can toss their long, lax, flower-laden branches. The lamb's ears won't like it much but I will.

L. 'White Fountain' is standing behind the lower purply species along with some taller asters and a froth of *Artemisia* 'Powis Castle'. The lespedeza is getting so big I'm going to have to rescue some of its neighbors on which it's beginning to impose. In spring, when the previous year's growth on the lespedezas has been cut to the ground, it always looks as if there's plenty of room, but by fall I wish I'd followed my better judgment and shifted things around.

Last September the prettiest spot in the border was that where *L.* 'Pink Fountain' stood beside *Caryopteris* 'Black Knight'. What an inspired combination! if I do say so, although some might call it banal. (What's new about putting such colors together?) Both plants are quite upright so they can mingle their blossoms without interfering with one another. The caryopteris flowers are darker than those of the more frequently seen C. 'Blue Mist', and the pink of this lespedeza has no blue or purple tones at all. A 'Ballerina' rose was holding its clusters of single pale white and pink in just the right places in back of the smaller shrubs, while some 'Hidcote' lavender was obligingly furnishing an echo of the caryopteris's deep grey-violet. More greys in dwarf sage and helianthemum, more rosy repetitions from various dianthus. Pure white in the crinkled petals of white-foliaged prickly poppies (*Argemone grandiflora*). It's moments like these that keep us gardeners trudging on.

ASTILBES

Some years ago I developed a passion for astilbes. I already had several, names unknown, given me by a friend and loved them for their ferny foliage composed of leaves several times divided into jagged little leaflets. I liked their slender wiry stems and their tapering fluffy plumes of cream and pink. I liked, too, the way they sent their leaf and flower stems straight up rather than lopping on their neighbors as is the wont of so many perennials. They had no problems with disease or insects and were easy to divide in spring. Furthermore, they were a great addition to my woods garden, providing color after the early bulbs, primroses, and most of the other shade-lovers had finished their big show. So now I wanted all the astilbes in the catalogues—short and tall, early, midsummer, and late, white, peach-colored, rose, and those copper-foliaged red ones that glow like torches and would light up the dark places under the trees.

I didn't acquire quite all of the astilbes available during the years that followed, but I did accumulate at least twenty different cultivars. And a great joy they are, despite their great fault of refusing (all but one or two) to remain green through the horrid hot days of July and August unless they receive generous amounts of water, either from the heavens or the hose, and this almost daily. Without it they will after flowering first shrivel, then turn yellow.

We gardeners hold this tendency against astilbes, calling it a fault, but actually it's not their fault but ours, or rather that of our climate. Those happy gardeners in our northwestern coastal regions don't have the problem of getting plants through the heat of summer, but the rest of us must find ways to solace and encourage delicate individuals that come to us from kinder and gentler climates.

Astilbes are members of the Saxifrage Family, and while there is one that is native to North America (*A. biternata*), a five-foot, white-flowering plant that resembles goatsbeard, most of the twelve to thirty-five species (the number depending on whether your authority is a "lumper" or a "splitter") come from the Far East—Japan, Korea, and China—from areas that are really temperate, with no great extremes of heat or cold. Luckily—and rather surprisingly—these fragile-looking plants seem to be unfazed by our winters, at least into areas that are classified as Zone 4. But the heat, whether dry or humid, they abhor. I've never known them to die of it, but if you have not given them the care they require, they will look so miserable in your August garden that you'll find yourself babbling apologies to garden visitors and wishing astilbes would go decently dormant and disappear underground until spring. It's no wonder that the work of breeding and hybridizing these lovely plants has been done mostly in cool, moist Germany, Holland, and England, rather than in Iowa, say, or Kansas. Or in upstate New York, for that matter. Still, even here, and perhaps in Iowa (although I'm not so sure about Kansas), if one has an ample supply of water and is willing to go to a little extra trouble, one can enjoy the aspect of astilbes all season long, even when they are growing in a sunny border rather than in the light shade they prefer.

In the first place, they must be planted in a fluffy humusy soil—no skimping if you want optimum results. But before planting them, examine their roots and you will see that they are shallow, wispy affairs attached to a woody base. Obviously, the plant will be sitting close to the surface and, not having powerful enterprising roots that can travel down and around in search of food and water, they will need a comforting and protective mulch that will not only help conserve moisture but will nourish them as well. The mulch could consist of sifted cow manure (old), compost, or woods soil. Even with such a mulch, astilbes can still use—and will respond with alacrity to—having a handful of organic fertilizer sprinkled around them when they emerge in early spring.

If the plants are sited so that they receive only morning or filtered sunlight, so much the better. No doubt a garden whose shade is provided by a building rather than by trees would be ideal, as trees soak up a tremendous amount of moisture during summer droughts, moisture that must be replaced by the gardener if his shade-loving plants are to be kept happy. Certainly, astilbes should never be planted under surface-rooting trees such as maple, catalpa, and poplar. In my woodland garden they do well under the sassafras trees, whose roots go down, but very poorly under metasequoia, locust, and white pine, whose roots are superficial and voracious.

People who write reference books tell us that astilbes should be divided every few years, and no doubt that would be beneficial, but I have wide clumps of them that have been sitting in the border undisturbed for eight or ten years, still putting on a dazzling performance every summer. In full sun, too, even though they would doubtless prefer to be standing in part shade on the banks of a pond or stream—so long, that is, as they did not have to fear being flooded; they are not among those few plants that can survive in standing water.

If you're interested in trying astilbes or in adding to your collection, you'll be confronted with a bewildering number of cultivars listed in the catalogues, all of them described so as to be nearly irresistible. And justifiably, for I think I've seen only one or two that I haven't liked; most of them really are perfectly beautiful, so it is difficult to choose.

Because they have been bred from many different species, astilbes vary as to height, color, form, texture of flower and foliage, and blooming time. The most thorough dissertation I've found on the origin of the cultivars is in *Hardy Herbaceous Perennials* by Leo Jelitto and Wilhelm Schacht.* But here, perhaps, I need only say that most of those listed as *A. arendsii* (the largest group) were bred by a man to whom all of us should be grateful—Georg Arends of Germany (1862–1952) who worked with various genera, including phlox, sedum, and campanulas, but whose greatest love was astilbes. His magnificent hybrids were the result of crossing such species as *A. chinensis* var. *davidii*, *A. thunbergii*, *A. japonica*, and *A. astilboides*. Although many of the best plants are in this group, other fine astilbes may be found listed under *A. simplicifolia*, *A. crispa*, *A. chinensis*, and *A. rosea* (*A. chinensis* x *A. japonica*). But astilbes have been classified and reclassified so often that one can find the same cultivar going under several different names—that of its breeder (*A. arendsii* 'Rheinland') or that of a parent (*A. japonica* 'Rheinland') or under one parent (*A. simplicifolia* 'Sprite') or the other (*A. glaberrima* 'Sprite'). Actually, the listing of these plants is apparently so whimsical that it might be best for gardeners who are easily joggled by botanical names that are in a state of confusion to concern themselves when ordering only with the cultivar name. Then they will have only to worry

---

*Leo Jelitto and Wilhelm Schacht, *Hardy Herbaceous Perennials* (Portland, Ore.: Timber Press, 1990).

about whether the nursery got the right marker on the right plant.

As you pore over books and catalogues (and order sheets) looking for whites, consider two-foot 'Deutschland', whose impressive dense showy trusses appear in early summer, or the airier 'Bridal Veil' of about the same height. 'Avalanche' makes a three-foot cloud of white in my garden, while 'Professor van der Weilen' rises to four feet and, having slender branched and curved inflorescences, produces an effect entirely different from that of astilbes with close-packed upright spikes such as 'Deutschland'.

As to pinks, Herr Arends's old hybrid 'Peach Blossom', a one-and-a-half- to two-foot mid-season plant, is still going strong, giving us all much pleasure, while taller 'Ostrich Plume', with its arching, drooping, coral-pink chains of tiny blossoms, gives grace to any shade garden. 'Rhineland' is a good two-foot early bright pink, but I'm most fond of a plant I got as 'Gloria Rosea', a tall elegant subject with especially pretty foliage. 'Gloria Purpurea' has plumes not of purple but of a rich raspberry. Some people like the big lusty cultivar that goes under the name of *A. tacquetii* 'Superba', but while I appreciate its dark red stems and its height (four feet), I find its narrow spikes of fuzzy magenta-pink flowers tolerable only when they first appear. Later on, the bottom sections of the spikes turn a particularly revolting shade of yellow-ochre-brown while the tops are still pink, making a dreadful color combination. Nor am I very fond of my colony of *A. chinensis*; the fact that their stiff narrow two-foot plumes appear in late summer when there's very little color in the shade garden is certainly in their favor, but, gracious, what a lugubrious shade of murky mulberry they are. Furthermore, their stout creeping roots make them a menace to their more diffident neighbors, so that, if the color of their flowers didn't echo that of some midsize hostas nearby, I think I'd have evicted them long since. They do have interesting brown fur on their stems, it's true. There are several forms of *chinensis* sold but the most common one is surely *A. c.* var. 'Pumila' of eight to fifteen inches, whose color and height vary depending on the nursery they come from. The color is often given as "lilac-pink" but that would be a charitable description of mine, which are more of a melancholy mauve. However, this plant has more to offer in some ways than most other astilbes; in addition to flowering in August (when almost any bloom is welcome) it manages to trudge on courageously through heat and drought, making, with its prettily incised leaves, a decorative and manageable ground cover in either sun or shade.

The only other member of this genus I know that does not turn yellow in late summer when not sluiced regularly with water is 'Sprite', my very favorite astilbe. To look at it you'd never divine its stamina; only a foot tall, it makes a lacy arrangement of dark green, copper-toned, delicately cut leaves that delight the eye all season. Its pale peachy-cream-pink blossoms on slender stems shoot out in fine sprays. No plumes, spears, or spikes, just a sort of froth of delicate tracery that is almost as pretty when the flower petals have disappeared and only seeds remain.

I've scarcely mentioned the red astilbes that provide so much drama in the garden, especially if they are sited so as to catch the rays of the late afternoon sun as it slants in under the tree branches. It is not for nothing that they have names such as 'Fanal' (meaning "beacon"), 'Etna', 'Fire', and 'Glow'. 'Fanal', probably the oldest and shortest, is still one of the best, although the taller 'Red Sentinel' and 'Spinell' cannot be faulted. Because red astilbes are crimson, that is, a deep blue-red rather than scarlet (orange-red), they harmonize with most border perennials. All of the reds I've seen have dark winey undertones to their shiny dark green leaves. Wonderful plants.

Every garden writer is supposed to say something about plant combinations. Well, in the sunny border I have astilbes combined with roses, geraniums, campanulas—everything. In the one area where I contrived to have some bright pink ones repeat in the foreground the spikes of *Lythrum* 'Morden's Pink' in the background I'm afraid it looks a bit too obvious. Still, it's good enough that I leave it. In the opposite border where I have masses of creamy white astilbes restating the creamy white explosion of goatsbeard behind them the effect is a bit classier, I think.

The fact is, astilbes harmonize with almost all other perennials, but it may be that I am right when I find them most glorious when they're all massed together: clumps of white, pink, cream, and red, lots and lots of them, in the cool, dappled shade of a woodland garden.

GAURA

ave you thought about getting seed for gaura? If you sent for it during the winter and planted a flat in March, you could have blooming plants by late summer. The seeds germinate as easily as annual seeds, yet the plant is perennial.

Oddly enough, considering all the garden literature one is exposed to, gaura first came to my attention only a few years ago when I was having a Willa Cather revival and found it referred to in her novel *One of Ours*. The homesick American soldier finds, growing in France, a gaura that reminds him of the ones he knew on his native Nebraska prairies. (The gaura in the French garden must have been imported, as the several species appear to be strictly North American.)

My second encounter with the plant was when a friend pointed one out in her garden—*Gaura lindheimeri*, she said it was. I wasn't terribly impressed, but I planted the two new seedlings she gave me, putting them out in the nursery because I didn't consider they merited a place in the perennial garden. How sorry I was later that I had been so blind to their beauty and ignorant of their virtues! The two gauras, although having come from seed that spring, began to bloom by June and went on exuberantly producing blossoms until late fall, when a really hard frost brought an end to their incredible performance. You can be sure I moved them into prime spots in the border the next year, where they started blooming again, earlier than the year before, naturally, and went on nonstop, until the beginning of winter.

The reference books I've consulted, except for Harper and McGourty's *Perennials,* are very cool about this plant. *Wyman's Gardening Encyclopedia* calls it "nice"; one English expert allows it "modest charm," and another rates it "not in the first flight of herbaceous plants" (but, like the others, he gives it points for its length of bloom). *Taylor's Guide to Perennials* says you can grow it in informal borders. L. H. Bailey's *Standard Cyclopedia of Horticulture* says gauras are unusual but that they probably wouldn't appeal to anyone other than a wildflower enthusiast.* What's the matter with these otherwise discerning people? It's a lovely plant—admittedly, you have to really look at it to enjoy it. It doesn't tower (at least not in my garden), it doesn't have large flowers, it doesn't knock you over from forty feet away with solid masses of aniline dye color.

Let me tell you what it does do. It makes a taproot from which it sends up many three foot long wiry stems, spraying out like broom plants and branching toward the top. These stems are clothed in small one- to three-inch lance-shaped, slender, alternate leaves and they swarm with what appear to be delicate white moths—one-inch flowers consisting of four un-equal, translucent petals above and below, a whisk of eight to ten white stamens tipped pink. Since the calyxes, pedicels, bracts, and buds are also pink, the effect is that of a fountain of floating pink-and-white flowers.

---

*Pamela Harper and Frederick McGourty, *Perennials: How to Select, Grow and Enjoy* (Tucson, Ariz.: HP Books, 1985); Donald Wyman, *Wyman's Gardening Encyclopedia* (London: Macmillan, 1986), p. 439; Barbara W. Ellis, *Taylor's Guide to Perennials* (Boston: Houghton Mifflin, 1990); L. H. Bailey, *Standard Cyclopedia of Horticulture* (London: Macmillan, 1935).

Have I persuaded you that you must obtain this elegant thing? If you don't want to bother to raise it yourself, several nurseries sell it and there are good pictures of it in the *Taylor's Guide*, and in the Harper/McGourty book. Pamela Harper says it grows tall to shoulder height or to seven feet; so far mine haven't attained more than three and one-half feet, perhaps because I live in the North.

Wildflower seed companies must offer the seed, and Park Seeds has listed it this year. Once you have a plant you're all set—you can gather your own seeds and grow any number of plants. You'll even have self-sown seedlings—you can start a gaura nursery. On second thought, you may need the seedlings yourself, as the parent plants may die in a severe winter if they don't have enough snow cover.

Since these are prairie plants, they prefer to grow in full sun. They might be satisfied with slightly less so long as they have perfect drainage. They can stand a lot of drought but do not want water sitting on their roots. If you have heavy clay soil, you should lighten it with peat and grit or coarse sand or raise the bed—or both. Otherwise there are no special requirements. Sometimes the leaves have maroon spots on them, but that seems to be a fancy rather than an affliction.

I should think gaura would look spectacular against a dark background. So far, I haven't been able to manage that but it looks awfully nice with its sprays of blossoms wafting over and among grey and plum-colored foliage (purple sage, heuchera 'Palace Purple', lavender) and *Geranium endressii* 'A. T. Johnson', whose clean pink blossoms bring out the touches of pink in the gaura.*

---

*There are some new gaura cultivars on the market now; the plant has ceased to be only a wildflower. I've found 'Come's Gold' and 'Whirling Butterflies' listed and a friend has just given me a delicious rose-colored one called *G. lindheimeri* 'Siskiyou Pink'.

CHRYSANTHEMUMS

I don't know whether many other people are as confused about chrysanthemums as I've been all these years.* We all know about "football mums" at the florist's, the so-called "hardy mums" in pots at the garden center, and we may not only know about but grow "cushion mums" and some taller ones in our gardens. But when we've seen shasta daisies, painted daisies, and even feverfew listed with chrysanthemums (and sometimes listed under something else) we've been joggled. And what about costmary, also classified as a chrysanthemum? The costmary in the herb corner of my garden is a far cry from those basketball-sized football chrysanthemums that probably represent the whole tribe to a lot of people. So let's straighten this thing out. I've been poking into books and making charts to the point where I think I've got the situation under control.

Chrysanthemums, of which there are about 160 species, be-

*Shortly after I finished writing this piece, I learned that the genus chrysanthemum had been shaken apart by the taxonomists. Since 1990 the Hardy Plant Society seed list has contained no chrysanthemums. *Chrysanthemum alpinum* is now *leucanthemopsis*. *C. maximum* (shasta daisy), earlier changed to *C. superbum*, became *Leucanthemum gayanum*. *C. corymbosum, macrophyllum,* and *parthenium* (feverfew), and even *coccineum* (painted daisy) are all called *tanacetum* now. That is, by the taxonomists. Since most reference books and nursery lists still use the old names this essay will still, I trust, be useful.

long to the daisy or Compositae Family and are native to the temperate regions of Europe, Asia, Africa, and America. They are annual or perennial herbs, often partly woody, with pungent foliage, their leaves ranging from nearly entire to much dissected. Their heads are many flowered; the flowers on the wild species all having single daisy petals. Hybrids may be (and usually are) doubled with many ray florets and few disk florets. In the wild, chrysanthemums come in white, yellow, and pink.

As one might have deduced from the designs on their fabrics, scrolls, and pottery, the Chinese and Japanese have had a long love affair with chrysanthemums. They appear to have been breeding the forms native to their part of the globe since five hundred years before Christ, developing blossoms of various shapes and sizes, in every color but blue. The Chinese varieties have been mostly tightly incurved and the Japanese reflexing or loosely incurved—shaggier, in short. The Chinese started it all but their productions weren't discovered by people in the West until 1688, when some were taken to Holland. They failed to survive there but showed up in France in 1789. England received them in 1795 and that was when they began to move west in earnest. Robert Fortune, working for the Royal Horticultural Society, in 1846 sent home from China many pompom varieties, which were so well received that when, in 1861, he sent back from Japan specimens of the fantastic varieties that the Japanese had been developing for over one thousand years, the English growers, considering the newcomers to be in poor taste, wouldn't accept them for about twenty years.

Most of these original chrysanthemum cultivars (bred, it is thought, from *C. indicum, morifolium,* and other species) have become—or perhaps I should say have remained—show flowers. They are grown to be sold to florists or to be entered in exhibitions, hence they reside in greenhouses where they are fed, disbudded, pruned, and cossetted so as to produce the largest, most astonishing creations possible. The National Chrysanthemum Society in this country lists thirteen divisions for these, such as "Regular or Chinese reflex," "Incurve," "Spoon," "Quill," "Spider"—on up to thirteen. However, with none of these will we be dealing in this piece but rather with the chrysanthemums that grow out in the sun, wind, and rain. Real garden flowers. There are many of them, but not so many as one would wish that are tough enough to be depended upon to win through our difficult winters in the northern part of the United States. Southern gardeners, especially those who live in the eastern states, can grow many chrysanthemums that we cannot; we treasure those we have, treat them as kindly as we can, and keep experimenting with different species and cultivars.

Some of the plants that do well in the South are hardy enough to live farther north, but they bloom so late they are seared by frost before their blooming period is well under way. *C. nipponicum*, the Nippon daisy, is one of these. I grew it happily here, enjoying its dark green foliage, its low, spreading compact shape, being grateful to it for having no diseases and no allure for insects, but grieving when its long-awaited white flowers were given no chance to perform. I might try it again in a different spot.

Chrysanthemum weyrichii looks very similar to *nipponicum*— low, nicely cut dark leaves. It comes as 'White Bomb' and 'Pink Bomb' and I'm embarrassed to report that I failed decisively with both of them. My robust-looking plants simply collapsed in a heap their first August, as if from a heart attack, while to the naked eye nothing was amiss. They are supposed to be able to endure cold and heat (Zones 3–8). Unfortunately, no one was by who could have performed an autopsy. If you are cleverer than I, you can use these chrysanthemums with the late-summer-blooming asters.

C. arcticum, the Arctic daisy, is another low spreading one (six inches by one foot), hardy to Zones 2 and 3, as well it might be, coming from Alaska and Kamchatka. It carries pinkish white starry single flowers on spreading branches. It is a fine plant for a rock garden or for the front of the border. The Royal Horticultural Society dictionary says it blooms in June and July but Clausen and Ekstrom in their reference book say it blooms extremely late and may be overtaken by frost.* My plants cover themselves with bloom in September, as it happens, to my great satisfaction.

A taller, wider (one foot by eighteen inch) species, *C. yezoense*, from Japan, is often sold as *arcticum*. It is also a good white-flowering rock garden plant and even comes in pink and yellow as well as white. It's said to be tougher than *arcticum* and might bloom earlier in the fall. Louise Beebe Wilder's description of her *arcticum* sounds like *yezoense* and she said it bloomed from late summer on.

If I lived in California or somewhere in the southern part of the country I'd try *C. frutescens*, the lovely pale lemon or white marguerite that looks, in pictures, to be all a flower should be— fresh, pure, and elegant. I could grow it as an annual, perhaps, if ever I saw the seed offered. One should try a few new annuals every summer, to change the scene.

There's an old plant that's much talked about called *Chrysanthemum corymbosum*—another low spreader with white single flowers. Nancy Goodwin formerly of Montrose Nursery in North Carolina describes it enticingly. She's not sure it will do in areas colder than Zone 6, but since it's from the Caucasus it would be worth trying farther north.

Mrs. Goodwin also likes the cultivar of the wild field or oxeye daisy, *C. leucanthemum* 'May Queen'. She says she's had it for

*Ruth Rogers Clausen and Nicholas H. Ekstrom, *Perennials for American Gardens* (New York: Randon House, 1989).

twenty years and can vouch for the fact that it's not weedy. It produces its white flowers from early summer until late fall, at least in North Carolina. Graham Stewart Thomas, in discussing this species, says it's strange that there is no garden form of it in England, although in Germany they have a good one called 'Maistern' (May Star). Do you suppose it is Mrs. Goodwin's 'May Queen'?

You'll be tired of hearing about small white flowers, but I have one more that belongs here—feverfew, often listed under *Matricaria* but rightly listed under *Chrysanthemum—C. parthenium*, an herb native to Europe and Asia, probably growing wild in America, too, by now. Heaven knows it's skilled at taking care of itself. Some people like the single-flowered feverfew but I love the double and am so glad that its seedlings retain the same form, although they *are* variable, some of them whiter and fuller than others. Often the parent plant, or half of it, dies in the winter, but there are always enough self-sown seedlings for the border, the cutting bed, and the compost heap. The pretty yellow-flowered feverfew, 'Golden Ball', didn't prove hardy here, nor did the charming miniature 'Santana'. The latter left some seedlings at least, so I can carry it along. There's a feverfew with golden foliage, an annual often used in bedding-out schemes in parks—in case you're interested. Also one with crimped green foliage, similar to that of restaurant parsley.

Feverfew was obviously used to quell fevers, but there are other herbs of the genus chrysanthemum that have been, and are still, of culinary importance. Costmary, *C. balsamita tanacetoides* from western Asia was used by the Egyptians, Greeks, and Romans and has always been part of the cuisine in Spain and the rest of Europe. We are told that the English and early Americans used it for brewing. They also laid the leaves in the bottom of cake pans to flavor cakes and in their Bibles to nibble on in church when trying to stay awake. It's not much for looks, costmary, with its large leathery leaves and yellow button flowers but it does have a heady aroma. Several different species of chrysanthemum, whose names I don't know, are used in Japanese cuisine, the leaves and/or flowers, fresh or dried, being pickled, boiled, or fried and eaten with raw fish or in salads and soups. Even I, in the spring, often put the leaves of the wild field daisy in my salad—they're pungent and refreshing.

I've always thought painted daisies were of the genus pyrethrum, but it appears there is no such thing and that they are *Chrysanthemum coccineum* from Persia and the Caucasus. Well —they don't *act* like chrysanthemums, I must say. I'll have to take the word of *Hortus Third* and the other authorities, even if I am secretly incredulous. Everything about painted daisies is wonderful except for their habit of going yellow and dead-looking in late summer. At least in my garden. A friend triumphantly claims that her plants bloom twice if cut back after the first blooming. It may be that mine need dividing and nourishing, but every year I have to cut the yellow foliage to the ground. I'm always sure they're dead, but early the following spring the scroll-shaped shoots emerge, announcing the imminent arrival of the lovely lacy foliage, and soon there are great two-and-one-half-foot clumps of wide-eyed daisies, single and semi-double, in shades from palest pink and medium rose to a deep vibrant crimson. As the double ones have not been bred to lose their character they remain daisies, with double rows of petals, some of them with crested centers. Mine all came, years ago, from a seed packet labeled Robinson's or Kelway's Double Mixture, I forget which. (Half the plants from seed for double flowers come out, as a rule, single.) Single or double named cultivars are offered in several colors and can be increased by division.

I grew the Dalmatian pyrethrum, *C. cinerariaefolium*, at one period. It's the one whose small white flowers are dried and ground for insecticide. With lacy grey-green foliage, it's a pretty thing, though one couldn't call it splendid.

Chrysanthemum 'Clara Curtis' is a great boon to us northerners; even if we lose some of the plants in a bad winter, there are usually enough pieces to reset for a good show in late summer. This is a special kind of chrysanthemum, called *C. rubellum* for as long as anyone can remember, but now, God alone knows why, appearing as *C. zawadskii* or *C. zawadskii latilobum*. The plant was found, recordless, in a Welsh nursery in 1929 and is believed to be a hybrid with *zawadskii* for one parent—but since no one is sure, why don't we let it alone? In Britain there are fifteen or more cultivars of this plant, but we deprived stateside gardeners have had to be grateful for Clara. 'Mary Stoker', in buff, has lately come to the United States. (I tried it and found it a bit too leggy.) The *rubellum* foliage is paler, thinner, and finer cut than that of ordinary garden chrysanthemums, but the plant's habits are the same, that is, it is shallow rooted and starts sending out its new underground shoots while it is still flowering. The single pale pink daisies of 'Clara Curtis' begin to open in late July or early August and make a most satisfying one-and-a-half-foot mass for many weeks. It is usually still blooming toward the front of the border when the rosy Japanese anemones come out further back. With luck, the pink boltonia, which I've found blooms much earlier than the white one, would perform at the same time, back near the anemones, with perhaps a big pouffe of *Artemisia* 'Powis Castle' between them. New plan for next summer.

I have several clumps of a chrysanthemum that I call "Dusty Double Pink". It's one of those old farmyard plants— everyone around here who has flowers at all has it. I got it from a neighbor who got it from her neighbor. You can't kill it, which is something you can't say for most of the chrysanthemums sold now. The center of the flower is deep wine red, especially as it is just opening, which it does so early that you can enjoy it for a month or two before winter puts it to sleep. I fondly hope it may be the old 'Emperor of China' the English talk about, but I'm not at all sure of it. The Emperor looks, in photographs, to have longer, more pointed petals than our Finger Lakes stalwart.

Have you seen the unusual Japanese chrysanthemum, C. *pacificum*, quite recently introduced to American gardeners? It's a foot tall, spreading out and making mats of grey-green scalloped leaves, edged white. The flowers aren't very jazzy—just yellow tansy buttons, but the foliage is so attractive it is worth growing for that alone. The vendors of this plant said it would tolerate dry lean soil and temperatures to minus 20 degrees F. Lots of us bought it, liked it very much, and were pretty cross when our plants died the first winter.

Chrysanthemum uliginosum is also said by its vendor, Carroll Gardens, to be able to endure the cold of Zone 3, but it lasted only a couple of years here. I'm going to try again. What a creature it is—a kind of super daisy! From four to six feet tall with four-inch leaves and three-inch white flowers with sulphur green eyes. Marvelous with monkshood.

Speaking of big white daisies, some wonderful ones are to be found among the many versions of *Chrysanthemum superbum* (*maximum*) or shasta daisies—tall and short, single or double. The doubles—most of them, that is—retain their daisy character since, like the pink pyrethrums, they haven't (yet) been doubled to a fare-thee-well, to the point where they have been turned into puffy spheres. Although some writers poke fun at it, I love C. 'Aglaya'—at least one of the versions I've had from nurseries, and they do differ. The one I've kept in my garden is beautifully fringed and crested without having lost its elegant shape. A similar but rather frenziedly feathered one is 'Stamm

Potschke'—too much, I thought when I saw it; they've gone too far.

If you'd like a noble-looking white daisy with a double row of non-fringed petals and a fluffy yet restrained cream crest in the center, try 'Wirral Pride'. There are many fringed and many crested ones, but of those that I've encountered 'Aglaya' and 'Wirral Pride' are the two best in those categories. The largest single shasta is 'Majestic' but 'Thomas Killen' is almost as large and has a cream crest as well. 'Cobham Gold' has been pictured and described as being yellow but is, in fact, creamy white with a yellowish crest. Nice, but not as tall and sturdy as 'Wirral Pride'.

I've been pleased through the years with the semi-double 'Little Miss Muffet', which although short (eight to twelve inches) doesn't look stunted, like some of the new dwarfs. If it sits in the same spot for several years it tends to grow taller—to fifteen inches or more, so it should be divided every other spring. While you're at it, you can put little colonies of it here and there, all down the front of the border. It's a clean, dependable, cheerful individual and adds sparkle to whatever group of plants it joins.

Shastas have the reputation of not being very hardy but I've not lost any to cold so far. I divide them only in spring, of course, and I do throw evergreen boughs over them in autumn, when I have enough to spare.

It's sad to have to admit that chrysanthemums, most of them, are plagued with many afflictions—aphids (various), caterpillars, tarnish bugs, leaf miners, gall midges, spider mites, thrips, and mealy bugs, besides various fungi, wilt, viruses, powdery mildew, and rust. If you don't use chemical sprays or dusts you'll have your work cut out for you trying to keep them in good shape. Naturally, the species are much less disease-prone than the hybrids, but even those you would have to keep an eye on. As with all plants, you can help them to fight their enemies if you give them what they want in the way of moisture and nourishment. Excepting the rock garden species, chrysanthemums want a good rich soil with plenty of organic matter—old cow manure or compost, ideally. They need deep watering during hot dry periods but good drainage is essential to prevent their roots from rotting. Full sun for most of them, at least sun all morning long.

As to the hardiness of morifolium chrysanthemums, alas! I've spent a small fortune on "hardy mums," various tall and short, gorgeously colored and doubled versions, and have found perhaps two that could be relied upon to come through the winter. The one I call "Dusty Double Pink" is one; 'Aztec', no longer listed in nursery catalogues, is another. There are, of course, the single and semi-double 'Korean' chrysanthemums, and C. *arcticum* and *weyrichii*, all of which are quite reliable.

I've learned that chrysanthemums have a better chance of making it if they are constantly divided. Lift the plants in the spring, shake them apart, extricate the stout young rooted shoots, and plant them, at least a foot apart, in refreshed soil. Each two-inch baby plant will make a mass of flowers in late summer or fall, hard as it is to believe. If you want to keep the taller ones from flopping and make them more bushy, pinch them back at six to eight inches and again when the new growth reaches the same height. At least in the north, don't pinch them back after the first part of July. In the fall, after the summer's growth has been frozen brown, cut them to the ground. You will see next spring's leaves emerging below the dead stems. Cover them with evergreen boughs or some other non-matting, non-weedy material.

I'm trying to finish this piece without lashing out against people who say "mums" and people who sell the colored chrysanthemums all year round, when they are, and surely should remain, the very essence of autumn. All right—I won't say any more about either of those things, but I simply must bring up something that I find both exasperating and mystifying—the peddling of chrysanthemums as *hardy* when most of them aren't. When I say hardy, of course I mean able to stand at least a few nights of minus 20 degrees. Just last year a woman told me she had had a local landscaping firm plant a garden for her, putting in, among other things, hundreds of dollars' worth of "hardy mums." They wouldn't have had much chance even if they had been planted in the spring, but being planted in the fall, of course, the following spring they were all dead. "What did I do wrong?" she asked. I think the chrysanthemum producers count on people's blaming themselves for garden failures.

Once, at a perennial conference in Ohio, I sat across the luncheon table from a young man who said he did nothing but raise garden chrysanthemums for garden centers. I asked, "Do you tell the vendors which ones are hardy and which are not?" He looked at me pityingly, shrugged, and said, "Lady, I have a family to support."

But are gardeners never going to weary of buying plants that die? Will they always blame themselves, or will they finally catch on? What will happen to the young man's income then?

GARDENING *with* PURPLE FOLIAGE

It seems to me that I am always having to recant, as I go through phases of hating, then loving, certain plants or categories of plants. For years I've disliked trees, shrubs, perennials, and annuals with purple foliage, and now their aspect fills me with admiration and a fierce desire to possess them. They look exotic, serene, soothing, and they combine so well with other plants—that is, if they are cannily placed and if, as in all good compositions, the theme is repeated. If this is not done the plant with purple foliage will look simply bizarre, out of place.

The artist-gardener who is interested in composing a "garden picture" will not stick one 'Palace Purple' coral bell in the front of the border and walk off. He—or she—will know that every plant put into the garden will relate to everything that is already there and that it had better relate harmoniously. Installing purple-foliaged plants entails a greater amount of time and trouble than planting those with green leaves because changes will have to be undertaken so that they can be made to look natural, to blend in.

Let's say I have a border consisting of plants with only green or grey foliage. There happens to be room for a twelve-inch wine-colored *Ajuga* 'Jungle Beauty Improved' for which I need a home. I plant it in front of a pale pink geranium whose deli-

cate color it immediately enhances. But since any picture or tapestry must have its colors repeated, I decide to divide a red-
leaved 'Husker Red' Penstemon from another part of the
garden and set half of it in the place of an old yarrow, behind
and to one side of the geranium. There's already a rose, 'The
Fairy', that repeats the clear pink of the geranium, so things are
shaping up. Warming to my work, I go out to a holding bed and
fork up a clump of black mondo grass and set it beside some
mounds of rosy dianthus on the other side of the ajuga—you
see? I shift a few more things around and by the time I've finished the eye can travel happily over an eight-foot stretch of
border, picking up pale pink and dark wine red combinations,
all slightly different in intensity and tone, very different in texture and form, but similar enough to give the beholder an assur-
ance, however unconscious, of consistency, order, and harmony.

Purple foliage is not really purple, you know—purple as we
know it in *Campanula glomerata*, *Delphinium* 'Black Knight', or in
a box of Crayolas. It's ruby or chianti or plum, cocoa, sometimes
almost black, and it can certainly provide new thrills for the
longtime perennial gardener who thought there were no new
thrills left in the way of color combinations. I have become tremendously intrigued with the ways one can use this color—or
perhaps I should say these colors, for purple foliage varies not
only from genus to genus but from plant to plant within the
same genus.

For example, the foliage of certain dahlias is a glossy burgundy while that of the sweet potato vine, *Ipomoea batatas*
'Blackie', is the color you would get if you mixed on a palette
alizarin crimson and ivory black. I don't know any other way to
describe it. Perhaps the color of a beet as you pull it from the
ground, the skin still coated with a light film of soil? And there
are many tones and shades between the colors of the two kinds
of leaves I've just tried to describe. Within the same genus, if it

is propagated by seed, you'll find great differences between the individual plants. Other gardeners, looking at my rather insipid specimen of *Clematis recta* 'Purpurea' often say (tactlessly), "*Mine* is much darker." They say the same in August of my *Lysimachia ciliata* 'Atropurpurea'. (Several people have offered to bring me a piece of their superior specimens, but so far . . .)

The weather, too, influences leaf color of certain perennial strains—for example, a *Heuchera* 'Palace Purple' that starts out ruby red in spring can become decidedly oak-leaf russet by August after having undergone dry periods and long days of scorching sun. In this same heuchera strain the individuals vary greatly, even in spring, as to the intensity of red in their leaves. Nevertheless, all of these coral bells seem to preserve their spring color until fall if the summer has been cool and rainy.

There are many subjects that display splendid red or "purple" leaves in May, then, no matter what the weather, gradually become greener as the summer wears on. *Lysimachia ciliata* 'Atropurpurea' is one of these, having such stunning oxblood foliage in spring that we gardeners, though exasperated at beholding its rosettes spread everywhere, far from the parent plant, shrug and forgive all and resignedly scoop up the unwanted progeny, sparing enough to preserve its presence in the border. By August or September, when the lysimachia forest we left behind has turned into a mass of tall red-tinged green plants, feebly decorated with inconsequential star-shaped, pale yellow flowers, we may well wonder at ourselves for having been so compassionate.

Penstemon digitalis 'Husker (or Husker's) Red' is also inclined to lose interest in preserving the red of its leaves as it begins to concentrate on making tall stems laden with whitish tubular blossoms—ill-advisedly say I, who value the early leaves more than the later flowers. I have a sempervivum (name unknown) that starts the season in flaming red only to subside into an undistinguished purple-grey later on. The weak purple leaves of my *Clematis recta* 'Purpurea' are sadly evanescent. There are these little tricks plants play on us and we can only submit.

Luckily not all purple-foliaged plants are so fickle. Most of them change color only slightly during a season, and many shrubs and trees such as Japanese maple turn an even more brilliant red in fall. The purple form of the smoke bush (*Cotinus coggygria*) remains stable, certainly, as does *Prunus x cistena*, the tough and useful sand cherry. The barberries are mutable but reliable in that they present you with slightly different versions of "purple" from month to month. Never do they do anything so dastardly as to turn green.

One of the great things about purple foliage is that it brings out the best in the colors of neighboring plants whether they are cool (grey, lavender, blue, pale pink, lemon yellow) or hot (orange, chrome yellow, vermilion). The cool colors when seen against dark, rich chianti-colored leaves are suddenly given form and character that had gone unnoticed when they were surrounded only by green. This is all the more true as the green leaves of perennials (unlike those of most evergreen shrubs and trees) are not only paler by comparison but tend to reflect sunlight, which whitens the whole effect, almost wiping out pale colors. Which is one reason gardens look more beautiful in the morning and evening and on cloudy days.

This passion for purple has led me to discover (probably after lots of other gardeners had long ago done so) how well it combines with hot colors. I had already used it in the border but had never thought of using it elsewhere. When first I started planting my new hot-color garden I thought to rest the eye from all the flaming colors by introducing a few white- and blue-flowering plants among the scarlets, oranges, and brassy yellows. But I found that instead of harmonizing, while bringing down the temperature, they simply looked as if they didn't belong—had wandered into the garden by accident. After giving the matter much serious thought I sent them packing and replaced them with cool plants that yet contained *red*, which would make them compatible with the brilliant red and orange dahlias and daylilies, monardas, and marigolds they'd be consorting with. Real purple flowers (heliotrope, *Campanula glomerata*, and the like) that contain red and dark crimson as found in *Clematis* 'Niobe' and *Gaillardia* 'Red Plume' rest the eyes as much as the "purple" foliage of perilla, opal basil, and that of some dahlias. The introduction of these colors, especially of a variety of shades and textures of burgundy purple foliage, made cool, quiet places in the hot-color garden and greatly enriched the garden picture.

Fierce, incandescent red, such as that found in the flowers of *Dahlia* 'Bishop of Llandaff' or *Lychnis arkwrightii* 'Vesuvius' take on, when set next to mahogany red, the sumptuous quality of an oriental rug—which may be why both those plants thought of decorating their stems with leaves of that color. A bright orange calendula is a pretty sight, but when it's standing in front of the intricately lobed, gleaming chocolate-colored leaves of *Hibiscus acetosella* 'Red Shield' what drama it assumes! The crimson explosions on dwarf double *Gaillardia* 'Red Plume' are fine by themselves, but against the lovely, palmate, almost sinister sepia leaves of *Ipomoea* 'Blackie' they are so glorified that they might be the crests of tropical birds.

But back to the cool border. As I write, in late May, I'm observing it carefully, glorying in the plant combinations and at the same time trying to suppress the suspicion that perhaps this time I've really gone too far. But look how beautiful it is! There is Nancy Goodwin's *Heuchera* 'Montrose Ruby' whose scalloped leaves are silvery deep red, if there is such a thing, with darker veins. The undersides, which show when the wind blows, are pure dark red with no smoky overtones. On its left is a lacy, grey rosette of that loveliest tansy, *Tanacetum niveum*. On the right is the small chartreuse *Hosta* 'Kabitchan' (sorely tried by hungry slugs, I must admit). Then a black-purple rosette with crimped and puckered leaves—*Ajuga pyramidalis* 'Metallica Crispa Purpurea' (at least that's what I *think* it is; I bought four purple ajugas at once and got the tags mixed up). The little ajuga is topped with blue flowers, a blue that is repeated by a few blue, red-veined cups on *Geranium grandiflorum alpinum* standing behind it. Another chartreuse hosta, this one slug-free and very elegant with green-edged leaves, is keeping company with another ajuga—'Pink Silver'—which is a faint echo of Nancy's heuchera since its plum-colored leaves have a grey overtone. 'Crimson Pygmy' barberry is at its best this time of year, its tiny leaves stained-glass red, made even more dramatic by the color of its neighbor, a graceful whirl of rose-tinged yellow and white grass: *Hakonechloa macra* 'Aureola'. After a low tuffet of grey-green geranium (*reynardii*) comes a colony of grey, almost white, *Artemisia stelleriana*; then another purple ajuga, this one rising to an almost one-foot cone—*A*. 'Purple Brocade'—also bearing blue flowers. Does it sound symphonic? Behind the smaller plants, clumps of amsonia are putting forth their restrained milky-blue stars while a stout stand of the roughneck *Lysimachia ciliata* 'Atropurpurea' is providing a repetition of wine-colored foliage amid not-as-yet-flowering perennials. Way back behind the wall, some *Prunus x cistena* are performing the same service, while the hue of the hostas is restated by *Euphorbia pilosa* in an enormous explosion of sulfur yellow. The plant is four or five feet tall and almost as wide. A splendid sight.

Contributions in an adjoining border are these: tall rosettes of *Penstemon* 'Husker Red' with long, pointed and polished, claret-colored leaves; a foam of *Artemisia* 'Lambrook Silver'; more silver in *Tanacetum niveum*; a white-and-green tuft of grass

(*Arrhenatherum elatius tuberosum* 'Nanum'); and a swirl of *Nepeta* 'White Wonder', blooming white. Nestled between the nepeta and the 'Lambrook Silver' is a mound of *Oxalis vulcanicola*—do you know it? Its rounded three-parted, garnet-red leaves are no more than three-quarters of an inch across and it bears continuously (summer outdoors, winter indoors) hundreds of tiny yellow flowers. An exuberant little thing, though not as volcanic as I expected it to be from its name. (Apparently when it is at home it grows on volcanic soil.)

You've got to imagine all these plants surrounded and backed by other green and gray individuals: blue-green dianthus, grey dwarf sage, grey veronicas and caryopteris, wonderful foamy calamintha (*C. cretica*), furry white mint that I think is *Mentha buddleoides*, and variegated pineapple mint. Red foliage appears again in some heucheras, in that sempervivum I mentioned earlier, and in purple *Salvia officinalis*, whose color one would really be hard put to it to define. The thick, opposite, elliptic, pebbled leaves seem to be charcoal grey over dark purple. Most mysterious. And so in this border we have purple foliage combined with greys and white and in the other border with sulfur yellow, a bit of grey, and touches of blue. I wonder—is anything more fun than gardening?

PURPLE-FOLIAGED PLANTS

Annuals

Atriplex hortensis 'Rubra' (purple
    orach)
Anthriscus sylvestris 'Raven's Wing'
Hibiscus acetosella 'Red Shield'
Ocimum basilicum 'Purple Ruffles'
    (purple basil)
Perilla frutescens (shiso)
Setcreasea pallida 'Purple Heart'

Perennials, Tubers, Bulbs, and Shrubs

Heuchera 'Palace Purple', 'Chocolate
    Ruffles', 'Montrose Ruby'

Ophiopogon planiscapus 'Nigrescens'
    (black mondo grass)
Lysimachia ciliata 'Purpurea'
Ajuga pyramidalis 'Metallica Crispa
    Purpurea', *A. reptans* 'Royalty',
    'Purple Brocade', 'Jungle Beauty
    Improved'
Clematis recta 'Purpurea'
Oxalis triangularis
Dahlia 'Ellen Houston', 'Bishop of
    Llandaff', 'Japanese Bishop'
Ipomoea batatas 'Blackie'
Prunus x cistena
Berberis 'Crimson Pygmy'
Berberis thunbergii 'Rosy Glow'

NEPETAS

For some years I've been growing, but not particularly enjoying, a catmint I got as *Nepeta faassenii* (*mussinii*) or *Nepeta mussinii* (*faassenii*)—the catalogues have always seemed to imply, by means of parentheses, that they were the same thing. I would look at my floppy little plant with its greyish-green leaves and idly wonder why the British gardening books made such a fuss about it; it wasn't even *grey*, as they said it was. I did like its pungent aroma and its spikes of lavender flowers. Then, a few years ago, I began to acquire different species of the genus and now I'm into nepetas, wanting to sort them out and find more of the garden-worthy kinds.

As soon as I got out the books I found that the situation is fairly muddled, with the same nepeta going by several names or even being listed alternatively under the dracocephalums, a closely related genus. I wouldn't dream of inflicting the confusion on a reader—in fact, I myself don't understand the difference between a nepeta and a dracocephalum—it has something to do with whether the calyx teeth of the blossom are straight or curved and whether the bracts are pinnately divided or entire. There's also a terminal apicule involved. Although I'm not versed in such things as terminal apicules I *do* want to find the right names of the plants I'm growing and looking for.

To begin, nepetas are aromatic perennial or annual herbs of

the family of Labiatae. They have square stems, opposite leaves, and small tubular flowers of lavender, white, or yellow in whorls borne on long racemes. They come from hot, sunny, well-drained areas in Europe, Asia, and North Africa, so, naturally, they want to be planted in light soil in well-drained, sunny parts of our gardens. Surprisingly, most of the garden varieties are hardy through Zone 4. There are about 250 species in the genus, of which probably the best known is catnip, *N. cataria*, a plant that has gone wild in America and elsewhere and is suitable exclusively for herb gardens, and that solely for its medicinal qualities. It's no beauty and its odor is revolting to some of us. (Garden catmints smell good to most of us.) Only a few nepetas are generally used in flower gardens, although many of them deserve to be. It's those I've been chasing down. We've got into a rut, as we so often do.

The most widely grown nepeta is the *mussinii?/faassenii?* I've been puzzling over and imagine my surprise when I found the following sentence in a scholarly article in an old volume of *Baileya* at Cornell: "For somewhat over 100 years it has been known to botanists and horticulturists that all was not well with the plants that were passing under the name *Nepeta mussinii*."* Well, wouldn't you think they would have done something about it?

It appears that the species *mussinii* was introduced into western Europe in 1803 by a Russian count named Apollos Apollosovich Mussin-Pushkin who brought it back from an expedition to the Caucasus. It was named in his honor (as were the spring-flowering bulbs puschkinia). *N. mussinii* later crossed with the small white-flowering *N. nepetella*, producing a plant that was superior to both of its parents and was called *N. faassenii*. When this hybrid began to be used in British gardens its name became confused with that of the species and they've been

---

*Gordon P. DeWolf Jr., "Nepeta," *Baileya* 3 (1955): 99–107.

confused ever since. That this should have happened is odd since in appearance and behavior they are quite different. (It's also odd that the British should be growing the real *faassenii* and we the inferior *mussinii*.)* *Faassenii* is twelve to eighteen inches tall while *mussinii* is around eight to ten inches. *Faassenii* has one and one-half inch narrow, wedge-shaped silvery leaves and *mussinii's* are one inch, rounded, and greyish green. *Faassenii* is sterile while *mussinii* sets seed and even self-sows. How could they possibly be confused? One of England's greatest plantsmen writes that *"faassenii* is the new name for *mussinii"* and the authors of the *The Color Dictionary of Flowers and Plants* imply that the names are interchangeable.† Although Carroll Gardens lists *mussinii* as an alternate specific they do say their N. *faassenii* is "the true sterile species (hybrid, they mean), propagated vegetatively." I'll try them next spring.

There's a larger form (or a hybrid) of *faassenii* called 'Six Hills Giant' (or N. *gigantea*) that a few U.S. nurseries are offering at last, and if the nursery sends you the right plant it will be a three-foot by three-foot upright silvery plant that should have a lot of eager gardeners lined up to buy it. I was lucky.

All three of these nepetas I've mentioned billow about a good deal, distributing their many lilac-colored blossoms generously on and around their neighbors. If they are sheared back halfway when the first flowering is over they'll do it again in late summer. There are a couple of special forms of *mussinii*—'Blue Wonder' and 'White Wonder'. I've got the white one and like it well enough but don't consider it a wonder.

A summer or two ago I grew several nepetas from seed-exchange seed. The plants from the packet labeled N. *sibirica* grew one and one-half feet tall (if you can call a flopping stem

*Written before the true *faassenii* finally trickled over to America.
†Roy Hay and Patrick M. Synge, *The Color Dictionary of Flowers and Plants for Home and Garden* (New York: Crown, 1974).

"tall"). The crenellated leaves are one and three-quarter inches long, and the lilac flowers grow in ten- to twelve-inch racemes on dark red stems. Not many flowers open at the same time.

Nepeta grandiflora is quite tall—two and one-half feet, upright, and its scalloped green leaves are two and three-quarter inches long. The stems are green, and the lilac-colored flowers on long open spikes are similar to those of *sibirica*.

These are both pleasant plants but don't, I feel, deserve a place in the border. I have raised several that do. One is N. *nervosa*. It is low (six to eight inches), compact, and has small, dark green lanceolate ribbed leaves. When it flowers it holds straight up, very close to the plant, dense spikes of lavender-blue blossoms with a paler lip. Their color is more nearly blue than that of any other nepeta I've seen and certainly *nervosa*'s growth habit is the best—at least the neatest. I find that while I enjoy the sight of plants intertwining with and embracing nearby plants I have a sneaking fondness for those that keep to themselves. They're so easy to tend, so controlled, so organized. I'm putting some of these small catmints in the front of the border with the mat dianthus, armerias, and other self-contained subjects.

Another fine nepeta came from seed labeled N. 'Souvenir d'André Chaudron' ('Blue Beauty'). Since cultivars rarely come true from seed I doubted the name, though I liked the way it rolled off the tongue. However, mine matches the descriptions of 'Souvenir' that I've found in books. Some people say that this plant is a form of *grandiflora*, others say *sibirica*, but it doesn't resemble either of them. It *does* resemble a plant described in L. H. Bailey's *Standard Cyclopedia of Horticulture*, one he calls *Nepeta veitchii*. My plant is around two feet tall (taller when flowering), has jagged pointed two- to three-inch-long smooth dark green leaves and tiered racemes of wonderful deep violet-blue flowers, one and one-half inches long each. The leaves have a strange wild aroma and the whole plant is a great success, unless you want to hold against it its tendency to sprawl. It sprawls only after a storm, say I, defensively. It *does* spread from the roots, but since every piece is welcome, who's to complain?*

Another seed-exchange nepeta is one that came as N. *camphorata*—a lovely pungent small-leaved, very silvery creature that produced cascades of pale lavender blossoms in its first year. I'm not sure how many years I'll be able to keep it as it's from southern Greece.† The temperature here two days ago went from 70 degrees F during the day to 19 at night. The next night it was 12 degrees. I did pot one of the plants and bring it in to the back porch that warm day, but I think I should have taken it to bed with me instead. It must have been about 20 on the porch. Are plants ever dealt such cruel blows in Greece?

One of the catmints in the garden is a real mystery. It was given to me as N. 'Dropmore', but looks very like *camphorata*—small cordate, stalked, and with deeply notched grey leaves and racemes of pale purply flowers flung about with complete abandon. Very floriferous, very long-blooming. It doesn't appear to be as hardy as *mussinii* but has staggered triumphantly through quite a few nasty winters with the help of evergreen boughs. Sometimes it doesn't pull itself together until the end of May. A year or so ago Wayside advertised a N. 'Dropmore' they said was from Manitoba and thrives in Zone 3! (This year they didn't list it). Their plant, as pictured, had roundish green leaves rather than long notched grey ones. Carroll Gardens has sold a N. 'Dropmore' they describe as having grey, toothed foliage, like mine. Do you see what I mean by muddled?

An almost white-foliaged little nepeta, N. *phyllochlamys*,

---

*Since writing this I've seen plants in other gardens labeled 'Souvenir d'André Chaudron' but none of them has looked (or smelled) like mine. I do wish Mr. Bailey were still here.

†As it happens, the plant lived for ten years in the garden.

came from seed. Its dear leaves on long petioles are perfect tri-
angles, not more than one-quarter inch on each side, crinkled,
soft, and furry. The plant huddles itself into a rosette about
three inches high. I have it in gritty soil in a raised bed. It
seemed to die the first winter, two years ago, then this summer
it rose from the dead, either from the old roots or from seed.
You can be sure I potted it up this fall before the hard frosts began and put it in the bay window in the parlor. It has pink and
white flowers and I don't know what part of the world it comes
from as I can't find it in the books.

The Hardy Plant Society seed exchange recently included
ten nepetas, several of which are described by garden authorities as being excellent candidates for the border. I'm hoping
their next list will repeat those offerings. Since nurseries don't
carry them, we'll have to raise our own.

For example, one writer says *N. nuda* is taller than but reminiscent of the white *Verbascum chaixii*, with greyish basal leaves
and five-foot branched stems carrying spikes of small lavender-
white or white flowers with bronzy lilac-colored calyxes. I wonder why such a fine plant isn't in circulation? Sounds like a
perfect subject for Beth Chatto's dry garden or a dry area in our
own gardens. All it wants is sunshine, apparently. I'm not so
smitten with my white *Verbascums chaixii* that I would mind replacing them with something else. I had been thinking of the
native moth mullein (*V. blattaria*), the one whose dusky white
blossoms have hairy violet stamens. They always seem too
pretty to leave out in the fields with the burdock and nettles. In
the border, however, they might seed themselves too liberally.

There is praise in the Clausen-Ekstrom perennial book for
a catmint from Spain and Portugal that bears spikes of purple
flowers with deep rose calyxes—*N. tuberosa*. Would it have a
chance of being hardy? The Hardy Plant Society had the seed,
as they had for a bushy three-by-two footer called *N. govaniana*

or *governiana*, a Kashmiri with rounded green leaves and racemes of small creamy yellow blossoms. This is one catmint that likes a cool moist spot. Graham Stuart Thomas uses the words "beautiful," "charming," and "graceful" when describing it and is mystified at its lack of popularity, since it's been growing for all to see, at Kew, for years. Perhaps I can get hold of the seed.*

None of the nepetas in my garden seem to concern themselves unduly with the confusion about nomenclature but get on cheerfully with their job of being decorative and aromatic. Well might they be cheerful as they seem not to suffer at all from any diseases or insects. They should probably be divided once in a while so as to liberate their crowns from crowded growth but other than that—no problems. When the taxonomists have finally succeeded in straightening out names and origins we gardeners will be relieved. Meanwhile, the plants couldn't be happier.

*Graham Stuart Thomas, *Perennial Garden Plants, or The Modern Florilegium* (London and Melbourne: J. M. Dent & Sons, 1982). As it turns out I didn't agree with Mr. Thomas as to *N. governiana* which, in my garden, was undistinguished and unappealing. There are several new nepetas in the trade nowadays, in addition to a plentiful supply of the grey-leaved 'Six Hills Giant'. I'm trying 'Walker's Low' this summer, having seen it making a great glorious bush in a friend's garden, as well as 'Dawn to Dusk', a plant that bears, I am assured, spikes of pink flowers with purple calyxes.

TWO SMALL PLANTS

I s it true for you that you don't always appreciate gift plants when you are given them? It seems to me that I'm always saying thank you, perfunctorily, for some horticultural donation or other and not learning to value it until months, even years later.

Not that all gift plants are a blessing! When you first start to garden, the neighbors often, under the guise of generosity, unload on you all the offspring of viciously prolific plants that they haven't the courage to compost. But as your gardening prowess grows and you begin to move in more exalted gardening circles (the American Rock Garden Society? the Hardy Plant Society?) so does the quality of the gift plants move upward. No more variegated goutweed, for example, no more gooseneck loosestrife. Nevertheless, human nature being what it is, it's the plant that has cost good money that often receives the most loving attention—at least at the outset. Gift plants have to try harder. Then, so often, they end up giving more joy and satisfaction than the high-priced item one had such hopes for.

Here I want to talk about two unsolicited, unassuming, undramatic but undeniably charming little creatures that are growing in my garden, donations for which I am being belatedly grateful.

The first comes originally from southwestern Europe—a very small plant with a very big name—two of them, in fact: *Chaenorrhinum origanifolium, var. crassifolia* or *Linaria origanifolia*. It makes a compact bush whose one-half-inch-long, dense, leathery, opposite leaves make it look like something in between thyme and sweet marjoram, except that the color is of a bluer green. One automatically rubs the leaves and is astonished to find it not pungent. The plant sends up, above the foliage, countless stems bearing clouds of tiny lipped lavender dragons-head flowers whose open mouths show a pale yellow bearded tongue. As they grow longer, seeds form on the stem, while two or three more flowers are continuously appearing on the top. The plant, including the flower stems, never surpasses eight or nine inches. Although the Royal Horticultural Society dictionary calls it a perennial, here it is not winter hardy. It's all the same, however, as it never fails to self-sow—not so much as to annoy, just enough to please. I have it growing in poorish soil in a raised bed where it's content.

My second pet these days is a cranesbill that was raised no doubt from seed-exchange seed, it being highly unlikely that a nursery would bother with such a non-flashy individual. When I first saw it, I myself was not impressed until the scales fell from my eyes. I did observe, even at first glance, that the leaves were attractive, but that is true of all cranesbills. The plant came to me as *Geranium pyrenaicum albiflorum*, but the deeply lobed leaf resembles that of *G. pusillum* in Dr. Peter Yeo's book *Hardy Geraniums*, a plant that he calls a weed and which he says is rumored to have hybridized with *pyrenaicum*.* Be that as it may, my cranesbill is a dear—it doesn't run, doesn't flop, but makes a neat bush about one foot high. From the outer edge of the base long, delicate, branching stems radiate, each with pairs of

*Peter Yeo, *Hardy Geraniums* (Portland, Ore.: Timber Press, 1984).

opposite leaves from whose axils shoot thready stalks that branch into pairs of peduncles, each holding aloft a one-half-inch flower with five pale lilac (not white) delicately veined and cleft petals. It is still blooming now, sparsely, in October, but for many weeks during the summer there appeared to be hundreds of blossoms floating above the plant. Lacy and lovely. It might not count for much in a perennial border but would be appreciated, certainly, on a wall, a raised bed, or in some other spot where it wouldn't be competing for attention with bigger and brighter subjects.

ANNUALS *for the* PERENNIAL BORDER

Rather an odd title for an essay, you may be thinking, but not so odd when you think again. Ever since the introduction of the herbaceous border in the days when William Robinson and Gertrude Jekyll ruled over the horticultural world in England and part of America, it has been considered legal to fill in gaps in a perennial or a mixed border (which may include bulbs, shrubs, and small trees as well as perennials) with annuals. It is almost inevitable that dull areas and even blank empty spots will occur in a perennial border as the summer wears on; plants with not much to contribute but flowers stop blooming, while others may even have the habit of disappearing underground to sleep the summer away. Then there are plants that don't concern themselves with keeping up appearances after they've had their fling and others that are subject to unsightly afflictions if the summer is too wet—or too dry.

Now some of these mid- or late-summer embarrassments can be avoided by not installing in the border subjects that look glorious in spring but take no responsibility for the rest of the season. Just don't *plant* tulips, daffodils, spring anemones, and oriental poppies in the border but put them out on the edge of the woods garden or this side of a group of shrubs. If you must have feckless, happy-go-lucky individuals such as columbine (and I, for one, must) try to place them so that stout and faithful late-bloomers will surge up and hide their untidy August foliage. Think ahead.

But even when one has thought ahead and planned carefully, putting the troublemakers elsewhere and orchestrating one's garden so that delicious combinations of color and texture will provide an ever-changing but ever-delightful symphony from early spring to late autumn, even when all that could be done has been done, those annoying gaps will occur. Perhaps your helper (or you) chopped to bits a group of dwarf balloon flowers or Japanese anemones during the spring cleanup (all their own fault, the wretched things, for taking so long to come up!) Or perhaps mice got into your heather during the winter. Perhaps rabbits ate the amsonia or deer the delphinium, or the wildly changing spring weather did in some of the roses and helianthemums, thus depriving your symphony of important notes and, in some cases, whole themes. It's then that you need annuals.

Annuals, yes, but not just any old annuals, mind. The solution is not to be found, unless you are amazingly lucky, in a few six-packs from your local garden center, and I'll tell you why. Most annuals that are raised for "the trade" are deliberately bred to be—if we don't say "garish" we must say "assertive." They are intended for quick front-yard planting, for window boxes, gas station containers, and park bedding. They're bred for maximum impact and minimum maintenance and they do their job well. They are not, however (with a few exceptions), calculated to harmonize with most perennials. They're bold, bouncy, bright, and sometimes beautiful but are not often compatible with the more delicately designed, more reticently tinted plants in the typical perennial garden. Think of campanulas, of dianthus, of lavender and flax, of artemisias and shastas and veronicas. Think of feathery astilbes, goatsbeards, and nepetas. Even delphiniums. Most borders, in the North at least, tend to be compositions in pink, lavender and grey, blue, white, and lemon yellow. In these borders strong yellow, orange, and flaming red can rarely be integrated successfully. (These colors should be kept for separate gardens, I've decided, after having spent many years attempting to incorporate them into my mixed border).

So what kind of annuals do we need? Those of restrained, refined, non-strident hues and, if possible, delicate or at any rate attractive foliage. Since this kind of annual is rarely to be found in garden centers, serious perennial gardeners will have to plan ahead, assuming that they'll need extra plants, either potted up or waiting in holding beds, that they can resort to in case of emergency. Seedlings can be raised in early spring at home under lights or possibly in a local greenhouse with an obliging manager.

Now let us consider the plants we might like to use. Of course there are countless genera to choose from, but here I'll discuss only those I've grown and used in my own garden. Let's start with yellows.

One of the best blenders I've ever found is an annual chrysanthemum, *C. coronarium* 'Primrose Gem', a twelve- to fifteen-inch plant with lacy foliage whose upright stems hold dense corymbs of small, soft yellow semi-double daisies with gold centers. Fresh and lovely, something to help carry you through the dog days of August when so much of the garden looks hot and discouraged. It would be hard to find a perennial with which it wouldn't harmonize.

Another yellow jewel is the Mexican tulip poppy, *Hunnemannia fumariifolia*. I'll admit it's not a very pale yellow, but since it has elegantly cut silver leaves and since its three-inch silky cups glisten so brilliantly in the sunlight, the total effect is that of delicacy and grace. *H. f.* 'Sunlite' is semi-double. As you know, members of the poppy family don't like to be moved, so their seeds must be planted in peat pots or directly in the ground early in May and the young plants subsequently thinned to stand seven to eight inches apart.

There are lemon yellow snapdragons that look at home in an established border even though they're only summer visitors. They come tall or short and, of course, in many other pretty colors that you might prefer, depending on your color scheme, all of them, so far as I know, reasonable, natural, easy-to-handle colors. (But what am I saying? By the time you read this there may be bright orange snapdragons, and double, to boot.)

As much can be said for the annual scabiosa whose two-and-a-half-inch fluffy round flowers are rose, violet, or an intriguing shade of plum. Their only fault is that without support they flop. The "dwarf" type, *S. atropurpurea* 'Dwarf Double Mixed', are still eighteen inches high, so I imagine they'll not be much more erect than the thirty-six-inch ones I used to raise for cut flowers.

The only other flower I know that has a color similar to that of the plum scabiosa is a species of verbascum, *V. phoeniceum*. This is really a short-lived perennial but must be considered an annual in the north. If it overwinters once or twice, you're lucky. This verbascum is not a big hairy creature but a two- to three-foot plant with a basal rosette of smooth, dark green toothed leaves from which rise straight slender stems set round with solitary flowers on slim pedicels, flowers in shades of lilac, rose, and that special smoky plum color. Very nice indeed.

More and more annual (and biennial) salvias are being used in borders and with good reason. I'm not speaking here of the fiercely red *Salvia splendens* but of tender perennials or annuals such as *S. farinacea*—a perennial in the South but an annual here in the North. This species gives us that fine branching eighteen-inch plant with never-ending spikes of purple-blue lipped flowers. There are several named varieties, but the best of the lot so far is 'Victoria'. I tried a "white" one one year but thought it dingy and undistinguished. The breeders may have improved on it by now and they have lately come out with a blue and white bicolor called, alternately, 'Strata' or 'Sea Breeze'. These may be somewhat different plants but they're both blue and white. I didn't think they did much for my border.

S. coccinea and its cultivar 'Lady in Red', are both superior subjects that seem to fit in anywhere. They are fifteen to eighteen inches high, and carry slender spires of small scarlet flowers. 'Lady in Red' is, without question, an improvement on the species, with somewhat larger blossoms and the ability to bloom in either full sun or light shade, all summer and fall until hard frost. They do benefit from a trimming that relieves them of their spent blossom stems in mid or late summer.

Now, here am I, after warning you away from bright red annuals, telling you to try 'Lady in Red'. My excuse is that these scarlet flowers are small and, being wafted about on long graceful stems, seem to add little sparks to the border combinations, rather than colliding with them. Naturally, they don't fit everywhere, but it's surprising how many groups of plants can accept this lively salvia with equanimity, even gratitude. There's a new pink and white *S. coccinea* called 'Cherry Blossom' that I tried and found wanting.

It's hard to stop talking about salvias but I must just add that every year I plant seed of *Salvia patens*, perhaps the bluest blue flower alive. I don't consider these to be temporary flowers but permanent residents of the border, even though they're not hardy here and I must gather their seeds every autumn. "Permanent" because they have their own section of the garden reserved for them every year.

I raised lots of annual baby's breath during the period when I was selling cut flowers—*Gypsophila elegans* 'Covent Garden', as I recall. The blossoms were single, white, and airy, the perfect mixer. *G. elegans* can also be had in shades of pink, which might be nice too.

One year I tried lavatera as a filler in the border, both 'Silver Cup', a pink one, and 'Mont Blanc'. They were dazzlingly pretty but I felt, not a success for two reasons. They were too exotic-looking, I thought, to blend with my northern plants, and the white one was *so* white that it jumped out ahead of all the other flowers, insisting on being the center of attention. There is such a thing as being *too* white, I discovered.

This is not to say that lavatera wouldn't work in your garden—it depends on what is already there—but only to warn you that it is quite a presence.

One spring I planted a flat of those sky blue forget-me-nots, *Cynoglossum amabile*. I believe mine were called 'Firmament'—Mrs. Burpee's favorite, said the catalogue, and there was Mrs. Burpee in a housedress, beaming over a bouquet. The plants, with their grey-blue leaves and cloud of tiny cobalt flowers were such a joy that I saved the seed and sprinkled it along the front of the border in the fall. They kept coming up all the next summer. As they finished blooming I pulled them up and other plants would come along and take their place. It was a wonderful system—free flowers all summer. I did this for years until, at length, I allowed them to be crowded out by some small bright blue delphinium that I now keep going the same way, gathering the seeds every fall. (These, however, I don't broadcast outdoors but plant in flats indoors in early March.) I believe this one-and-a-half-foot delphinium to be a form of *D. grandiflorum* var. *chinense*, perhaps the one sold as 'Blue Butterfly'. I can't be sure—a friend pulled off some seeds and dropped them into my pocket some years ago when I admired the plant in his garden. Now the seedlings I raise are labeled simply, "Allen's delphinium." Since *D. grandiflorum* comes from Siberia and western China and is classified as a perennial, one would think it would come through our winters without a hitch, but it rarely does for me.

The frankly annual *Delphinium ajacis*, known to all of us as larkspur, is a lovely thing and is, with its spikes of soft pastel blossoms, eminently fitted to associate with hardy plants. I'd love to use it, but here, where we have hot humid summers, it is sadly prone to mildew and depression. I imagine it does beautifully in Denver and other high, dry blowy places. I must add, though, that a friend who lives farther away from our lake grows it successfully.

If you've not found, among these plants I've been discussing, something you'd like for the very edge of your garden, how about annual dianthus? You can find the cushion or taller twelve- to fifteen-inch tufted sorts in white, pink, rose, either solid or bicolors, with either green or silvery blue-grey foliage. Nearly all of them are spicily fragrant. Most of them come from *D. chinensis* or *D. heddewigii* but there are a couple of new hybrid strains resulting from crossing *D. chinensis* with *D. barbatus*, the biennial sweet william. They are the 'Ideal' and 'Telstar' dianthus and are said by their vendors to bloom the first year from seed but to behave otherwise like proper, rather tender biennials—that is, they should go on through at least a second season where winters are not very severe. You can get seeds for separate colors. Last summer I tried 'Ideal Crimson' and 'Telstar Dark Purple' and found them to be as attractive as described.

Having been dazzled by the sight of sea-blue *Anagallis linifolia* growing gloriously among the grey rocks of the Kabylia

Mountains in Algeria, I once tried them on the edge of my border. That happened to be the summer we broke all records in
heat, humidity, and drought and before we had an adequate
supply of water here at the farm. My poor anagallis wished
themselves back on their mountains and eventually they pined
away and died. However, I mean to try again and I recommend
them to you as most desirable plants, especially made for the
gardener who is always searching for pure blue. Thompson &
Morgan is showing one they call *A. monelli,* apparently the
same one, for the books tell me that the name has been changed
to *A. linifolia monelli.* It makes a nine-inch mound that will sit
chummily among your clumps of dianthus without discom-
moding them in any way.

If space permitted, we could consider the qualifications of
such cooperative subjects as spiderflower (cleome), bachelor's
button, oxypetalum, with its cerulean stars, love-in-a-mist,
especially the pure blue *Nigella* 'Miss Jekyll', and that fine, old-
fashioned green and white euphorbia (*E. marginata*), snow-on-
the-mountain.

To conclude this discussion of annuals for the perennial
border, let's consider how to place these temporary tenants of
established gardens. When designing and planting my perennial or mixed borders, I not only tried to combine color, form,
and texture felicitously, but kept in mind rule number one of
any successful composition, whether it be a written work, a
painting, a piece of music, or a garden—repetition of theme. I
sited the plants so that the eye of the observer, as it traveled
down or around the garden, could pick up the same colors,
shapes, and textures throughout, even though they might be
provided by different plants. For example, there might be a
clump of pale yellow iris, with a pale yellow rose further on,
then a bouquet of *Oenothera missouriensis.* Spires of lavender delphinium could stand in the back of the border, a froth of grey-

and-lavender nepeta this way, then veronicas that echo the color of the delphinium. Vertical lines of Japanese iris can be repeated by lythrum and cimicifuga; the hemispherical shapes of santolina will recur in dwarf box and helianthemum; frothy clouds of gypsophila will be echoed by misty *Galium aristatum.* And so on. All of the repetitions and reminiscences that satisfy the eye although the brain may not know why.

So we must hold to this rule of repetition when placing annuals. We don't want clumps of brilliant blue anagallis where there is no color nearby that is even faintly related to such a blue. It would be perfect if we had a group of *Salvia patens* somewhere nearby or the single *Delphinium grandiflorum* or tall *Delphinium* 'Bluebird' or five-foot *D. bellamosum* in the background. We can use soft yellow snapdragons here and there throughout the garden where they will make a recurring note as well as picking up that of the non-brassy yarrows such as *Achillea* 'Moonshine' or, better yet, *A. x taygetea. Chrysanthemum* 'Primrose Gem' can be used in the same way. Cynoglossum, from seeds sprinkled along the front of the border, will stitch the whole composition together. Above all, we must not plant isolated, irrelevant batches of annuals but must try to weave them in and out so that they will not only repeat the colors and/or forms of the permanent border residents but repeat themselves as well.

VARIEGATED PLANTS

Variegated plants seem to have something in common with succulents: people either love them or loathe them. And even variegated plant freaks don't fall for all of them. Some of the plants look fresh, harmonious, dramatic, distinguished, and others merely speckled, indecisive, hectic—I might even add *sick*. All, I suppose, depends on who is looking at them and how they are being grown. I've seen several new variegated perennials I do not covet. Merely to be variegated is not enough.

But perhaps we should define "variegated." Wyman's *Gardening Encyclopedia* says it means "having marks, stripes or blotches of some color other than the basic ground color, in plants which are green." The marks, stripes, or blotches come in white, cream, yellow, grey, red, and shades of pink. While some say that such variegations are caused by an affliction, the *Royal Horticultural Society Dictionary* says it is not so. However, many variegated plants are less robust than their solid green siblings or cousins and tend to develop afflictions more readily— infectious chlorosis, for one—and to be more liable to succumb to drought or severe weather conditions. Not that such a tendency discourages their collectors who would go to any amount of trouble to preserve in good health a choice variegated plant.

Plants with variegated leaves are found in all categories—annuals and perennials, grasses, vines, shrubs, and trees. Because they are popular with a growing number of gardeners, the breeders are constantly endeavoring to produce more of them. As a rule, they must be reproduced by vegetative means, that is by buds, cuttings, or divisions, rather than by seed. Even then the plants will sometimes revert to plain green, to the exasperation of their growers, who value them not only for their intrinsic beauty but because they contribute color and variety of pattern to the garden all season long, instead of being effective only during a brief flowering period. Owners of recherché variegated plants get in the habit of looking at them sharply as they make the rounds of the garden, readying themselves to swoop down and pinch out any leaves that show signs of reversion, which is the only way to save them from backsliding. And even that doesn't always work.

There are a few plants that have variegated leaves in the spring but change to solid color later on, alarming the person who bought them without being informed of their habits. *Hosta fortunei* 'Albo-picta' (*viridis marginata*) is one of these, having bright chartreuse leaves edged with deep green in spring but looking like any other plain hosta during the summer. There are, of course, many fine variegated hostas that retain their yellow or white markings all summer.

A friend brought me a large coarse-looking astrantia one September, assuring me that I would find it sensational the following May. I couldn't believe it but poked it into my garden for the sake of friendship and forgot about it. The following spring as I was weeding and tidying up in that area I encountered what appeared to be a most exotic greenhouse plant growing in my garden, displaying with great dramatic effect glossy, deeply cut leaves of cream, yellow, and green. Only after I had examined it closely did I realize that, although it looked scarcely related to my ordinary *Astrantias major* and *maxima*, it was indeed an astrantia. I later found the marker which said *Astr. major* 'Sunningdale Variegated'. My friend was right—it's really sensational. But only until summer comes along, when the color disappears slowly, and there you finally are with a rather common-looking green plant. I find that if you place it close to a group of *Helleborus orientalis* (and it looks splendid near the jade green speckled ones) their handsome new leaves spread out and get all the attention when the astrantia has lost its allure.

Some of the old standby ground covers come with interestingly varied leaves—there's a *Vinca minor* called 'Sterling Silver', a *Pachysandra terminalis* 'Silver Edge', and various ajugas. I like *A. reptans* 'Silver Beauty' and the rose, pink, and cream one known as *A. r.* 'Burgundy Glow' or 'Burgundy Lace', especially when planted with Japanese painted fern, which is variegated itself in shades of grey and wine red. In this country aubrietas behave more like rock garden plants than ground covers, especially the variegated one I found at Stonecrop Nurseries. Its small, jagged holly-shaped leaves are edged with pure white, which makes a very pretty picture with grey rocks, particularly when the blue flowers appear. There's also a variegated antennaria or pussytoes. We think of arabis as being an all-too-common green-leaved plant with pink—or more often white—blossoms, a creeper that travels around among the spring bulbs. Reliable but not very classy. There is an *Arabis caucasica* 'Variegata' with cream-edged leaves, and while it's an improvement on the ordinary one, it is still not what one would call distinguished. But last spring I met an elegant arabis, *A. ferdinandi-coburgi* 'Variegata', a small rock plant with flat glossy chartreuse-and-white oblong leaves that form a tight rosette *composed* of rosettes. The flowers are small and white. Since the plant comes from Macedonia, I was afraid my specimen would be longing for its native mountain air during our summer heat, but it's come through its first trial with flying colors and is still with me, perched serenely on top of a raised bed in soil that is mostly sand and grit with a little garden soil and old manure added.

When the ground covers *Lamium maculatum* 'Beacon Silver' and 'White Nancy' finally arrived here from England, those of us who had become fed up with seeing pictures of them without being able to get our hands on them were finally gratified. Their green-edged silver foliage has, especially in part shade, a sheen that makes it one of the few greys we're truly justified in calling silver. They are identical plants as to foliage but 'White Nancy' produces white flowers and 'Beacon Silver' pink. These are much finer plants than the common *L. maculatum*, whose splotchy leaves are not particularly attractive and whose traveling urge is hard to curb. A pink-flowered *L. m.* 'Aureum' is available whose green and yellow leaves with white mid-veins will appeal to those who like yellow foliage.

For a while I liked *Houttuynia cordata* 'Chameleon' ('Variegata'), and understandably, for it has green leaves painted with swirls of cream, rose, and deep red, all colors varying according to the season and site. The plant had been launched with great éclat by the major nurseries and I took the bait. Now, years later, I'm still fighting the beautiful vandal whose conquering hordes don't know the meaning of defeat. It's true, I haven't used Roundup on it, but that's what will be needed for the final solution.

Woodland plants with variegated foliage are particularly welcome both because the patterns are especially effective in part shade and because, since there is very little flower color from shade-loving perennials after spring has passed, the patterned foliage provides interest where it is needed.

Several of our American woodland natives have patterned leaves. Two of the prettiest are *Goodyeara pubescens*, the downy rattlesnake plantain or orchid, and *Chimaphila maculata*, known as pipsissewa in Virginia where I first saw it, but as spotted wintergreen in some regions. The goodyeara is really an orchid, although its small white flowers on tall bare stems don't live up to what one thinks an orchid should be. The beauty is in the tapered oval leaves that circle the flower stem near the ground. In addition to a white midrib, the leaves are marked with an interlocking netlike white veining that must have reminded someone of the scales of a rattlesnake, accounting for its threatening name. (As if "goodyeara" weren't enough of a handicap!) The fragrant, nodding, waxy, white flowers of pipsissewa are borne on ten-inch woody stems, well above the whorls of sharply toothed shiny, pointed leaves with white midribs and veins. They grow in dry woods, often near pines, but, like the rattlesnake plantain, are difficult to domesticate. How wonderful it would be to have colonies of these two plants in a woodland garden!

I've just read an article by an English visitor to this country who, upon seeing large expanses of our mottle-leaved *Erythronium americanum* (dogtooth violet or trout lily) was told that the reason for the scarcity of flowers in these plant colonies was that they have running roots that take time to produce flower stalks. She was misinformed, for actually each leaf comes from an offset bulb that will not produce its yellow flower until it is several years old, hence one sees many leaves and only a few flowers. But the leaves, thick, smooth, and splotched with brown or purple, are attractive in themselves. There is a splendid erythronium from Oregon, *E. revolutum*, with large ten-inch creamy mottled leaves that do, I must admit, go dormant in the heat of summer, but are impressive in spring, surmounted by their winged, reflexed flowers. *E. r.* 'White Beauty' is the one sold by most nurseries.

Some native trilliums have fine, smooth, mottled leaves that disappear in July and August like those of the erythroniums.

A relative of our Solomon's seal, *Polygonatum odoratum thunbergii* 'Variegatum' comes from Japan. It has the same graceful growth habits as ours, with small flowers hanging from arching stems. It's not as tall as the American giant Solomon's seal, attaining a height of only three feet, but its leaves are edged with yellow so that it seems to bring flickers of sunlight into the woods.

There are several variegated lamiastrums on the market, most of them too energetic for a restricted shady area but good for covering a lot of otherwise waste space. The foot-tall *Lamiastrum galeobdolon* 'Herman's Pride' is of a different order, confining itself to making clumps of small silver-patterned leaves that are extremely attractive. It has clusters of small butter-yellow hooded and lipped flowers in spring and is a good untemperamental plant that doesn't worry you with all kinds of mysterious needs that you don't know how to fulfill.

The same could be said for all of the pulmonarias. I wouldn't bother with the species if I were you. *Pulmonaria officinalis* (lungwort, Jerusalem sage, or, as it's known in England, soldiers and sailors or spotted dog) may be greeted with enthusiasm when it puts out its pink and blue bells before any other plant has caught on to the fact that it's spring, but later on when its dusty splotched leaves turn mildewy it fails to move the soul. Besides, it spreads too fast. *P. saccharata* 'Mrs. Moon' is nicer, having similar pink and blue bell flowers but larger, cleaner, more clearly heavily spotted grey and green leaves. I have a white-flowering *saccharata* as well as 'Mrs. Moon'.

During the last few years, breeders have been creating quite wonderful pulmonarias. Have you seen 'Roy Davidson' by any chance? A handsome plant—its long, pointed white-flecked, non-mildewy leaves form a large rosette that is effective in a shade garden long after its pink and blue blossoms are gone. *P. saccharata* and *P. longifolia* are its parents. Another descendant of *longifolia* is 'Bertram Anderson', whose extremely narrow speckled leaves give it an odd attenuated look. The breeders may have gone a little too far on this one. Silver-splotched 'Excalibur' and 'Spilled Milk' are still too new in my garden for me to judge them, but *Pulmonaria* 'Argentea' is already the joy of my life, so luminous it lights up the woods around it. The good-sized leaves are of beaten silver and are delicately embroidered around the edges with pale green. Awfully nice planted with clumps of Japanese painted fern.

I haven't seen *Disporum sessile* 'Variegatum' so I shouldn't presume to write about it. I do have *D. flavum*, but would like to have the one whose lance-shaped leaves are "cleanly striped with white" because Graham Stuart Thomas says it's worth growing. He also says it has a "far-questing root stock" so I assume one would have to give it plenty of room.

I know of several variegated perennials for full sun (there are no doubt many more)—the gold and silver-edged thymes, pineapple mint (*Mentha suaveolens* 'Variegata'), and a physostegia or false dragonhead. As to the physostegia, I'm not sure whether I like it or not, even after harboring it for six or eight years. I've tried it in several places but it doesn't seem to fit in with any of my other plants. I wonder if other people have solved the siting of this good-looking individual?* Another problem child was a gift from someone. It is a large, variegated *Sedum spectabile*, that (and I hope the donor does not see this) I find perfectly revolting. Fleshiness and smears of a sickly yellow

---

*I finally gave mine away.

are a bit too much for my taste, which I realize is not always that of the next person; I'm hoping to be able to make a gift of it to him or her.

Touches of cream, rose, wine, and plum on the grainy, leathery, pungent leaves of tricolor sage are another matter altogether. When this plant is burgeoning in midsummer, surrounded by grey-green plants with rose, plum-colored, or white flowers, I would give it first prize. I'm cheating, of course, to indicate that it's a perennial, which it certainly is not in the cold edge of Zone 5. I pot it and bring divisions of it in to the unheated back porch or an unheated upstairs bedroom for the winter. I'm probably cheating, too, to mention a dear plant I have called *Ballota nigra* 'Variegata', because it was also a gift, from my astrantia friend, who probably brought it back from England in his suitcase. I didn't dare ask. The plant consists of a foot-tall mound of rounded, puckered, and crimped one- to one-and-one-half-inch leaves that show innumerable variations of variegations in palest creamy chartreuse on medium green. There are spots, edgings, fan designs, each leaf different from its fellow. I've had this ballota for several years and it never shows the least distress during our wild extremes of heat and cold. It has small lavender-pink labiate flowers that are not the point, really. *Ballota nigra* is related to marrubium (horehound) and is found in Britain, Europe, North Africa, and western Asia and has become naturalized in the northeastern United States, the books say.

There are many striped grasses and bamboos for your selection—you can even choose between horizontal or vertical stripes. Now that grasses are enjoying a great vogue you will have no trouble locating striped *Miscanthus sinensis*, *Molinia caerulea*, *Carex morrowii*, and many more, all most effective when they are properly placed, which is not so easy as is generally supposed. Some people are plopping them, willy-nilly, into their flower borders among the perennials, while some of the rest of us are holding back and saying no. They seem, especially the tall striped ones, to be too large and too insistent to combine well with all but the most imposing perennials. If your flower garden is composed of big globe thistles, daylilies, rudbeckia, and the like, striped or solid-color grasses might join them harmoniously. But for the more modest, small-leaved, small-flowered perennials such as the cranesbills, campanulas, and dianthus, the large grasses seem to be inappropriate companions. There are a few small ones, it's true, that one might try, including a striped green and white one, *Arrhenatherum bulbosum variegatum*, that looks good among clumps of dianthus, coral bells, and other restrained garden inmates. The arrhenatherum, commonly known as bulbous oat grass, never grows above a foot tall, makes a neat clump of almost white leaves, and doesn't romp recklessly around the border as do many grasses. After it flowers it turns a bit yellow, when it should be cut to the ground. It will then re-emerge looking white and clean.

Tall grasses, striped and otherwise, look best to me in windswept places—by fences on the edge of a field, by the sea, on the edge of a pond—where they might be growing naturally.

The same vertical lines that gardeners are looking for when they plant grasses may be obtained by the use of iris, several of which exist in handome two-tone forms. One Japanese iris has bold cream-white stripes on its leaves, and *Iris laevigata* 'Variegata' or *I. foetidissima* come in green and white. Look for the green and white *I. pallida* 'Albo-variegata' and the yellow and green form of *Iris pseudacorus*, the tall swamp-lover with yellow flowers. The contrasting markings on this plant last only through the spring but those on *Iris pallida* remain beautiful all season. My clump, of which I was so fond, seems to have been lost to borers and root rot or some other iris enemy that I didn't immediately detect. I should have planted it in higher, sandier ground. It was happy for some years, multiplying itself and carrying its pale lavender flowers in season—I didn't realize trouble was afoot.

Variegated shrubs are not tricky and they come in what appears to be every genus, from the wide-leaved evergreen shrubs such as leucothoe, pieris, holly, boxwood, and euonymus to the narrow-leaved juniper, hemlock, arborvitae, and chamaecyparis. Since many broad-leaved evergreens cannot be grown in cold climates, it is those gardeners who live where the thermometer doesn't drop below zero who will be able to regale themselves with hollies that sport gold or silver margins on their dark green leaves (*Ilex aquifolium* 'Golden King' and 'Silver Queen'), a variegated pittosporum, or a Japanese osmanthus whose glossy oval leaves are edged in white. For the same gardeners there is aucuba with large gold-speckled leaves, which are effective against a dark background. We further north can have a *Pieris japonica* with white edges as well as variously edged and splotched evergreen euonymus that come as upright shrubs or in a sprawling form that can be trained as a shrub, a vine, or a ground cover. One of the latter type, *E. fortunei coloratus*, has leaves with red and purple areas and is the one frequently used as a ground cover by landscape designers.

I bought my 'Rainbow' leucothoe (*L. catesbaei* 'Folia Multicolor') from the man that bred it, but I've never been satisfied with it. The leaves are supposed to show shades of yellow, pink, deep red, and copper at different times of the year, but they don't do it for me. They merely look muddled and undecided. Not only is it not as pretty as my ordinary leucothoes, it is not as sturdy. I've been on the point of tossing it on the compost for some time, restrained only by seeing pictures of it looking handsome in other people's gardens.

The narrow-leaved evergreens can be grown by northerners as well as southerners and are to be had with either frosty white or yellow tips, when they are not solid green, yellow, "blue," or almost white. There's a 'Gold Tip' juniper, a white-tipped dwarf hemlock, a Leyland cypress with white edges, and various chamaecyparis. I have one of these, *C.* 'Snow', a compact globe that has attained one and one-half feet after five or six years. The center of the shrub is a very pale green but the outer few inches are nearly white during much of the year. Its only fault is that it has a sad yellowish aspect for the first weeks of spring.

Daphne burkwoodii seems to be almost evergreen in the north but does eventually drop all its leaves. No doubt it retains them year round down south. There is a much-prized version of this subject, *D. b.* 'Carol Mackie' with gold borders on its tiny leaves. All the passionate gardeners I know either have it or wish they had it. It comes easily from cuttings so I make lots of them from my plant as well as from the plain-leaved *D. b.* 'Somerset' so I'll have little plants to give away as well as to use as replacements when parent plants leave the scene (these daphnes have the regrettable habit, in their maturity, of splitting open in the center).

Of the deciduous variegated shrubs, I have only two—the old green and cream dogwood sold as *Cornus alba* 'Elegantissima' and a single-flowered *Kerria japonica* whose slender, pointed leaves are decorated with white. It's an airy delicate thing, never rising above three feet, making it a good candidate for a mixed border. The dogwood is taller, more robust, very pretty, and would also be good in a border if it didn't form mats of surface roots and stolons, which is all very well for a specimen that is planted singly or in a shrub border, but not for one planted as a neighbor to perennials. My dogwood may be a freak: others who have shrubs of the same name have no such trouble with theirs. There is another *Cornus alba* called 'Gouchaultii' whose foliage is described as being green, creamy yellow, and rose. All *alba* dogwoods have red, varnished branches in winter that are as enjoyable as their foliage is in summer. One should keep renewing the stems in order to have the best color, by cutting to the ground several of the stoutest of them very early in spring.

As I look through books and catalogues I learn that old familiar shrubs such as deutzia and abelia now come in variegated forms. Weigela too, and cotoneaster. I'm toying with the idea of trying *Hydrangea macrophylla* 'Variegated Mariesii', but I know I might lose it in a hard winter. The catalogue pictures have been tempting me for a long time, even though I know better than to believe in photographs.

I *have* taken a chance on three variegated vines—the first, a Japanese honeysuckle that has fine yellow webbing patterned on its round leaves. It's still too small to be judged, but the second vine, a very expensive *Actinidia kolomikta*, was three years old last summer and made only the most offhand attempt to live up to what was expected of it. I'd been mooning over pictures and descriptions of it for several years, as who would not upon reading: "... its heart-shaped leaves, which are purplish on their first appearance, can then develop vivid pink and pure white bands. Working from the tip backwards, you will first get a white area, then pink and then (if any of the leaf remains) green."* However, the author goes on, plants sometimes fail to perform and no one knows why. And sometimes they will climb to the top of two-story buildings in Sweden. Well mine, planted against a tool shed in New York, grew many solid green leaves the first summer. The second summer, as I rounded the corner of the shed on my riding mower, I very nearly capsized from the joyful shock of seeing a wide white band and a touch of pink on one of its leaves. Ha, thought I, it's got the idea and is on its way!

*Christopher Lloyd, *Foliage Plants* (New York: Random House, 1985), p. 108.

But no such thing. That was that for the summer. The fourth summer finally produced the long-awaited foliage in white, pink, and green. Patience, apparently, is required. This vine is planted against the weathered grey boards of the old shed, and next to it there is an uninhibited specimen of a rose called 'Ballerina', whose large sprays of small single pink white-centered flowers are displayed continuously during the summer. The pink of the rose is almost identical to that in the actinidia leaves, so the combination looks to have been perfectly planned. I don't tell approving visitors that it was an accident.

My third vine is a variegated porcelain berry, *Ampelopsis brevipedunculata* 'Elegans', which, I have just learned, will die to the ground in winter. Let us hope it resurges, for it is indeed extremely elegant with twists and curls of fine rosy thread and, along the points of its ivy-like leaves, soft hints of white. I had to keep watch over it last summer as the Japanese beetles attack porcelain berry relentlessly.

Those who can grow osmanthus can also choose among a wide selection of patterned ivies, some of which I wish I could plant in a shady part of the garden. There actually is one that its vendors say will survive in Zone 5, but their extra little note, "needs protection in cold areas," gives me pause. Besides, how can you protect something that's climbing up a tree? Which is what I would want it to do.

I have news for those people who, like me, thought that real trees had green leaves, or at the most red, as in the case of the small Japanese maples, some Norway maples, and purple beech. I don't know how long it's been going on but that is no longer the case. Now there are tulip trees (liriodendron) whose leaves have yellow margins and beech trees whose leaves are edged with pink, white, or yellow, or, in the case of *Fagus* 'Tricolor', marked with purple, pink, and cream all at once. You can buy a Norway maple with white edges, a variegated oak and dogwood trees with white variegations (*Cornus florida* 'Welchii' or 'Daybreak') or yellow (*C. f.* 'Sunset' or 'First Lady'). As I write this, no doubt more new forms are being born.

The real field for breeders of varied leaf forms and colors, however, is the Japanese maple, *Acer palmatum*. Greer Gardens lists 105 cultivars, not all of which have variegated leaves, of course, but many of which do. Most of them have Japanese names and each description sounds more intriguing than the last. I haven't read all 105 descriptions but if I had a place to put it and a movable greenhouse with which to cover it in the winter, I'd buy 'Butterfly'. In the picture it is beautiful enough to bring tears of longing to the eyes. Unfortunately—or perhaps fortunately—for me, most of them won't tolerate temperatures more severe than minus 12 degrees F and many, not more than minus 3 degrees F. Otherwise I might want to buy half a dozen and redesign my whole garden around them.

Here I have come to the end of my piece without more than mentioning variegated annuals, of which there are many—but actually, I think that the flashiest ones are pretty well known, plants such as coleus, caladiums, and the geraniums (pelargoniums) with fancy leaves. Some of the color combinations are so outrageous they make some of us shudder, those of us who are looking for serenity rather than frenzy in the garden. But there are others that would do very well with proper handling. Every time I get Park's seed catalogue I think I'll allow myself to try a few—but then I pass them by, knowing I'd have to arrange a special separate area for them as they don't fit into a perennial garden easily. Some of them are splendid, especially the caladiums. If I had a stone-paved court I'd have pots of them standing around—white ones with green veins or pale grey-green ones with red veins. The new impatiens from New Guinea are wildly exotic as to design and color. I almost think they'd require a tropical setting in order to look at home. Perhaps, though, away

from perennials with their mauves and pinks, say in an area enclosed by dark yew hedges or against a grey wall, they could be
managed. Some of the newer, brighter, more aggressively colored rex begonias need almost as careful placing. Easier for
most of us to use would be the new plum-colored coleus and the
annual *Euphorbia marginata* 'Summer Icicle', which comes in
cool grey, green, and white and associates well with almost any
other plant.

PART THREE

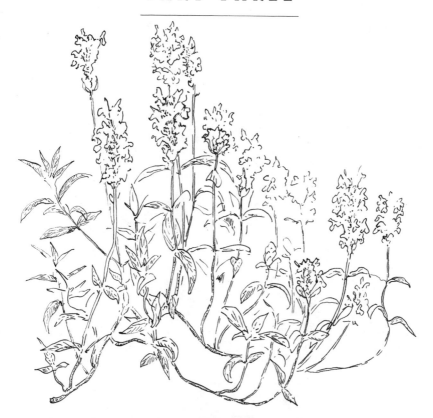

GARDENERS OF OTHER
TIMES

MISS JEKYLL

During the last few years most gardeners have heard about Miss Gertrude Jekyll—some, of course, have known about her for a long time. Keen gardeners or students of garden history have been collecting her books from secondhand dealers and borrowing them from libraries. Now, the copyrights having finally run out, they have all been reprinted and are easily come by. Next the television producers will be considering doing a series on her— but no. She wouldn't really do for a television show. The producers couldn't possibly make her glamorous, like George Sand, for she was a dumpy woman who wore thick spectacles, sometimes two pairs at once, a shapeless garment of stout blue serge, often covered by a heavy gardener's apron, and thick boots. Furthermore, her apparent lack of amorous adventures would disqualify her immediately for the typical biography. But her books are as valuable and just as good reading now as when they were written. She was an amazing woman, a person to whom everyone who is seriously involved in making flower gardens in England and America, at least, is in debt.

Her approach to gardening has added much to the joy of those who find nourishment in the contemplation of plants, particularly plants as related to the landscape. For she was a landscape painter herself, who, when she had to give up painting due to increasing myopia, developed her gardening interest in compensation and was still, as she said, "making pictures"— living three-dimensional ones.

When we consider the lives of exceptional people we often observe that all the circumstances that surrounded them seem to have been calculated to produce just the result that occurred—except that they don't produce it until the person comes along who has that spark, that flame we never can analyze, and who can put the circumstances to good use.

Gertrude Jekyll was born in England in 1843 into a notable family, where interest in the arts, letters, and politics prevailed. Her mother, in addition to being a musician and a pupil of Mendelssohn, drew and painted.

When Gertrude was very young the family moved to a large house with extensive gardens in West Surrey. There she was given remarkable freedom, presumably when not having lessons with her governess. Her only sister was seven years older than she and her four brothers being away at school, she grew up almost as an only child. Far from being lonely she reveled in the opportunity to wander with her pony and dog all over the immediate countryside, exploring woods, ponds, and streams. During these years she developed not only a love for plants and the landscape but an abiding affection for the country people with whom she made friends. She learned a lot about country crafts as well, spending long hours in the workshops of the local carpenter, blacksmith, saddler, and other craftsmen.

At this time a governess gave her a copy of *Flowers of the Field* by a Rev. C. A. Johns, a book that had a great influence on her life. She began to bring home plants and look them up in her book. During her life she possessed three copies of this book, wearing out the first two. She said that the original was the most precious gift she had ever received.

Another felicitous element in Gertrude's early environment was that she was able to have a "hut" of her own in the garden where she painted, read, studied, and wrote. When I learned of this I thought of Virginia Woolf's *A Room of One's Own*, in which she proposes that one of the reasons for women's failure to accomplish much of lasting creative value is that they so seldom have had a place all their own, where they could be alone. Gertrude even laid the path from the house to her hut with cinders when she discovered that her father couldn't stand the noise cinders made when walked upon.

At age seventeen she enrolled in the Kensington School of Art, living at home and going back and forth to classes. This was very daring for those times, when girls of her class were expected to stay at home with their mothers, embroidering in the parlor until they married.

Three years later she had the great opportunity of taking a trip to the Greek islands, Rhodes, and Turkey with friends, the Charles Newtons. Newton was in charge of Greek and Roman antiquities at the British Museum and was a distinguished Orientalist and the excavator of Halicarnassus. His wife Mary, daughter of the painter Joseph Severn, was herself an artist. The journey was a marvelously enriching experience, with all of them visiting and studying Greek ruins and architecture, drawing and painting, and even collecting plants.

From 1863 through the 1870s Miss Jekyll's life was full enough. Although, as a young unmarried woman she still lived properly at home, she was often in London, meeting such people as Watts, Ruskin, and Morris, who was a lifelong friend of Mary Newton's brother. She went to Paris with a cousin and took voice lessons, to Rome with a friend from art school where she studied not only art but the carving and gilding of frames. During the 1870s she was often a house guest of the pianist Jacques Blumenthal and his wife who had a home in London and a chalet in France. Her fellow guests were French and En glish musicians, artists, and writers, so that days and evenings were spent reading aloud, performing amateur theatricals, making music, writing verse, painting, and, in France, plant collecting. At these gatherings she became the friend of Queen Victoria's daughter Princess Louise and more significantly, the painter Brabazon. This friendship lasted a lifetime and Miss Jekyll attributed any sensitivity and skill she might have in the use of color to having studied painting with Brabazon.

In her late twenties Miss Jekyll was designing interiors, the most notable of her commissions being that of furnishing Eaton Hall for the Duke of Westminster. She was getting orders for silver repoussé work, for embroidered hangings, and for garden alterations. George Leslie, an artist who met her at that time, wrote:

> I became acquainted with Miss Jekyll ... a young lady of such singular accomplishments that I cannot resist giving my readers some account of her various occupations and pursuits. Clever and witty in conversation, active and energetic in mind and body, and possessed of artistic talents of no common order, she would at all times shine conspicuously bright amongst the other ladies. The variety of her accomplishments, however, is far more extensive; there is hardly any useful handicraft the mysteries of which she has not mastered—carving, modeling, house painting, carpentry, smith's work, repoussé work, gilding, wood-inlaying, embroidery, gardening and all manner of herb culture. . . . Her artistic taste is very great.*

She also painted several inn signs in her neighborhood! Later she acquired a new skill, photography, of course do-

*Betty Massingham, *Miss Jekyll* (Devon, England: David & Charles/Newton Abbot, 1973), pp. 28–29.

ing a thorough job of it, setting up sinks and a dark room and becoming so adept that she was later able to furnish the photographs for all of her books.

The Jekyll family in 1876 bought some property on Munstead Heath in West Surrey and proceeded to build a new house. Remaining at home there were Gertrude's brother Sir Henry Jekyll and his wife, Gertrude, and her mother. In 1882 they bought an additional fifteen acres adjacent to the property, planning to build a separate residence on it for Gertrude and her mother, since the comings and goings of Henry and his guests made the house too lively for the old lady. Gertrude must have enjoyed the guests, among whom were the pre-Raphaelites Rossetti, Burne-Jones, H. Hunt, and Ruskin. Even though it was some years before the new house went up she began to lay out and plant her own garden.

What a life it must have been for her, full of good conversation, song and dance, hard work at her painting and crafts of various kinds, gardening, and frequent trips to Europe!

Miss Jekyll had always had trouble with short-sightedness but as a painter she ignored it as long as she could. However, in 1891 an eye specialist in Wiesbaden told her she should stop painting and embroidering in order to retain as long as possible the sight that remained to her, which, without glasses, enabled her to see objects about two inches away. It was this advice that caused her, while not abandoning painting entirely, to turn more and more to gardening and to associate with people in the gardening world.

Luckily she had just met a young architect, Edwin Lutyens, with whom she was to form a friendship and an informal partnership that was to last the rest of Miss Jekyll's life. Lutyens was twenty-two at the time, twenty-six years younger than she, just getting started on his career with his first commission. As the years went by those two designed buildings and gardens that changed the course of landscape design not only in England but in Europe and America as well. She was able to introduce him to influential people such as Princess Louise and help him to get commissions, but even more valuable was her advice and guidance. She had always been interested in architecture and had good common sense as well as taste. He submitted his plans for her comments even when she wasn't to design a garden to go with the building, and he testified later as to how much he had learned from her. Christopher Hussey wrote of one of their cooperative ventures, "Miss Jekyll's naturalistic planting wedded Lutyen's geometry in a balanced union of both principles."*

Lutyens had a workshop at Miss Jekyll's house, which was a second home to him. Both he and his wife loved her dearly and she them. They always referred to her as "Bumps" when speaking to one another and her nephew says she was "Auntie Bumps" to the children of the family. I'm unable to find out whether she was ever actually addressed as "Bumps" or even whether she knew about it. Everyone who knew her said that she had a wonderful sense of humor but one doesn't know that she could apply it to herself. Her character seemed to be a combination of opposites, not unusual, perhaps. She was meek and modest, yet on occasion autocratic, firm, and fierce. A formidable lady, who was at the same time gentle. Further, she was a no-nonsense, down-to-earth soul who was full of poetic feeling. She saw the big picture, yet dwelt lovingly on small details.

Gertrude Jekyll had a good year in 1897, as she not only received the Victoria Medal of Honour from the Royal Horticultural Society but moved into her new house, Munstead Wood, designed by Lutyens. Her garden was already well known by then, visited by gardening enthusiasts from all over Great Britain, and she was a contributor to various publications—*The*

*Massingham, *Miss Jekyll*, p. 83.

Garden, National Review, the *Edinburgh Review,* and *The Guardian.* The next few years saw the publication of her first two books, *Wood and Garden* and *Home and Garden.*

From 1900 to 1908 Gertrude Jekyll published almost a book a year, including a children's gardening book. She was asked for advice from all over Great Britain and abroad and designed gardens of all sizes—from a window box for a factory boy to extensive gardens for large estates. When she was over seventy she was asked to plan a piece of ground two miles from Munstead Wood as a memorial for a founder of the National Trust. Miss Jekyll worked two days a week during spring and summer with a patrol of Boy Scouts, clearing undergrowth and arranging paths on hills that went up to five hundred feet. In her eighties she was still collaborating with Lutyens, writing, collecting seeds, and supervising garden projects. She published *Old English Household Life* during this period, painted another inn sign, and continued to publish articles until her death at age eighty-nine.

In trying to evaluate Gertrude Jekyll's contribution to the art of gardening I must first mention William Robinson, editor of *The Garden* and author of *The English Flower Garden,* which came out in 1883. Robinson and Miss Jekyll were friends and were writing about gardening in the same period and must share the credit for many of the revolutionary ideas that had such an influence on the gardening world. At the time they began to write, gardens of middle-upper-class people were usually formal and were filled every spring with hundreds of bright annuals from the greenhouse, planted in rigid designs or rows. This practice was known as "bedding out" and was deplored by both Robinson and Miss Jekyll, who brought back into use the more subtly colored perennials or hardy plants. They promoted a more natural look in gardens; that is, they felt that the planting should not be stiff and geometrical even if the overall design of the garden was formal. Miss Jekyll was imbued with a strong respect for nature and endeavored to preserve the character of any place she planted, to beautify, with restraint, without destroying or clashing with what was already there. She loved the old cottage gardens of the working people, crammed as they were with berry bushes, fruit trees, vegetables, and the old-fashioned roses, vines, and humble flowers. She taught people to appreciate green, grey and brown foliage as well as bright-colored flowers; she taught all of us who garden to think of values, line, leaf shape, and contrast of foreground and background. She worked out in detail, in her books, sophisticated and subtle color harmonies possible for every season of the year. One of her most important themes was that no color stands alone but has real value only if thought of in relation to the colors around it. Someone called her the first horticultural Impressionist.

Miss Jekyll's influence can be seen in most of the great gardens of today. One in particular comes to mind—that of Sissinghurst Castle, where gardens of special coloring, the roses climbing up into trees, the use of grey plants, the nut walk planted to primroses, just to name a few, are all ideas that were first tried out at Munstead Wood and were written about (and in beautiful English) in Miss Jekyll's books.

Her creed in all departments of her work could be summed up in a quotation from *Home and Garden*: "sound work done with the right intention, . . . material used according to the capability of its nature and the purpose intended, with due regard to beauty of proportion and simplicity of effect."[*]

---

[*]Gertrude Jekyll, *Home and Garden. Notes and Thoughts, Practical and Critical, of a Worker in Both* (1900; reprint, Wizzingers Falls, N.Y.: Antique Collectors Club, 1982).

FIRST LADY *of* GARDENING: JANE LOUDON

We hear and read a lot these days about women who have distinguished themselves in the field of horticulture—Gertrude Jekyll, Ellen Willmott, Vita Sackville-West, Beatrix Farrand. But of the very first professional woman gardener, Jane Webb Loudon, not much has been said. This may be because her light was outshone by that of her brilliant and tremendously productive husband, John Claudius Loudon. However, Jane wrote magazine articles and as a journalist "covered" the first big horticultural shows in England. Besides a novel and several books of stories she wrote sixteen excellent books on gardening, botany, and natural history, books that were very popular in her day and were much admired by William Robinson who reedited and published her *Amateur Gardener's Calendar* in 1870. Most of the material in her *Gardening for Ladies* and the *Ladies' Companion to the Flower Garden* would be just as helpful today as it was when she wrote it, if the books were obtainable.

Jane Webb came into the world at a time when women were beginning seriously to question their assigned role. There had, of course, been cries of feminine rebellion raised in the seventeenth and eighteenth centuries, demands for equal education and equal treatment. Jane Austen (who died when Jane Webb was ten) had driven her fine little wedge into the established system; George Eliot, Elizabeth Gaskell, and the Brontë sisters were shortly to add their quiet contribution to the feminist movement. Women in the nineteenth century would soon be organizing in an effort to gain control of their own money, to have bank accounts (Mrs. Gaskell had to ask her husband for the money she earned from her novels), to be allowed to vote, and to enter the professions. Changes were in the air. Jane Webb Loudon was never to be a flaming feminist but she did champion women breadwinners, being one herself, and did what she could in her gardening books to get Victorian women to lay down their eternal needlework, to get out of their stuffy drawing rooms, to observe and study natural history, to design and plant gardens, and to *dig*. And the last editorial she wrote as editor of one of the first women's magazines was entitled "A Few Words on the Condition of Women." It was an intelligent assessment of the problems of her day in which she expressed her confidence in women's imminent emancipation.

Although it was true that Jane Loudon was the first professional woman garden writer, women had been involved in gardening, one way or another, from the beginning of time. Country women and farmers' wives certainly tended the earliest kitchen gardens. Nuns in the Middle Ages were adept at growing the fruits, vegetables, and herbs they needed for food and medicine. Later, ladies in castles would have similar walled gardens for use and pleasure. Women in every establishment were expected to be skilled in cookery and in the uses of healing herbs, being responsible to a degree for the health and well-being of their families and servants. By the sixteenth century gardens had begun to move outside the castle walls and became so extensive that "weeding women" were employed on many estates. (At Cardinal's College, Oxford, weeding women were given free bread, ale, and herrings as well as a few pence a day.) In 1618 a William Lawson wrote *The Countrie Housewife's Gar-*

den, in which he gave instructions for planting gardens of herbs, vegetables, and flowers. William Coles, in 1656, wrote in his *The Art of Simpling:* "Gentlewomen, if the ground be not too wet, may doe themselves much good by kneeling upon a cushion and Weeding." Many aristocratic ladies, including members of the royal family, gained reknown as gifted gardeners, interesting themselves passionately in their flower gardens, and in the late 1700s several books on botany were published by lady gardeners.

But Jane Webb's early years foreshadowed no career in garden writing. She was born in 1807 in Birmingham, England, into a nonliterary, non-gardening family. Her businessman father was well enough off to provide a governess for his daughter and she was allowed to read the books in his library. Upon the death of her mother when she was twelve Jane and her father spent a period on the continent where she studied German, French, and Italian. When they returned to England and lived in the country she ran the house for her father, drove about in her pony chaise, studied languages, sketched, and wrote verses like any other well-bred young girl. At seventeen, when her father died leaving her not very well off, she undertook to write books to augment her sparse income. Occupations that were open to young gentlewomen at that time were not numerous. She could, heaven help her, hire herself out as a governess or paint miniatures and card racks. She could become some great lady's "companion," a fate sometimes even more grim than that of being a governess. She could open a school, if she knew enough wealthy people who would undertake to send her their children. Or she could write. Some years later, the Brontë girls, unable to tolerate life as governesses and failing as schoolteachers, would try the same thing as an answer to their financial predicament. But Jane needed special courage to attempt it, alone and at an earlier age.

Her first little volume consisted of one original story and translations from German, Spanish, and Italian verses. In 1827, when she was twenty, she published her second book, *The Mummy*, a kind of sci-fi novel that was not without merit. In it a mummy of one of the Egyptian pharaohs, who has been revitalized by a scientist, stalks through England in the year 2126. The book is remarkable for its foresight, as it contains accounts of a welfare state in which education is universal and leisure available to all. Travel is by air, albeit by means of balloons, and communication is handled by letters and telegraphs that flash through the air to special receiving towers. Houses are air-conditioned, commodities are mass-produced, and the fields are worked by steam ploughs. There are even some Espresso-type machines that roast and grind fresh coffee beans, then serve cups of hot coffee with milk!

Jane's book was so well received that she proceeded to write *Stories of a Bride*, which appeared in 1829. But in 1830, John Claudius Loudon had just read *The Mummy* and, impressed by the author's ingenuity, especially in predicting not only steam-powered ploughs but milking machines, reviewed the "fantastic and witty novel" in his *Gardener's Magazine*. He wangled an introduction to the author, was impressed by her, too, and married her within several months. Thus began what must have been one of the most strenuous partnerships in recorded history.

Here we must give a brief account of the earlier years of the extraordinary man Jane Webb married.

The son of a Scotch farmer, he was an extremely handsome man, who had been educated in Edinburgh. There he assiduously studied Latin, French, and Italian, arithmetic, botany, chemistry, and agriculture. So bent was he on self-improvement that he established what became a regular practice of sitting up all night twice a week studying and keeping himself awake by means of strong green tea. Having decided that he wanted to go into landscape gardening, he apprenticed himself as draughtsman and assistant to several nurserymen in succession, then went off to London to seek his fortune.

From 1803, when he first arrived in London, until the day, twenty-seven years later, when he met Jane Webb, he had cut quite a swath in the horticultural world. He had worked with great success as a landscape gardener and had been involved in the replanting of London's parks. He was a member of the Linnean Society and a friend of the naturalist Sir Joseph Banks. He had published numerous articles and twelve or thirteen books including encyclopedias of agriculture, gardening, and plants. His *Hortus Brittanicus* came out in 1830, the year of his marriage. (He was dictating to his secretary as he was being dressed for the ceremony, the day of his wedding.) He was also "conducting" or editing two magazines at the time he and Jane met, one on gardening and the other on natural history. Besides his literary and designing work Loudon had run a school at which he taught Scottish methods of agriculture, had made a small fortune and lost it in investments, had traveled widely in Europe, even through Russia, studying gardens and methods of agriculture, and had come home to build a duplex on Porchester Terrace in semi-rural Bayswater near London, in half of which he had installed his widowed mother and two sisters.

All of this production had been accomplished in spite of tremendous physical handicaps. Loudon suffered attacks of what was thought to be rheumatism. The pain in his right arm was so intense that he submitted to treatment by some bungling *masseurs* who succeeded, over a period of months, in breaking the arm in two places. In 1824, when it had failed to mend, it was amputated. His left arm also was affected by the rheumatism to the point where he could use only two fingers of his remaining hand. He, who had been so skilled a draughtsman and painter, had henceforth to employ draughtsmen and amanuenses for all of his work. One of his knees was also giving him a great deal of trouble. During these trials, however, he forged full speed ahead, never breaking his pace. He had, during the years of greatest pain, resorted to laudanum to the point where he was taking a wineglassful every eight hours. After the amputation he broke himself of his addiction by pouring a wineglassful of water into the laudanum bottle after taking his dose, until finally he was taking pure water.

Her new life at Porchester Terrace must have been something of a shock to Jane Loudon, plunged as she was into a world of horticulture and hard work for which she could scarcely have been prepared. Docile and adoring wife that she was, she left no record, at least, of any feelings that she might have had of distress, rebellion, or even exhaustion, but it would seem inevitable that they should have existed to some degree.

The Loudon house, complete with a domed conservatory, stood on about one quarter acre of land in which grew somewhere near three thousand species of plants—annuals, bulbs, perennials, vines, trees, and shrubs, besides a saltwater tank containing a named collection of seaweeds and a border of—no doubt named—mosses. On a stone shelf in one of the garden sheds stood a collection of six hundred alpines in small pots. The year of his marriage John planted fifty-eight new trees and shrubs with the idea of keeping them under control by means of drastic root pruning in alternate years!

When Jane arrived the house was already organized efficiently and running smoothly, two servants being employed besides John's valet/coachman. Jane was already accustomed to being housekeeper, but that was only one of her duties. During daylight hours there was constant work in the garden, the conservatory and the potting sheds, caring for indoor and outdoor plants. There was only one part-time gardener to help. Jane's meticulous husband hated untidiness in a room and "tawdriness" in the garden, so every object indoors had to be kept clean and in its proper place and in the garden plants had to be trimmed, staked, labeled, and kept free of weeds. (In the house Loudon expected to be able to lay his hand on the book or paper he was looking for, even in the dark.) The lawn had to be cut with hand shears so as not to damage the thousands of bulbs that inhabited it. One wonders what Jane's secret feelings were when John remarked to her in later years, "If we had only confined ourselves to herbaceous plants from the first, instead of growing 3,000 species, then we might have had 10,000 plants in our limited space"!*

During dry periods or during a crisis in one of Loudon's horticultural experiments all the women in the house had to pitch in, including the two servants, Jane's sisters-in-law, and little Agnes Loudon, when she joined the group. But, as Loudon said, "The end we had in view was scientific knowledge rather than ordinary enjoyment."† That didn't leave much time for sitting down and smelling the flowers. Perhaps if Jane had seen an entry in an early section of John's journal before she married him it might have given her pause. It read: "Alas! How have I neglected the important task of improving myself! . . . I am now twenty-three years of age, . . . and yet what have I done to benefit my fellow men?"

Still, the worst of the routine at Porchester Terrace was not the feverish activity of the daylight hours but the demands of the night shift. Jane became her husband's writing hand, and they sat up every evening, working on the next issue of *The Gardener's Magazine* or on whatever book Loudon had in hand, until midnight. In 1832, the year of the birth of Agnes, the Lou-

*B. Howe, *Lady with Green Fingers: The Life of Jane Loudon* (London: Country Life Limited, 1961), p. 66.
†Geoffrey Taylor, *Some Nineteenth Century Gardeners* (London: Skeffington, 1951).

dons' only child, John began his *Encyclopedia of Cottage, Farm, and Villa Architecture* and the pace increased. Wrote Jane in *Gardening for Ladies:* "The labour that attended this work was immense; and for several months he and I used to sit up the greater part of every night, never having more than four hours' sleep, drinking strong coffee to keep ourselves awake."

In order to help maintain the garden and help her husband, Jane set herself to learn about plants and how to grow them. She said later in the introduction to *Gardening for Ladies:*

> When I married Mr. Loudon, it is scarcely possible to imagine any person more completely ignorant than I was, of every thing relating to plants and gardening; and, as may be easily imagined, I found every one about me so well acquainted with the subject, that I was soon heartily ashamed of my ignorance. My husband, of course, was quite as anxious to teach me as I was to learn, and it is the result of his instructions that I now (after ten years' experience of their efficacy) wish to make public for the benefit of others.

Nevertheless, she wrote elsewhere that during that learning period she tried to improve her knowledge of gardening by reading gardening books, only to find that they didn't teach what an amateur needed to know, and as for her husband in the role of instructor: "We both found unanticipated difficulties at every step. It is so difficult for a person who has been acquainted with a subject all his life to imagine the state of ignorance in those who know nothing of it, that a professional gardener has rarely patience to teach anything to an amateur."*

But what with reading and doing and by attending a course of botany lectures at the Horticultural Society Mrs. Loudon eventually became a horticultural authority herself.

*B. Howe, *Lady with Green Fingers,* p. 48.

In 1831, when John Loudon was asked by the city of Birmingham to design a new botanic garden, the couple set off in their phaeton together for what Jane thought would be a kind of belated honeymoon. She was soon disabused of that notion however; it was to be, like all their future trips together, a "learning experience." "Sit up, my love," said John, "and observe the flora and fauna of the passing countryside."* He himself missed nothing and wrote up his tours in issues of his magazines. They provide a wonderful picture of the English countryside in the nineteenth century, as he noted the trees, wildflowers, agricultural practices, and the condition of the laborers' cottages along the way. It occurs to one, however, that when one reads that "Loudon made endless notes" and later "wrote them up in article form" it was Jane who was making the notes and doing the writing later.†

On his many trips John Loudon studied palatial residences and gardens, smaller country houses, inns, factories, public buildings, cemeteries, and schools, dispensing praise or condemnation afterwards as he saw fit in the pages of *The Gardener's Magazine*. He was interested in improvements of every kind in gardening, architecture, work methods, and people's characters. How touching, it seems to us, that nineteenth-century faith in everything and everyone as improvable if not improving. The first issue of *The Gardener's Magazine* in 1826 contained the announcement that its two principal objectives were "to disseminate new and important information on all topics connected with horticulture, and to raise the intellect and the character of those engaged in this art."

In his observations of people and places John Loudon was certainly generous with his praise but pitiless in his condemna-

*Ibid., p. 8.
†Ibid., p. 49.

tion. Of the Earl of Shrewsbury's Alton Towers, a sort of pre-cursor to Disneyland in the form of a garden containing, among many other horrors, pagodas, caves, grottoes (in one of which was a huge stone serpent with a spear-shaped iron tongue and glass eyes), an imitation of Stonehenge, an Indian temple cut out of solid rock, a lofty Gothic tower, and a fake cottage for a blind harper, Loudon wrote that it was "the work of a morbid imagination joined to the command of unlimited resources." Inevitably, he made not a few enemies in the course of his career.

John Loudon's greatest work, which has not yet been sup-planted, was his *Arboretum Brittanicum*, a book that lists and de-scribes all of the trees in Great Britain, native and introduced, with a vast amount of information as to their history and other attributes. Miles Hadfield says in his *History of British Gardening* that the *Arboretum Brittanicum* book alone would have been enough to immortalize him.* It was produced in monthly num-bers with no financial backing except what Loudon could ob-tain from subscriptions. He was resolved that all of the draw-ings of trees should be made from nature and that the work should be perfect, in spite of the immense labor and expense in-volved. Jane Loudon writes:

> From the year 1833 to Midsummer 1838 Mr. Loudon under-went the most extraordinary exertions both of mind and body ... he had seven artists constantly employed and he was frequently in the open air with them from his breakfast at 7:00 in the morning till he came home to dinner at 8:00 in the evening, having remained the whole of that time without taking the slightest refreshment, and generally without even sitting down.†

*Miles Hadfield, *History of British Gardening* (London: John Murray, 1979).
†B. Howe, *Lady with Green Fingers*, p. 50.

After dinner he dictated to Jane until 2 or 3 in the morning. He also started *The Architectural Magazine* and *The Suburban Gardener* during that period. This meant that he was "conducting" four periodicals that came out every month simultaneously.

But after all his efforts, the *Arboretum*, far from making money, left the Loudons £10,000 in debt, a staggering sum in those days. Since, in addition to this calamity, her husband could no longer walk without assistance, Jane began to write books, while her sister-in-law took up wood engraving. The women hoped to be able to earn enough money so that John wouldn't have to resume working as a landscape gardener. But notwithstanding Jane's pleas, John slugged on, visiting gardens, taking on assignments, not stopped by sleet, rain, and physical suffering.

In the autumn of 1839, Jane brought out two children's books, one of which was natural history in the form of a story. Early in 1840 she started working on *Gardening for Ladies* and had it finished in May. When it appeared in that same year, it was an immediate success and soon found a place in the homes of all the wives of successful merchants and professional men who were interested in creating beautiful gardens around their properties. A few ladies' gardening books had already appeared but they were neither so helpful nor so charmingly written as Jane's. And as she said, she, having been a late learner herself, knew exactly what other amateurs needed to know. Further, instead of using the usual flowery and poetic language of her fellow Victorians, Mrs. Loudon spoke out clearly and directly; the sun was the sun, not "that bright luminary," a spade was a spade, and manure was manure. She told her readers not only how to do things but *why* they should be done, from "stirring the soil" to grafting and budding, dividing and pruning. One can learn from her, perhaps for the first time, why one is told to move plants from a small pot into one only slightly larger, and why plants should be shaded after transplanting. Her chapter on sowing seeds should be required reading for all gardeners. Her book also provided instructions on how to dress practically for garden work, what kind of lightweight tools to use, and how to make the necessary motions efficiently. After her dissertation on digging, she says that a lady, when she has succeeded in doing with her own hands all the digging that can be required in a small garden, "will not only have the satisfaction of seeing the garden created . . . by the labour of her own hands, but she will find her health and spirits wonderfully improved by the exercise, and by the reviving smell of the fresh earth." At the end of another section of the book she writes: "The great point is to exercise our own skill and ingenuity, for we all feel so much more interested in what we do ourselves than in what is done for us, that no Lady is likely to become fond of gardening who does not do a great deal with her own hands."

In 1840 also appeared the first volume of Jane Loudon's magnum opus, *The Ladies' Flower Garden*, which was to be comprised of five separate volumes dealing with annuals, biennials, bulbs, perennials, roses and shrubs, and hothouse plants. It is still collected today, partly for its very fine colored illustrations, which were drawn from nature, on zinc. When John Loudon announced its future appearance he wrote, "Though the production of a member of our family, we think it but justice to state that this is an elegant work, and one which will be found no less beautiful than it is useful." Jane Loudon must have been pleased to have such praise from that "perfectionist and ruthless critic of others," her husband. He was proud, too, of her *Botany for Ladies*, which was published in 1842, calling it the best introduction to botany for women or men that had ever been written.

One wonders how Jane managed to work on books of her

own as well as her husband's, to say nothing of helping with the magazines. Nevertheless, after her debut as a horticultural writer, her books came thick and fast—two in 1841—*The Ladies' Companion to the Flower Garden* and the second volume of the *Ladies' Flower Garden* series, this one on bulbous plants. That her books were not strictly how-to manuals is illustrated by a section in the bulb book where she speaks of small gladiolas "the colours of whose petals at sunset take a curiously shifting hue like that of shot silk when held up to the light." She suggests that they be placed where the rays of the setting sun can illuminate them and points out that they are "sweeter-smelling by far at dusk."*

In spite of the great pleasure that the Loudons obviously took in gardening, it is almost agonizing to consider them flailing away year after year, trying to pay off their tremendous debt, caring for the plants and publishing book after book. The cheerful easy tone of Jane's writing belies the facts of her situation. One of the worst aspects of her dilemma must have been that she had no control over her husband who took on one assignment after another, working like one possessed. On one trip they made to the north he marched with Agnes and Jane all over a botanic garden in the pouring rain. Then on to the next stop by train to inspect another botanic garden, again in heavy rain. John fell ill. In the morning they went on to the next city but he couldn't descend from the carriage to visit *that* botanic garden so he sent Jane, who examined it and reported. That night they sailed to Scotland. After traveling by rail to the house of friends Loudon collapsed. His life was in danger for some time, but after six weeks he struggled to his feet and went off to work again.

By 1843 Loudon was in very bad shape indeed, but he was

---

*B. Howe, *Lady with Green Fingers*, p. 64.

laying out cemeteries and grounds for new clients that he had to inspect from a wheelchair. His doctors thought his lungs were affected and that he was incurable. The race to beat death began then, with John working all day and dictating to Jane most of every night. One of his creditors began to harass him, threatening him with debtor's prison. Jane wrote, "Nothing could be more awful than to watch him during the few weeks that yet remained of his life. His body was rapidly wasting away; but his mind remained in all its vigor, and he scarcely allowed himself any rest in his eagerness to complete the works that he had in hand." He died on his feet while dictating to his wife and she caught him in her arms.

After spending some months recuperating, both physically and emotionally, Jane began slowly to set herself to work again, but never, one hopes, at the frenzied tempo of former times. That jam-packed garden, however, was a tremendous burden to her; she felt obliged to keep it up for her husband's sake but couldn't afford even a part-time gardener. Eventually, after heroic efforts, she had to get rid of all but the essentials. She devoted a lot of time to little Agnes, who had probably had precious little of her time up until then. She saw her husband's last book through the press and contributed to it, as foreword, a short, simple, and moving biography. She finished a book of her own, *The Lady's Country Companion; or How to Enjoy a Country Life Rationally*, which appeals to some readers more than all her other books; and several years later she brought out *British Wild Flowers*. *The Amateur Gardener's Calendar* appeared in 1847, the book so much admired by that giant of British gardening, William Robinson, that he re-edited it.

In 1848 Mrs. Loudon finished the last volume of the *Ladies' Flower Garden* series, which was the handsomest of all, since it dealt with ornamental greenhouse plants. Plant hunters were sending exotic plants home to England from all corners of the globe during the 1800s and the passion for greenhouses was at its peak, so the volume must have been greeted with enthusiasm.

The knowledge we have of the rest of Jane Loudon's life comes mostly from her daughter Agnes's diary. We know that, through her own writings, through editions of her husband's work which she reedited and reissued, through a very small government pension, which was given her as the widow of an eminent horticulturist, she managed to hang on at Porchester Terrace. She had what must have been an interesting social life as her friends were, among others, the Dickens family, Mrs. Gaskell, the Landseer brothers, the Millais and Wilkie Collins and his brother. There were great parties as Agnes grew to be a young woman. When money was scarce Jane and Agnes would rent the house and go to the Continent where living was cheap, a solution often adopted by their fellow countrymen.

For a while Mrs. Loudon was editor of a new magazine launched by *Punch*—*The Ladies' Companion: At Home and Abroad* (that is, away from home), a weekly periodical that provided a refreshing change from the syrupy highly sentimental ladies' journals of the day. Editing was work that Jane was familiar with, having helped her husband with his magazines for fifteen years. So, once again, the house was headquarters for a publication and she loved it. She was responsible for the entire layout and contributed many general articles herself, as well as being her own drama critic and book reviewer. She attended opera and theater performances, concerts and flower shows. There was a garden column as well, due to the insistence of readers. And she seized the opportunity to write articles pointing out the distressing situation of seamstresses and other working women. However, even though the journal was well received, her editorship was terminated after less than a year, and although she desperately needed the money the job had provided, the worst part of losing it was that she never could find out whether her employers had been dissatisfied with her performance or whether it was press politics. It was a terrible blow, in any case. She and Agnes rented the house again and sadly headed for Europe.

Agnes was a pretty girl and a lively one but was not distinguished for strong-mindedness. She always seemed to fall in love with the wrong fellow and gave her mother no little uneasiness through the years. One can't keep track of all the men, all romantic-looking bounders, apparently—an Italian, a Greek, other Italians. Well, it doesn't matter, nothing ever came of any of her adventures except tears and heartbreak. No doubt her mother suffered vicariously.

Finally, when Mrs. Loudon was only fifty she fell seriously ill. Inflammation of the lungs said the doctor and ordered one dozen leeches applied. (Maddening to read of medical practices of former times.) She became worse. Inflammation of the kidneys said the doctor and ordered more leeches. After a few months Jane knew it was the end. She spent one day alone sitting by the fire burning all her personal papers, to the regret of her biographers, and not long afterwards quietly died.

As one thinks of Jane Loudon lying on her sofa in her last days one wonders if, in thinking over her life, she had any desire to live it over again. Perhaps not. Perhaps even she, who was made of sterner stuff than most of us, couldn't have taken on that assignment twice. But most assuredly she knew that she had helped a great man to great accomplishments and that she herself had contributed much to the horticultural world. She was *the* authority on gardening for women all over Britain and America and would be a source of inspiration for women gardeners to come. As garden historian Geoffrey Taylor said, she died throwing the trowel to Gertrude Jekyll, who was at that moment at age eleven furbishing her first garden.*

As for Jane's relationship with her husband, she was obviously blissfully blind, since she could write, "He had not a single particle of selfishness in his disposition." This after her thousand and one nights of taking dictation—and those gardening *corvées*, and those inspection tours in the pelting rain.

In many ways Jane Loudon was more fortunate in her marriage than most women of her time in that she and her husband were companions. Very few men of that period, one gathers, especially in England, looked to their wives for companionship but rather found it in association with other men. Women were supposed to amuse themselves with their houses, their children, and one another. Further, she had the good fortune to marry one of the few men around who believed in encouraging women to develop all of their intellectual and artistic capacities. John Loudon not only encouraged her to branch out on her own, he took great pride in her accomplishments. So she had, at the end, what must be one of the greatest satisfactions possible, the conviction that she had used well the time and talents that had been given her.

*Geoffrey Taylor, *Some Nineteenth Century Gardeners* (Essex, England: Anchor Press, 1951).

LADY MARY'S GARDEN

Those to whom the name of Lady Mary Wortley Montagu is familiar probably remember her as the eighteenth-century wit she was—as a friend, then enemy, of Pope; as a famous letter writer; perhaps even as a writer of very good essays and poetry. They no doubt associate her with unconventional, even wicked, behavior. A few people might recall that it was she who, after having accompanied her ambassador husband to Turkey, brought back to England the Turkish practice of inoculation (later improved by Jenner) against the dread disease smallpox. But it is unlikely that many people will remember her as a gardener. It is indeed remarkable that she ever became a gardener; if ever there was a completely urban type it was she.

She was born Lady Mary Pierrepont in London in 1659, during the reign of Queen Anne, to an aristocratic father who was to become Duke of Kingston under the first King George. Her mother, Lady Mary Fielding, cousin of the novelist Henry Fielding, died when Mary was four. The child and her younger siblings were raised by various relatives, not including her father who was too busy with politics and his social life to oversee his children's upbringing. Parenting was not something many men were into at the time, one must add in all fairness.

Lady Mary, unlike her brother and sisters, was fascinated

by words, by literature, and by ideas. Her father did provide her with a French tutor, but only her brother was taught Latin. Since the knowledge of Latin was considered to be essential for anyone who aspired to the world of the intellect, Lady Mary in her teens taught it to herself over a period of two years. She later became more or less proficient at several more languages. She read books in her father's large library and wrote verses to amuse herself.

As she grew older she moved in the usual gilded circles of her class—attending balls and concerts in London and spending time at the family estate in the country during the summer. That Lady Mary was not drawn to bucolic pleasures is shown in a letter she wrote to a friend in the do-it-yourself spelling of that era from a secluded house in Wiltshire to which her father had sent her:

> Yes, yes, my dear, Here is Woods and Shades and Groves in abundance; you are in the right on't. Tis not the place, but the solitude of the place that is intollerable. Tis a horrid thing to see nothing but trees in a wood, and to walk by a purling stream to ogle the Gudgeons in it. . . . In this Hidious Country tis not the fashion to visit, and the few Neighbours there are, keep as far from one another as ever they can. The Diversion here is walking, indeed [the walks] are very pritty all about the house, but then you may walk a mile without meeting a living creature but a few straggling cows.*

At twenty-three she ran off with an educated, intelligent, but very dour man of thirty-four, Edward Wortley Montagu, with whom she had been carrying on a quarrelsome correspon-

*Montagu, Lady Mary Wortley, *Complete Letters*, 3 vols., ed. Robert Halsband (Oxford: Clarendon Press, 1965–1967).

dence for three years. Apparently she eloped in order to avoid marrying an unbearable fellow her father was trying to force on her. However it was, after they married, Lady Mary fell in love with Wortley and Wortley fell out of love with her, so their venture was not a success and Lady Mary's love for her husband died from lack of sustenance. They had a son who was to turn out a most flagrant scoundrel and a daughter who would become the staid, painfully proper wife of John Stuart, Earl of Bute, the unpopular prime minister of King George III. (When the young couple were married the union was opposed by Lady Mary and her husband because the Scottish lord had property but no money.)

For some years the Montagus lived separate lives together, he involved in parliament and politics, she moving in literary and artistic circles. Her beauty and wit drew many people to her, including, before their falling out, Pope. But her lack of discretion, her clever, sharp tongue—and pen—made her many enemies. Her friend Pope, whom she had offended in some way, and that pitiless little viper Horace Walpole, by using *their* clever pens, contrived to ruin her reputation in her day and for all time.

Of the forty-nine years of the Montagus' marriage, one half of it was spent apart, as fifty-year-old Lady Mary went off to Europe shortly after the marriage of her daughter in 1739 and didn't return until the death of her husband in 1762. (She may have agreed to stay overseas if he would send her an allowance.) She had gone to Europe to join a lover who subsequently rejected her, so she had had to cope with a broken heart as well as with the loneliness of exile. She *had* coped, valorously, but she died shortly after her return to England, to what must have been the vast relief of the Butes, who didn't appreciate her brilliance and who were intensely embarrassed by her eccentricities.

Those of us who are interested in Lady Mary will never forgive her daughter for having burned her mother's journal before she herself died. She tried to burn Lady Mary's most famous letters as well (those written on the journey to and from Turkey) but luckily was unable to get her hands on all of the copies.

"But what has all this to do with gardens?" you are asking yourself. Just this. After wandering about Europe for eight years Lady Mary bought a house in the Italian town of Gottolengo, about eighteen miles from Brescia. Then, not far from Gottolengo, she discovered some land for sale, one hundred acres or more, on the bank of a wide river. It was a beautiful spot and as she looked at it Lady Mary was suddenly possessed by the longing to make a garden. She bought the land, rounded up some helpers, and began to plan and plant.

The only building on the property was a rustic one she called her "Dairy House." Read what she writes to her daughter on July 10, 1748:

> I have been this six weeks and still am, at my Dairy House, which joins to my Garden. I believe I have allready told you it is a long mile from the Castle [her house], which is situate in the midst of a very large village ... and has not vacant ground enough about it to make a Garden, which is my greatest amusement; and it being now troublesome to walk or even go in the chaise till the Evening [because of the heat], I have fitted up in this farm house a room for my selfe, that is to say, strewd the floor with Rushes, cover'd the chimney with moss and branches, and adorn'd the Room with Basons of earthen ware (which is made here to great perfection) fill'd with Flowers, and put in some straw chairs and a Couch Bed, which is my whole Furniture.
>
> This Spot of Ground is so Beautifull I am afraid you will scarce credit the Description, which, however, I can as-

sure you shall be very litteral, without any embellishment from Imagination. It is on a Bank forming a kind of Peninsula rais'd from the River Oglio 50 foot, to which you may descend by easy stairs cut in the Turf, and either take the air on the River . . . or by walking an avenu two hundred yards on the side of it you find a Wood of a hundred acres, which was allready cut into walks and rideings when I took it. I have only added 15 Bowers in different views, with seats of Turf. . . . I am now writeing to you in one of these arbours, which is so thick shaded the Sun is not troublesome even at Noon. Another is on the side of the river, where I have made a camp Kitchin, that I may take the Fish, dress and eat it immediately, and at the same time see the Barks which ascend or Descend every day, to or from Mantua, Guastalia or Pont de Vic [Pontevico]. . . . This little Wood is carpetted (in their succeeding seasons) with violets and strawberrys, inhabited by a nation of Nightingales, and fill'd with Game of all kinds. . . .

My Garden was a plain Vineyard when it came into my hands not two years ago. . . . The Italian Vineyards are not planted like those in France, but in clumps fasten'd to Trees planted in equal Ranks (commonly fruit Trees) and continu'd in festoons from one to another, which I have turn'd into cover'd Gallerys of shade, that I can walk in the heat without being incommoded by it. . . . The whole ground is 317 feet in length and 200 in Breadth. You see it is far from large, but so prettily disposed (tho I say it) that I never saw a more agreable rustic garden, abounding with all sort of fruit, and produces a variety of Wines. . . . I believe my Description give you but an imperfect idea of my Garden.

Perhaps I shall succeed better in describing my manner of life, which is as regular as that of any Monastery. I generally rise at six, and as soon as I have breakfasted put my selfe at the head of my Weeder Women, and work with them till nine. I then inspect my Dairy and take a Turn amongst my Poultry, which is a very large enquiry. I have at present 200 chicken, besides Turkys, Geese, Ducks, and Peacocks. All things have hitherto prosper'd under my Care. My Bees and silk worms are doubl'd, and I am told that, without accidents, my Capital will be so in two years time. At 11 o'clock I retire to my Books.

She then gives the schedule for the rest of her day—dining, playing piquet, with some old priests to whom she has taught the game, riding or walking in the woods, going out on the river to fish. In another letter she writes to Lady Bute:

I am realy as fond of my garden as a young Author of his first play when it has been well receiv'd by the Town, and can no more forbear teizing my Acquaintance for their aprobation. Tho' I gave you a long account of it in my last, I must tell you I have made 2 little Terrasses, rais'd 12 steps each, at the end of my great walk. They are just finish'd and a great addition to the beauty of my garden. I enclose to you a rough draught of it ... I have mix'd in my espaliers as many Rose and jessamin Trees as I can cram in, and in the squares designed for the use of the Kitchin have avoided puting any thing disagreable either to sight or smell (having another garden below for Cabbage, Onions, Garlick [et]c.) All the walks are garnish'd with beds of Flowers, beside the parterres which are for a more distinguish'd sort. I have neither Brick nor stone walls; all my fence is a high Hedge, mingl'd with Trees, but fruit [is] so plenty[ful] in this Country nobody thinks it worth stealing. Gardening is certainly the next amusement to Reading.

Lady Mary asked her daughter if Lord Bute could send her a small model of a garden chair she could show to the Italian carpenters and also if he "would be so good to chuse me the best Book of practical Gardening extant." She asked for the garden book several times, perhaps in vain, and also for one by Collen Campbell on English Seats (country estates).

Another question she asked Lady Bute many times, with no result, was the price of raw silk in London. Since her little farm was producing so much silk she wanted to sell it at the best price—raw silk was one of the chief exports of her area in Italy. Naturally her daughter would have shuddered at the idea of her mother's being "in trade" even more than she did at the idea of her possibly publishing her writing. (Upper class people might circulate their works of prose and poetry among themselves but to publish for profit was considered unacceptable.)

The Countess of Bute apparently never even commented on her mother's account of her garden, as Lady Mary offered to repeat the description if the letters had been lost.

It is sad to think of Lady Mary's not being able to share her gardening enthusiasm and experience with any of her countrymen and women. Her son-in-law, as it happens, was more of a success as a botanist and gardener than he was as a statesman. He became a patron of horticulture and was influential in the founding of Kew Gardens. Linnaeus named the plant stewartia after him, misspelling Lord Bute's family name of Stuart. After retirement he wrote a nine-volume work on the flora of Britain and commissioned Lancelot Brown to redesign the grounds of Luton Hoo, his estate in Bedfordshire. The house and gardens were eventually so impressive that Dr. Johnson, who never exactly bubbled over with praise, remarked after visiting them, "This is one of the places I do not regret having come to see."

If only Lady Mary had been able to see into the future back in 1736, when she so strenuously tried to prevent her daughter's marriage. She might have laid up a store of good will in young John Stuart, who might then, in 1748, have sent her promptly the "best Book on practical Gardening extant" and much more besides.

He did send her a set of china, which she had asked her daughter to purchase for her, and her longing for home was such that she wrote in her letter of thanks, "Everything that comes from England is precious to me, even to the very hay that is employ'd in packing."

It is good to know that during one period, at least, in her long years of exile, Lady Mary Wortley Montagu experienced the stimulus, the fascination, and the intense gratification that gardening can provide.

TWO MORE
EIGHTEENTH-CENTURY
GARDENERS

Having said that it was a pity Lady Mary didn't ingratiate herself with her botanist son-in-law early in their acquaintance so that later she would have had help from him in her gardening projects, it occurred to me that she might have gone down in history with no stains on her reputation at all if she had interested herself in gardening earlier in her career. As it happened, both men who succeeded in blackening her name became passionate gardeners. They could all perhaps have forgotten one another's offenses in discussing their favorite plants.

Pope and Lady Mary, who was his neighbor in Twickenham, might have exchanged seeds and perennial roots instead of venomous verses. Then, if Pope hadn't made her name a byword for immorality, Lady Mary might not so readily have exiled herself and would have been in England when Horace Walpole bought Strawberry Hill (also in Twickenham) and could have wandered over to discuss with him the laying out of his gardens. She would have been fifty-eight by then and, with any luck, somewhat mellowed by long association with roses and lilies (it could happen, I suppose). Walpole, who had a penchant for dowagers, might have decided he could forgive her for having been a friend of his father's mistress—for that is the only offense she committed against him, as far as we know.

If, instead of flirting and quarreling for five years, she and Pope had gone into gardening together, she could have learned much from him. He began creating his garden shortly after her return from Turkey and eventually became a landscape designer of near professional caliber.

Pope was undeniably a great force in the evolution of "natural" landscape gardening that took place in England in the eighteenth century. His poetry and letters testify to the vital interest he took in his second important pursuit. He collaborated with Charles Bridgeman, the king's garden designer, on several of his assignments, including that of the gardens of the Earl of Oxford. He corresponded on horticultural subjects with many noblemen and country gentlemen who were creating gardens and was on familiar terms with William Kent, who changed the English countryside so radically, most notably with his work at Stowe.

Pope's own garden contained formal areas and certainly was designed around a central axis with cross allées or walks accented by statuary and urns. There was a bowling green between two thick groves of regularly aligned trees, but on the periphery there were curved sweeps and informal paths to break up the geometry and there were no parterres, no clipped trees or hedges. It would seem to have been an excellent combination of basic formal structure and informality. Pope had strong convictions as to how a garden should blend with and exploit its surroundings and strong feelings for the romantic landscape, as can be seen from his detailed descriptions of some large estate gardens. When he describes the play of light and shadow, the repetition of masses, of line, his words are almost those that a painter would use. His artistic sensibility was such that he is credited with having influenced Kent. Walpole, among others, believed it and wrote:

Mr. Pope undoubtedly 'contributed to form Kent's taste. The design of the Prince of Wales's garden at Carleton House was evidently borrowed from the poet's at Twickenham. There was little affected modesty in the latter, when he said, of all his works he was most proud of his garden. And yet it was a singular effort of art and taste to impress so much variety and scenery on a spot of five acres. The passing through the gloom from the grotto to the opening day, the retiring and again assembling shades, the dusky groves, the larger lawn and the solemnity of the termination of the cypresses that led up to his mother's tomb, are managed with exquisite judgement.*

In one of the more charming lines from a letter Pope wrote to a gardening friend, he says he has been planting shrubs and trees and thinks that they "will indeed outlive me, if they do not die in their travels from place to place, for my garden, like my life, seems to me every year to want correction and require alteration, I hope, at least, [it is] for the better."† So he, like all the rest of us, had his plants playing musical chairs!

Pope had been dead three years when Walpole bought the house he was to call Strawberry Hill. Writing about it to one of his many correspondents, he says: "Richmond Hill and Ham Walks bound my prospect. . . . Dowagers as plenty as flounders inhabit all around and Pope's ghost is just now skimming under my window by a most poetical moonlight."‡

No doubt that ghost was with him as he himself began to think about gardening.

Horace Walpole is generally agreed to have written the

---

*Horace Walpole, *On Modern Gardening* (Canton, Pa.: Lewis Buddy III, The Kirgate Press, 1904), p. 63.
†In Miles Hadfield, *History of British Gardening* (London: John Murray, 1979), p. 187.
‡To Conway, June 8, 1747, in *Letters of Horace Walpole*, ed. Mrs. Paget Toynbee, Vol. 2 (Oxford: Clarendon Press, 1903).

cleverest letters in the world but was admittedly a dilettante—something of a politician, something of an historian, a connoisseur of art, architecture, literature, antiques, and gardens. However, a long essay, "On Modern Gardening," that he wrote and had printed on his own press at Strawberry Hill in 1770 had an important influence on gardening in England and especially on the continent, where "English" gardens became the rage. It has been said that it is the sole instance of English taste in design affecting Europe. In the horticultural field, at least, everything had been going the other way for centuries, with the British importing both garden ideas and gardeners from Italy, France, and Holland. Now, in the late 1700s, Europeans began to send for Scottish and English gardeners and to try to imitate English landscape gardens.

I encountered, in the 1960s, a trace of this fashionable movement still visible when my daughters were day students at a convent school on a hill above Florence. The school occupied an old Medici villa whose formal gardens had been designed by the man who created the famous Boboli Gardens in the city. When I first looked out over the neatly raked paths, the parterres, the lemon trees in containers, I asked one of the sisters, "Is it *here* that the girls play?" "Oh no!" she answered, laughing. "They play in what we call the *English* garden, over there." She gestured toward a wild untended area of trees and grass. I knew nothing of gardens and garden history so I missed the joke.

In "On Modern Gardening," Walpole reveals a curious ambivalence toward formal gardens, both deriding and praising them. In much of the essay, he cleverly pokes fun at the French—at the Le Nôtre/Versailles style of gardening—at gardens where the compass and square are used to achieve symmetry; at geometric patterns accentuated by fountains, urns, and statuary; at walling in the garden and walling out the landscape (after which mounts are constructed so that people can climb up and peer out). He laughs at "parterres embroidered in patterns like a petticoat" and at topiary, at hedges and trees clipped and trimmed into unnatural shapes. He says, "Many French groves seem green chests set upon poles"—a marvelous description of what we've all seen or have seen pictures of. He quotes Pope:

> each alley has a brother,
> And half the garden just reflects the other.

I was entertained by Walpole's description of one Parisian garden where "every walk is buttoned on each side by lines of flower pots." (He says there were nine thousand pots of asters.)

Then come Walpole's ideas of the ideal garden, which he begins by quoting from Milton's description of paradise, the herald of modern gardening, according to him. He thinks that what is necessary is "a plan . . . that would embellish nature and restore art to its proper office, the just improvement or *imitation* of it." (Italics mine.) He certainly goes too far when he says that art should be an imitation of nature. Luckily neither he nor the other "modern" gardeners of his day came very close to imitating nature, except for Kent when, later in his career, he began planting dead trees in order to give a more "natural" effect. (His clients thought that was exaggerating so he gave it up.)

Walpole discusses Charles Bridgeman's contributions to garden design. His gardens, like Pope's, were part formal and part "wilderness." Bridgeman is given credit (mistakenly) for inventing the ha-ha or sunken fence that in some of the new gardens replaced walls. Walpole considered it to have been the biggest step toward integrating the garden with its surroundings. Then comes the most quoted sentence in the essay, when he says that Kent came along, "leaped the fence and saw that all nature was a garden."

Kent composed landscapes like a painter, breaking up

empty spaces with groves of trees, leaving broad sweeps where needed, playing with light, shade, and perspective. He borrowed the distant landscape where it enhanced the composition and blotted it out where it detracted from it. He added buildings (temples) and seats where "objects were wanting to animate his horizon." Walpole compares his handling of water with that found in Europe, where cascades tumbled down marble steps—"that last absurd magnificence of Italian and French villas." But in the new English garden the "forced elevation of cataracts was no more," says Mr. Walpole. "The gentle stream was taught to serpentize seemingly at its pleasure. . . . The living landscape was chastened and polished, not transformed." Trees were liberated so that they could stretch their branches, and nearby bushes and brambles were removed to reveal the shapes of the trees. Kent thinned the nearest trees in a forest to make a checkered light that led gradually to the deep gloom of the trees behind. (Reminiscent of Gertrude Jekyll where she talks of making the transition gradually from the garden to the woodland.)

It's perfectly obvious that Walpole didn't really want art to copy nature; he admired landscapes that looked like Claude Lorrain's paintings, and Lorrain didn't copy nature. As someone has said, nature is sometimes a slut and needs to be tidied up.

And here's where the ambivalence comes in. Walpole really wants it both ways. After damning formal gardens he still clings to "neatness" around a house, which in new designs is "frequently left gazing by itself in the middle of a park."* He thinks enclosed, even covered walks very convenient near a house, given the English climate. He actually pleads for "something of

---

History of the Modern Taste in Gardening (New York: Ursus Press, 1995), originally published in 1780.

an old fashioned garden." After condemning fountains, now he defends them for use at least in the courts of great houses and in cities, happily recalling the fountains at Saint Peter's and the Piazza Navona.

The designers of natural or landscape gardens, after arranging their trees, lakes, and streams still felt the need for what I am afraid we call "focal points" nowadays. The old allées with a statue or fountain at the end, a sundial where the allées crossed, large urns to accent the geometry—all these devices were ruled out. Instead, the focal points in the free-flowing landscape gardens were perhaps an old Greek or Roman temple (newly made), an ancient ruin (ditto), a picturesque cottage or a hermitage, which sometimes included a resident hermit. Walpole in his essay jeers justifiably at "hermitages," saying, "It is almost comic to set aside a quarter of one's garden to be melancholy in." And (in 1756 in an essay in *The World Magazine*) he remarked that the reviving taste for nature and realism was reflected in fashions everywhere, in gardens and on dinner tables alike. "There is not a citizen who does not take more pains to torture his acre and a half into irregularities than he formerly would have employed to make it as regular as his cravat." At dessert one sees "cottages and temples arise in barley-sugar." But his own garden, before he was finished, included, if not a hermitage, a rustic thatched cottage, a "chapel" in the woods, and a garden seat carved in the form of a sea shell. And, after criticizing walls, he himself, following the addition of a rounded tower to his house, had a walled enclosure constructed close to it with a round pool in its center. He also created what he called the Prior's Garden, with high protecting walls, between the house and the road.

Probably, by the end of his life, Walpole would have agreed with Miss Jekyll who, by the end of *her* life, had decided that the

very best gardens were made by combining good formal structure with informal planting.

Whatever his theories, and however sophisticated and urban his outlook, Walpole did indeed love gardens and old-
fashioned scented flowers. His enthusiasm for his own garden
is revealed throughout his letters. Slid in between accounts
of the latest scandal, recent parliamentary scrimmages, and re-
views of the current best-selling book are lines such as these to
a friend in Florence:

> The weather is excessively stormy, but has been so warm,
> and so entirely free from frosts the whole winter, that not
> only several of my honeysuckles are come out, but I have lit-
> erally a blossom upon a nectarine tree. . . . I am extremely
> busy here planting . . . I have now about fourteen acres, and
> am making a terrace the whole breadth of my garden on the
> brow of a natural hill, with meadows at the foot and com-
> manding the river, the village, Richmond Hill, and the
> Park.

And there I leave him, sniffing the scent of his honeysuckle
blossoms, on December 26, 1748, while I, in December of this
quite other year in quite another place, look out over my snow-
covered and scentless garden.

THE ILL-TEMPERED
GARDENER

I have a friend who is persuaded that working with plants improves the character. She thinks it even operated on V. Sackville-West and hunts eagerly, almost pathetically in biographical accounts of that talented and formidable lady for indications that a certain mellowing manifested itself in her later years. I cannot agree that Miss Sackville-West ever underwent a personality change and am certain that all evidence points to the fact that she remained more preoccupied with her plants than with her progeny and more charitable to her flowers than to her friends. In fact, as she grew older, she withdrew more and more from the world and the people in it, taking refuge in her garden.

My theory is that most gardeners are exceptionally gentle people but that the ones who are not will not find salvation in the soil. Think of all the gardening curmudgeons there have been, starting with Alexander Pope, the gardening poet, who treated Lady Mary Wortley Montagu so cruelly. Consider truculent William Robinson who settled a score with an employer one cold winter night by putting out all the stoves in the greenhouses and opening the windows. During his life he made false claims of having innovated various garden trends and stole credit for the work of contributors to his book, *The English Flower Garden*. He ceaselessly attacked Sir Joseph Hooker, director of Kew, and fought lustily with all of his neighbors at Gravetye. As Geoffrey Taylor said in *Some 18th Century Gardeners*: "Robinson had in him a combative, not to say quarrelsome streak.... He wielded a decidedly blunt instrument, but he wielded it with gusto; and by belabouring the whole surface of the target, he naturally from time to time hit the nail on the head." He demonstrated a prickly pugnacious nature even as an old man in a wheelchair, when, if only out of prudence, he should have been making peace with the world and his Maker.

Remember, too, Ellen Willmott, who not only missed the bull's-eye but shot at the wrong target when, at the Chelsea Flower Show, she hurled diatribes at poor dear E. A. Bowles. (She should have attacked that mischievous Reginald Farrer, if anyone. He was the one who wrote the foreword to Bowles's book, containing remarks she found objectionable.) And Miss Willmott drove the publisher of her book, *The Genus Rosa*, almost into bankruptcy and the grave—yet she was nothing if not a gardener.

Our own Doretta Klaber is said to have been very, very good when she was good, but quite peremptory with those who would have taken up her time to no purpose. And would one willingly have rushed into a conflict with that imperious lady, Beatrix Farrand?

To counterbalance the curmudgeons there are countless gardeners of historically recorded kindliness and generosity, beginning with a whole bevy of benevolent churchmen (who seemed to turn to horticulture as a constructive way of expending the energy that must have accumulated in their necessarily restricted lives). Canon Ellacombe comes first to mind, he who gardened so lovingly and wrote *In a Gloucestershire Garden* and *In My Vicarage Garden and Elsewhere*, small collections of very fine garden essays. The Reverend Samuel R. Hole, who eventually became Dean of Rochester, was another genial gardener who wrote on many subjects but most notably on roses. There was a vicar called Engleheart who did a lot for daffodils, as did a Canon Meyer. A pink linaria is named 'Canon Went'. Among other mild-mannered ecclesiastical gardeners was the Reverend William Wilks, vicar of Shirley, who bequeathed us that delicious strain of poppies.

E. A. Bowles, whose charitable sunny nature was well known, wrote three books about his garden—in spring, summer, and winter—that reveal and transmit the tremendous joy he took not just in raising plants but in living with them as well—all kinds of plants but particularly those grown from bulbs. Miles Hadfield ends his account of the dear fellow with this sentence: "We can aptly close this section with a glimpse of him, past his eightieth year, wading about the pond in a bathing dress to supervise the thinning of his water lilies."* Bowles, by the way, would himself have been a clergyman except that family circumstances prevented him from entering into holy orders.

Not that gardeners have to take holy orders in order to be nice. Jane Loudon, a layman, lived a life of great horticultural and literary accomplishment and personal sacrifice, never, so far as we know, having said a sharp word to anyone. She must have been sorely tempted, too, on those nights when she had to stay up until three or four, taking dictation from her imperious horticultural husband John.

Louise Beebe Wilder was a gentle creature, wasn't she, as well as being a fine plantswoman and writer—and I can find no accounts of irascibility on the part of Liberty Hyde Bailey, although, admittedly a thorough biography of that great plant expert has yet to be written.

And so I wind up my case for gardening's having very little

---

*Hadfield, *History of British Gardening*.

effect on the character of the gardener. If the question were: Is gardening of use in easing the gardener through periods of stress due to personal relationships? it would be a different matter entirely. One could immediately cite Margery Fish and the Countess von Arnim (Elizabeth of the German Garden) as women whose gardens probably kept them from shooting their husbands. And I have friends in the same situation.

As for people like V. Sackville-West who tend to retreat increasingly into their gardens as the years go by—their inclination is easily understood. In fact, might not the company of solacing plants woo one almost completely from the need for association with one's fellow human beings? Plants are alive, yet make no shrill demands on us. They don't damn, judge, accuse, imply, or betray. They accept one's ministrations gratefully and reward the minister with gifts of color, scent, and beauty of form. It's true one can't *discuss* things with them, but in many ways, one has to admit, they seem to give the human race strong competition.

PLANT INDEX

Plant Index